JACQUES RANCIÈRE: AN INTRODUCTION

Also available from Continuum:

Chronicles, Jacques Rancière
Dissensus, Jacques Rancière
The Politics of Aesthetics, Jacques Rancière
Jacques Rancière: Education, Truth, Emancipation, edited by Gert Biesta and Charles Bingham

Forthcoming:

Althusser's Lesson, Jacques Rancière
Mallarmé, Jacques Rancière
Jacques Rancière and the Contemporary Scene, edited by Jean-Philippe Deranty and Alison Ross
Reading Rancière, edited by Paul Bowman and Richard Stamp

JACQUES RANCIÈRE: AN INTRODUCTION

JOSEPH J. TANKE

continuum

Continuum International Publishing Group
The Tower Building 80 Maiden Lane
11 York Road   Suite 704
London SE1 7NX   New York, NY 10038

www.continuumbooks.com

© Joseph J. Tanke, 2011

All rights reserved. No part of this publication may be reproduced or transmitted in any form or by any means, electronic or mechanical, including photocopying, recording, or any information storage or retrieval system, without prior permission in writing from the publishers.

British Library Cataloguing-in-Publication Data
A catalogue record for this book is available from the British Library.

ISBN: HB: 978-1-4411-6770-5
      PB: 978-1-4411-5208-4

Library of Congress Cataloging-in-Publication Data
Tanke, Joseph J.
Jacques Rancière : an introduction / Joseph J. Tanke.
p. cm.
Includes bibliographical references and index.
ISBN 978-1-4411-6770-5 – ISBN 978-1-4411-5208-4
1. Rancière, Jacques. I. Title.
B2430.R27T36 2011
194–dc22

2010038361

Typeset by Newgen Imaging Systems Pvt Ltd, Chennai, India

For My Grandparents, Frank and Wilma Szomoru

CONTENTS

Acknowledgments ix

Introduction 1

Chapter 1: For a Critique of Philosophy 7

  Introduction 7
  1.1 The Lesson of Althusser 10
  1.2 The Lessons of May 15
  1.3 Lessons from the Archives 22
  1.4 Lessons on Philosopher-Kings 27
  1.5 Lessons from Equality 35
  Conclusion 40

Chapter 2: Politics by Process of Elimination 43

  Introduction 43
  2.1 On the Terrain of Policed Consensus 45
  2.2 The Aesthetics of Counting 48
  2.3 Supposing, Verifying, and Demonstrating Equality 55
  2.4 Disputing Subjects and Litigious Objects:
      Politics as Dissensus 61
  2.5 The Subjective Process of Politics 65
  Conclusion 70

Chapter 3: Retrieving the Politics of Aesthetics 73

  Introduction 73
  3.1 Analyzing the Part of Art 74

CONTENTS

3.2 Three Regimes of Art — 77
3.3 Equality in Art — 85
3.4 In Place of Modernity — 93
3.5 Against Postmodernity — 99
3.6 Art as Dissensus — 103
Conclusion — 108

Chapter 4: Regimes of Cinema — 110

Introduction — 110
4.1 A Historical Poetics of Cinema — 112
4.2 Cinema, the Dream of the Aesthetic Age — 115
4.3 The Logic of the Thwarted Fable — 121
4.4 Allegories of Modernity: Deleuze and the Use of Hitchcock — 128
4.5 Cinema and Its Century: Godard and the Abuse of Hitchcock — 136
Conclusion — 139

Chapter 5: Beyond Rancière — 142

Introduction — 142
5.1 Sensing Equality? — 143
5.2 The Centrality of the Imagination — 148
5.3 Inventing the Trans-Subjective Imagination — 155
Conclusion — 160

Notes — 163
Bibliography — 178
Index — 183

ACKNOWLEDGMENTS

Books rarely have simple origins. They emerge from multiple contexts, respond to various conversations, and bespeak numerous relationships only too fleetingly hinted at in their pages. This book is no exception. It was undertaken with the support of the Chalsty Initiative in Aesthetics and Philosophy, the Provost's Office, and the Division of Humanities and Sciences at California College of the Arts. While working on this study, I profited greatly from conversations with colleagues, students, and friends, many of whom were generous enough to read and discuss portions of what I wrote. In particular, I would like to thank Jim Bernauer, Ignacio Valero, Fred Dolan, Brenda Wirkus, David Rasmussen, Emiliano Battista, Marie-Eve Morin, Jon Meyer, Tzuchien Tho, Doug Hall, Mat Foust, Dan Russell, Tirza Latimer, Tina Takemoto, Anthony Marcellini, Elyse Mallouk, Lynne McCabe, Rob Marks, Matthew Rana, and Paola Santoscoy. Cody Hennesy's time and talents greatly facilitated the research conducted for this book. An extra expression of gratitude is owed to Colin McQuillan. During the book's final stages, he played for me the part of the ignorant schoolmaster. His careful readings forced me to improve my arguments and to refine my forms of expression. I am grateful as well to the editorial staff at Continuum for their enthusiasm for this project, especially Sarah Campbell, Tom Crick, and David Avital. Finally, I would like to thank Professor Rancière for his encouragement, time in conversation, and responses to questions regarding his position.

My work would not have been possible without the support of my parents, Jim and Claire Blanca, and my partner, Molly Slota.

This book is dedicated to my grandparents, Frank and Wilma Szomoru, who have been an inspiration for as long as I can remember.

INTRODUCTION

What follows is an introduction to the thought of Jacques Rancière. While introductory studies of philosophers often proceed by means of commentary, it would be perhaps the height of irony to offer readers good enough to expend energy on the pages I have composed an exegesis of texts. Rancière is quite critical of explication and the assumptions it makes regarding the intelligences of students, readers, and, in artistic contexts, spectators. In many instances, he views such procedures as hostile to what is the defining element of his thought, be it in a philosophical, political, or aesthetic context, that of equality. Rather than an exegetical introduction, I hope that my text will be viewed as a "reading." It is no doubt one among many, and it recounts the course I have been tracking through Rancière's works for a number of years now. Throughout, I have analyzed and commented on portions of Rancière's texts, not, I hope, to achieve the satisfaction of the one who knows, but to set in motion and clarify my intellectual adventure. In many places I have made arguments about how certain texts should be read, and how many concepts can prove useful for conversations on topics as diverse as the history of philosophy, critical pedagogy, politics, art, and cinema. These operations were necessary for me to find my way through the forest of signs Rancière has been scattering for over forty years, and they may prove useful to others. I do not view arguments or textual analysis as undermining the supposition of equality. On the contrary, most forms of expression want to be understood, and for this reason posit a community of equals.

This study follows Rancière as he attempts to analyze what he calls the "distribution of the sensible" [*le partage du sensible*]. This is the key concept in our story, for it unites the discussions of philosophy, politics, art, aesthetics, and cinema, all of which are conceived as practices of creating, distributing, contesting, and redistributing the sensible world. The French formulation, *"partage,"* has two senses that are easily lost in English, but which are nevertheless essential for the analysis Rancière conducts. In the first instance, it describes how partitions or divisions of the sensible structure what is seen and unseen, audible and inaudible, how certain objects and phenomena can be related or not, and also who, at the level of subjectivity, can appear in certain times and places. The distribution of the sensible is thus a general distribution of bodies and voices, as well as an implicit estimation of what they are capable of. In the second sense, *"partage"* indicates that these distributions are shared. The distribution of the sensible is a sharing of the sensible that refers itself to the principles and forms of relation that are part of a common world. To *partage* the sensible is thus to parcel out spaces and times, so as to create a shared or common world containing different allotments. Depending upon the context, and to avoid repetitiveness, I have employed a series of related words—distribution, division, partition, configuration, and so on—to refer to this idea. For Rancière, it is important to attend to the sensible, for its distinctions and divisions anticipate what becomes thinkable and possible. The sensible's distribution provides to thought its picture of the world, supplying the evidence of what can be conceived, discussed, and disputed. The conceivable in turn structures what presents itself to thought as a possibility for further thought and/or action. In its very givenness, it supplies possible courses of action, forms of relation, as well as new thoughts and sensible configurations. The distribution of the sensible thus ultimately defines, for Rancière, the field of possibility and impossibility. One can unite these three domains quite simply by noting that in French *"sens"* means at once sense, meaning, and direction. Throughout, we are analyzing the sense that is made of sense, or the meanings that are made of what appears to our senses, with the aim of instituting breaches so that other possible meanings, configurations, and directions can be created.

The key question with respect to any distribution of the sensible is to know whether it is founded upon equality or inequality. A division is always a division into parts, and it is essential for Rancière to determine the metric according to which this takes place. Whether it is the distribution of parts, objects, the arts, or the relationships between speech and visibility, these operations define worlds that are either compatible or incompatible with equality. What is often at stake in educational, political, and even artistic discourses is the attempt to divide the world into two different types of intelligences, one deemed capable of difficult thought and the other not. The primary goal of any analysis of the sensible is thus to determine what type of world it defines, and whether or not equality is there present.

In the chapters that follow, it is argued that Rancière's writings initiate a twofold movement with respect to the distribution of the sensible. In the first instance, they offer what I call a "topographical analysis" of the sensible. This form of analysis should be understood as sidestepping a "hermeneutics of depth," that is, interpretations premised upon meanings thought to reside below the surface of texts, political arrangements, or artistic forms. In addition to their inescapable theological residue, depth hermeneutics silently weave the pedagogical space of the explicative master, the one who knows the true meaning of things and is gracious enough to impart it to others. The hermeneutics of depth divides the world into two: minds capable of detecting in words and forms their correct meaning, and those who are dependent upon others for such discoveries. Topographical analysis, on the other hand, sticks to the surface of things. It offers a description of the relationships between elements in the common world. This form of analysis does not claim to strike upon the ultimate meaning of these forms, only to indicate how they appear, the logic of their relations, the conditions of their historical possibility, the meanings they have been given, and the overall picture to which they give rise. Since the sensible world is itself shared, and these elements are detectable on the surfaces of texts, images, and political arrangements, topographical analysis employs a supposition opposed to the hermeneutics of depth: it credits its addressees with being already in possession of capacities for making sense of sense. Topographical analysis thus frames its analyses as being verifiable inter-subjectively. The second moment of Rancière's project entails evaluating these arrangements in terms of the version of the possible they define. What we find is that he attempts to analyze how the constitution of a sensible given—in philosophical discourses, political practices, and artistic arrangements—defines forms of openness or closure. An essential part of Rancière's output can be viewed as a series of interventions designed to break apart the sense of inevitability attached to many forms of intellectual, political, and artistic labor. He takes particular exception with those positions, such as political realism or the ethical turn in aesthetics, that close the possible with discourses of necessity. This second movement contained in Rancière's writings is thus an intervention into the sensible configuration of our common world designed to create space for the implementation of equality.

In Chapter 1, we see Rancière creating a distance with respect to the traditional practice of philosophy. We follow his thought from his initial break with former teacher Louis Althusser up to the series of counter-assumptions forged in *The Ignorant Schoolmaster*. Essential for our account of the practice of philosophy he inevitably designs is a close reading of *The Nights of Labor* and *The Philosopher and His Poor*. In both instances, we see Rancière attending to the sensible and the means by which it is either controlled or contested. The readings of philosophy he offers in the latter text attend to the means by which philosophy monopolizes the discourse on the sensible. It is argued that the very framing of this analysis in terms of sensible practices allows a different understanding of philosophy to emerge. Essential to this project is an understanding of the destabilizing and generative force of equality Rancière reads from both the history of aesthetics, at the end of *The Philosopher and His Poor*, and the writings of the nineteenth-century pedagogical theorist, Joseph Jacotot in *The Ignorant Schoolmaster*. Equality is the primary means of contesting hierarchical and exclusionary distributions of the sensible. It allows us to imagine other forms of arrangement. Equality is what preserves the possible as possible.

The analysis and contestation of the sensible is extended in Chapter 2 through a reading of the texts Rancière has devoted to politics. We look at how he formulates his analysis in terms of the differences between the inegalitarian world of the police and the egalitarian world outlined by equality. Politics is, for Rancière, the process of placing these two worlds in conflict so as to define new forms of taking part in a community. Politics, understood as dissensus, is the process of making manifest the gap between the sensible and itself. Essential to this endeavor is a reading of Rancière's account of Greek democracy. With this reading we attempt to isolate the essential structures of politics: the advent of the *dēmos*, its creation of the polemical universal of equality, the logic of class struggle, and the process of subjectivation. Rancière's analysis of the aesthetic dimension of politics enables us to describe more intimately the processes, categories, and inventions of democracy, as well as to see how a certain historically constituted form of art can become active in the redistribution of the sensible. It is this latter project that we undertake in Chapter 3. We follow Rancière's discussion of the different regimes of art, with special attention directed at the identification he terms "aesthetic." Rancière understands aesthetics in three specialized and intermingled senses that we explore throughout this study. It does not, despite the importance he ascribes to the emergence of the discipline carrying that name, first and foremost designate the field often conflated with the philosophy of art. This is a meaning aesthetics assumes rather late in its history through the meeting of German idealism and romanticism. Rancière defends this form of thought against its detractors, inasmuch as it connects with other senses of the aesthetic. With the idea of the distribution of the sensible, aesthetics should be understood in an expanded sense so to include the factors—space and time—structuring the ways things appear. The *aisthēsis* defined through the partitioning of space and time is political because it sketches the boundaries of what is sensible, intelligible, and possible. It is in terms of the formation and contestation of space and time that art can be said to have a political capacity, and it is thus within this broader notion of the aesthetic as *aisthēsis* that the relationship between art and politics must be situated. The third understanding of aesthetics is contained in the notion of the aesthetic regime. It designates the identity art created for itself in literature, music, visual art, and design at the end of the eighteenth and start of the nineteenth centuries. The aesthetic regime is a particular identification of art, which can be distinguished from other regimes based on the relationships they sustain between art and other ways of doing and making. It is with respect to this identification that the first sense of aesthetics as a sub-discipline of philosophy becomes significant. It emerges in order to interpret the new forms of experience generated by these practices. Rancière argues that aesthetic art gives rise to a new sensible experience wherein equality can be discerned. He formulates the notion of the aesthetic regime in order to highlight art's capacity for dissensus, the manifestation of the fundamental separation of sense from sense. Chapter 3 attempts to clarify the politics contained in the aesthetic identification of art, and preserve it against two historical-theoretical edifices that threaten to efface it, modernism and post-modernism. Chapter 4 deepens our picture of the significance of art and aesthetics with an extended exploration of Rancière's writings on film. It argues that the analysis of film is quite central to Rancière's endeavor, and that in his discussions of the medium we can witness both the subtlety and the efficacy of his form of analysis.

The final chapter challenges Rancière's presentation of the history of aesthetic philosophy. It argues that the central experience codified by the texts of the aesthetic regime is that of freedom, and that as a result more argumentation is required to support the connection between aesthetics and equality. Second, I highlight the elision of the imagination in Rancière's reading of the texts in question, indicating that an investigation and retrieval of this capacity could prove indispensable to the intellectual-practical projects Rancière has set in motion. On the basis of the similarities between Kant's account of the imagination and Rancière's notion of dissensus, I contend that a version of the Kantian faculty can be seen as operative in the latter, with both thinkers describing instances in which the sensible is broken and redistributed. Rather, however, than framing the imagination in terms of the subject, I describe it as a trans-subjective capacity sustained by the supposition of equality. As we will see, the imagination is a capacity sustained by equality that is both disruptive and generative.

As these introductory remarks indicate, I am in agreement with the assessment commonly expressed today that Rancière is an exciting and important voice in discussions of politics and art. He has provided a new language of democratic politics that avoids the problematic tendencies of identity politics and the dead-end consensus of liberalism. He has given new life to the frequently disparaged form of thought known as aesthetics and shown how the experiences it defined over two hundred years ago remain relevant, and potentially subversive. Significantly, he has provided meaningful analyses of the historical conditions that allow for these two forms of redistributing the sensible to be joined. Much of Rancière's work can be understood as justifying our pleasures, whether philosophical, political, or aesthetic, and showing how they, at some point, rely upon the presupposition of equality. It remains an open question of course to what extent this clarification of the terrain on which philosophy, politics, and art meet can occasion the reinvigoration of their respective practices.

CHAPTER 1

FOR A CRITIQUE OF PHILOSOPHY

INTRODUCTION

Can philosophy enter into meaningful dialogue with the arts and political practice or is it irredeemably marred by the space and time of its production? Does its historical and institutional positioning put it at odds with the assumptions, actions, and discourses that might transform our world for the better? Does its refusal to think the site of its own production prevent it from entering into collaboration with other arts and practices, compelling it to monopolize the discourse on social-political reality? Are its procedures fundamentally inimical to equality, and are they themselves reliant upon its repudiation? Does philosophy's long history endow it with an orientation that requires us to find a new idiom for theorizing art and politics?

Essential for our study will be determining how one should read the early works of Jacques Rancière with respect to this line of questioning. Do the analyses conducted in *La leçon d'Althusser* (hereafter, *La leçon*) and *The Philosopher and His Poor* (hereafter, *The Philosopher*) announce a departure from philosophy as such or just philosophy as it is traditionally conceived and practiced? Should one interpret the archival texts *The Nights of Labor* (hereafter, *Nights*) and *The Ignorant Schoolmaster* (hereafter, *Schoolmaster*) as the embodiment of a fundamental suspicion regarding this reactionary science? And, what do these early texts teach about the eventual nature of Rancière's endeavor? Does his discourse ultimately dispense with philosophy entirely or are there some profitable connections to be found with it?

We would do well to consider the possibility broached at the end of *The Philosopher*, a trenchant critique of the elitist nature of philosophy. After over two hundred damning pages in which philosophy was exposed as constituting itself through the castigation of those who perform manual labor, Rancière writes:

> It remains important today to be able to judge if what our institutions, our images, and our discourses imitate is democratic hope or its mourning. Reflections in which philosophy can find itself implicated without pretending to give lessons about it.[1]

In this slight opening, Rancière gives voice to the possibility that, despite its "traditional aristocratic requirement," philosophy might play a part in the democratic adjudication of forms, statements, and arrangements.[2] Moreover, he indicates that there is a need for what I call a "topographical analysis" of our world, that is, the clarification and critique of the lines dividing those with the right to think from those deemed incapable of it. Can philosophy offer strong evaluations regarding what is better and worse, while maintaining a fundamental commitment to the equality of persons? Can it content itself with *taking part* in a conversation about our shared sensible world, without reviving the violence of its past?

This chapter elaborates this challenge and this possibility, reading the major works Rancière devoted to contesting philosophical privilege. It defends a thesis that might seem untenable given the thoroughgoing critique to which Rancière subjects philosophy. It argues that Rancière's distinct form of analysis maintains a productive relationship with philosophy, even as it continually exposes the moments of exclusion that have defined the discipline. Moreover, I argue that a limited, self-critical version of philosophy remains central to Rancière's attempts to disrupt the lines of division operative in our world. His practice is, in the first instance, dedicated to rooting out the moments of inequality that structure philosophy's discourses, and, in the second, a refusal to occupy the place traditionally reserved for it. What emerges is a form of philosophy that continually displaces itself in order to make room for other practices working to create the distribution of the sensible. It is a form of thinking content to take part in a conversation with other efforts to clarify and critique our world.

When philosophy gives up its efforts to monopolize the interpretation of the sensible, it enters into unprecedented relationships with other forms of thought. This is a key aspect of Rancière's unique mode of philosophizing: it refuses to recognize the boundaries that have traditionally separated philosophy from other practices. This results in an output that bears greater resemblance to the knowledges of autodidacts than the specialized publications of university professors.[3] Rancière has described this practice as "indisciplinary," a method of analysis that works in explicit defiance of customary divisions. Whereas interdisciplinarity keeps existing disciplines in place and shuttles between them, indisciplinarity aims to show how the disciplines themselves are constituted. The stakes of this analysis are political, for the delimitation of a discourse simultaneously creates the criteria for who can speak it. "My problem," Rancière explains, "has always been to escape the division between disciplines, because what interests me is the question of the distribution of territories, which is always a way of deciding who is qualified to speak about what."[4] Needless to say, it is this critique Rancière applies to philosophy, where he attends to the manner in which philosophical discourse attempts to naturalize a demarcation between those possessing knowledge and those condemned to remain its object. He analyzes how this discursive practice fashions for itself the spaces from which the few guide the many and the learned instruct the ignorant. In attempting to twist free from this distribution, he confronts the contemporary practice of philosophy with the history of its exclusions. The indisciplinary practice of philosophy is thus the attempt to break with these distinctions by thinking their history, measuring their effects, and indicating other possible configurations.

If philosophy remains central to Rancière's enterprise, it is not simply because it is the field in which he obtained his academic formation. Philosophy, as many of its historical sources attest, remains too problematic to be endorsed wholesale, and Rancière is compelled to reject not only many of its positions, but the position it assumes for itself in articulating those positions. One element he takes from philosophy, however, is its respect for logic. Logic is operative in his investigations in two major ways. First, his writings retain powers of formalization, supplying appropriate levels of abstraction from historical events as well as literary and artistic forms in order to achieve the insights we have come to expect from philosophy. In the second instance, this form of presentation is related to Rancière's attempt to discern the various logics at stake within a given historical space. His work frequently follows presuppositions, positions, and distributions through to their conclusions in order to evaluate their practical consequences. This involves comparing them in terms of the possibilities they create or foreclose. His writings reveal how ostensibly radical viewpoints often rely upon and reinforce antiegalitarian presuppositions, how discourses that appear quite traditional, such as aesthetics, can work in a progressive manner, and how these two tendencies are never found in pure states. Rancière analyzes the logics and counter-logics by means of which the distribution of the sensible is constructed and contested. His goal is to avoid inegalitarian positions and bolster egalitarian suppositions.

Rancière's form of philosophizing, which situates itself squarely on the side of human emancipation, is based on an unorthodox premise: people are not lacking in knowledge or the ability to think; what they require is confidence in their capacities for change. In this sense, it is tempting to view Rancière's trajectory as already contained in the early works announcing a break with former teacher Louis Althusser. "I began by moving outside of the boundaries of the discipline of 'philosophy,'" Rancière recalls, "because the questions I was concerned with revolved around Marxist conceptions of ideology—the issue of why people found themselves in a particular place and what they could or couldn't think in that place."[5] Indeed, the differences between Althusser and Rancière are so pronounced that one might read many of Rancière's core convictions, especially with respect to philosophy, as emerging through a reversal of his former teacher's positions. While such a simplistic formulation fails to capture the complexity of the relationship between Althusser's position and Rancière's thought, it will be indispensable for us to chart these divergences at the outset. In these early writings, what takes root are many of the notions that we follow throughout our study: the sense in which theoretical propositions rely upon and perpetuate sensible-practical divisions, the need to curb philosophy's scientific pretensions, and the manner in which the supposition of equality enables us to articulate new connections between the sensible, the thinkable, and the possible.

1.1 THE LESSON OF ALTHUSSER

It would be difficult to overestimate the influence of Louis Althusser on the French philosophical scene of the 1960s. In 1948, upon passing his *agrégation* in philosophy, Althusser was awarded a position as *agrégé répétiteur* at the *École Normale Supérieure* (ENS) in Paris.

As *caïman*—a term of endearment among *normaliens*—he was responsible for preparing students for their *agrégation* in philosophy. In this role, he participated in the intellectual formation of many who would become France's most distinguished intellectuals in the twentieth century.[6] 1948 was also the year Althusser became a member of the *Parti communiste français* (PCF). The cold war placed students under pressure to choose sides in an ideological battle, and many would join the Party under Althusser's influence. Depending upon the accounts one reads, Althusser was alternately an enormously charismatic teacher capable of winning over students or something of an intellectual bully who manipulated them with guilt over their class privilege. Regardless of one's perspective, it is the case that Althusser was indispensable for opening the school to new theoretical perspectives, such as linguistics, Lévi-Strauss' structural anthropology, and the readings of Freud pioneered by Jacques Lacan.[7] Étienne Balibar explains that Althusser made ENS a "centre for a philosophy that was 'living,' not 'academic,'" and compared the atmosphere to "a proper 'philosophical life,'" in the sense which the ancients would have understood it.[8] Rancière himself recalls fondly the "intellectual dynamism" centered around Althusser, and credits the differences he articulated with phenomenology as offering "a kind of liberation from university culture."[9]

At the beginning of the 1960s, Althusser became known to readers beyond the rue d'Ulm through a series of journal articles (later collected in *For Marx*) in which he advanced an original, if idiosyncratic interpretation of Marx. His reading hinged on what he construed as the radical break between Marx's early, ideological writings, and the mature, scientific project of *Capital*. The early writings, in Althusser's assessment, are marred by their reliance on the vocabulary of German idealism, thus preventing the development of a scientific understanding of social, political, and economic reality. Later, however, Marx developed a scientific perspective by quitting the terrain of philosophy. The "epistemological rupture," a notion borrowed from Gaston Bachelard's histories of science, was announced in *The German Ideology* of 1845, where Marx and Engels resolved to "settle accounts" with their "erstwhile philosophical consciousness."[10] According to Althusser, the later works belong to a fundamentally different "problematic," his word for the general conceptual framework in which concepts gain their meaning and applicability.[11] Although it would undergo subsequent revision, Althusser's position in *For Marx* was that Marx's thought could be parsed according to the following schema:

1840–44: early works
1845: the works of the break
1845–57: transitional works
1857–83: mature works[12]

This science/ideology distinction is central to nearly all of Althusser's thought, and much of his work consists of separating properly scientific notions from the vestiges of idealism hampering Marxist thought. The rupture, Althusser cautioned, must be continually produced if Marxism is not to lapse into the speculative thought that preceded it. Activating this break thus involved scrubbing Marx's corpus of concepts such as labor, alienation, consciousness, species-being, and the vague anthropology they define. Althusser can be read as attempting to distance Marxism from the humanist platform espoused by the PCF, as well as working to undermine its attempt to find common cause with socialists, social democrats, and the Catholic left. One part of this strategy involved distancing Marx from his predecessors. For example, he opposed the interpretation, spawned by Marx and Engels themselves, according to which historical materialism would be Hegelianism in inverted form.[13] Readers should take seriously, Althusser counseled, the famous XIth thesis on Feuerbach in which philosophy was condemned for *only* having interpreted the world. This proclamation signals not the transformation of philosophy, "but a long philosophical silence during which only the new science speaks."[14] The science inaugurated by the break is of course the science of history, likened by Althusser to the discoveries of mathematics and physics.[15]

According to *Reading Capital*, the scientific status of Marx's analysis follows not simply from a different interpretation of economic facts, but the delimitation of a new object. Marx starts by treating as questions what bourgeois political economists regarded as solutions. His method, as Althusser describes it, consists of working through the blind spots in their writings in order to supply concepts for the economic phenomena they left unexplained. Marx, for example, applies the name "surplus-value" to what Smith and Ricardo could think only as profit, rent, and interest. While Marx was not the first to isolate this concept, Althusser contends he was the first to handle it properly, using it to reconstruct the causal nexus to which it belongs. After identifying surplus-value as the key to the explanation of capital, Marx used it to elaborate the entirety of the capitalist mode of production, itself viewed as a historically variable system of effects. Crucially for Althusser, this understanding of the mode of production is what allowed Marx to describe capitalism's distinct form of structural causality, that is, the manner in which the capitalist system is determined by the reciprocal functioning of economic, political, ideological, and scientific components.[16] This, in Althusser's estimation, is the object of Marx's science: the structural relations of partial effects governing a given society at a particular moment in history. The scientificity of Marx's analysis thus results from the identification of a concept-problem, and the rigorous analysis of the causal system to which it belongs. The first volume of *Capital* (1867) was, for Althusser, the creation of both a new object and theoretical problematic. When both are pursued systematically such that the object's nuances become known in greater detail, one is operating on the plane of science.[17] It would be a mistake to think that all aspects of the object must be elaborated in order to claim the status of science for a given discourse. As Althusser explains, "a science progresses, that is, lives only by an extreme attention to its points of theoretical fragility. As such, it takes less of its life from what it knows than what it *does not know.*"[18]

Just as the advent of mathematics and physics gave rise to new theoretical developments, Marxist science also generates a new philosophy: dialectical materialism. In this sense, Althusser emphatically opposed the historicist desire to collapse the distinction between historical and dialectical materialism. Historical materialism, for Althusser, should be understood as the science of history, with dialectical materialism the theory of its practice. Unfortunately, Marx was not in a position to fully articulate the philosophical presuppositions upon which his endeavor relied, and it is therefore necessary to elaborate them from his late works. It is this task that Althusser and his students set themselves in the famous seminar devoted to *Reading Capital.*[19]

By Althusser's hypothesis, Marx's philosophy could not be gleaned from the anthropological positions of his earlier writings, but produced only through a "symptomatic reading" of *Capital,* that is, by exploiting the method Marx himself employed with respect to bourgeois political economy. Althusser describes this method as restoring to the text its unconscious, and cites, in addition to Marx's own method, Lacan's interpretation of Freud and various currents within French epistemology, such as the approaches of Bachelard, Canguilhem, and the early Foucault. Symptomatic reading conceives of a theoretical text as the necessary *combination* of sightings [*vues*], lacks [*manques*], and oversights [*bévues*], whose relationships it attempts to make explicit. It begins with present terms, identifies the absent concepts upon which the text nevertheless relies, and attempts to reconstruct the mechanism their interactions bespeak. With respect to *Capital*, this involves attending to those analyses that exploit, but do not articulate, a philosophical concept. This symptomatic reading of *Capital* thus tries to reconstruct the theoretical problematic to which it belongs, while distinguishing it from the ideological problematic from which it departs.

This project of drawing a dividing line between science and ideology is the obligation Althusser assigns to "philosophical practice." He asserts, "Philosophy represents the people's class struggle in theory. In return it helps the people to distinguish in *theory* and in all *ideas* (political, ethical, aesthetic, etc.) between true ideas and false ideas."[20] For Althusser, it is impossible to imagine a society without ideology; even a classless one would rely on it for achieving social integration. It is necessary, therefore, for philosophy to separate the truth of economic, political and scientific practices from their mystifications. Philosophy is "class struggle in theory" inasmuch as it prevents knowledge from being exploited by bourgeois tendencies. "The ultimate stake of philosophical struggle is the struggle for the *hegemony* between the two great tendencies in world outlook (materialist and idealist)."[21] Philosophy, despite its relative autonomy from the sphere of economic practice, has, for Althusser, an indispensable part to play in politics: the education of those enmeshed in the economic sector. For these practitioners, philosophy unmasks the false representations governing their lived relations to existence. It struggles on behalf of the non-ideological concepts produced by science, using them to clarify political thought and action.[22] Theory's perspicacity is predicated upon its deliberate remove from the spheres of economic and political practice. It provides those so engaged with the reality of what they cannot see because of their positions within the division of labor.

In this outline we see what would prove to be intolerable for some of Althusser's former students after the events of May 1968. In the sections that follow, it is argued that many of Rancière's political notions are developed in opposition to these propositions about the incapacity of material producers to think for themselves, and the concomitant heroic vocation of theory. From the vantage point of May, Rancière undertakes a genealogical exposition of the pedagogical space employed by the Althusserian apparatus. This break leads him to set in place a radically different set of methodological assumptions, and to engage in a historical critique of philosophy more generally. While the Althusserian strategy was at bottom founded upon incapacity, the thought that those engaged in the sphere of production require specialists to arrive at its truth, Rancière's approach is founded on the assumption of radically equal capacities. Rancière warns—and this will be central—one cannot start with inequality and work progressively towards its elimination. "Equality is a presupposition, an initial axiom—or it is nothing."[23] In this sense, the hypothesis Rancière invites us to entertain is that politics is hampered not by a lack of knowledge, the malformation of the marginalized classes, or the inopportunity of the moment, but by the failure to embody *in advance* the equality we endeavor to bring into the world. The postulate that workers are capable of thought requires us to abandon Althusser's manner of defining the relationship between political and theoretical practice, just as the supposition of equality more generally necessitates new forms of reading, writing, and organizing. Nothing is more troubling to those who would draw lines and erect hierarchies, whether between theory and practice, science and ideology, intellectuals and workers, than the contention that the world is not divisible on the basis of intelligence. Perhaps, however, it is necessary to draw one final dividing line and distinguish the lessons of May from the lesson of Althusser.

1.2 THE LESSONS OF MAY

Rancière's break with Althusser was precipitated in part by the ensuing differences with respect to the significance of the events of May. Rancière has recounted that his Althusserian perspective began to crumble when faced with the mass revolt in which 9 million people, without the support of the Party or trade unions, went on strike across France. Is there a need for a detour through science when the stakes of a struggle can be clarified in the street? One can perhaps imagine the intellectual turmoil of the former Althusserian.

Rancière explains, "A whole system of certainties was shaken."[24] The events were nevertheless propitious for the course Rancière was to follow. They indicated that it was time to revisit the tenets of Marxism articulated by Althusser.

La leçon is this reappraisal of an Althusserian Marxism that "died on the barricades of May."[25] It alternates between a critical analysis of Althusser's theoretical positions and the effects generated within the political field, taking aim at a more general constellation called "Althusserianism." Throughout, Rancière opposes to Althusserianism the new forms of politics emerging in its wake. The direction of this early book is largely critical; it works to prevent emerging forms of revolt from being subordinated to old forms of theory. At issue is the place allotted to theoretical practice in political struggle. Rancière articulates the suspicion that granting undue priority to the former has conservative consequences for the latter. In the discourses, actions, and organizational forms engendered by workers and students in May, as well as those undertaken by workers at the LIP watch factory in 1973, Rancière isolates the elements of a politics that has superseded Althusserianism. While *La leçon* lacks what becomes the central element of Rancière's mature politics, that of equality, one can nevertheless view the critique of Althusserianism as motivated by Rancière's concern for it. Large portions of *La leçon* contest the divisions between intellectual and manual work, as well as the hierarchical distributions operative in work, school, and political organizations.

This entails the repudiation of Althusser's notion of ideology, first articulated by Rancière in a trenchant article of 1969, "*Sur la théorie de l'idéologie: Politique d'Althusser.*"[26] Rancière claims that the ideology/science distinction facilitates a twofold repression of politics. In the first instance, Rancière accuses Althusser of construing ideology in non-Marxian terms when he suggests that ideology is inevitable. He provocatively terms Althusser's contention that even a classless society would rely on ideology the "myth of an ideological State of Nature."[27] This sociological thesis, Rancière explains, strips the concept of all political efficacy, placing ideology prior to class struggle. The consequence is that ideology is thought not as the clash of class-specific ideas, but as timeless.[28] This sociological suppression is joined, in the second instance, to the metaphysical structure of science. Althusser's notion of science also prevents an analysis of the specific functions of ideology. Rancière here observes that the science that counters ideology maintains an unacknowledged debt to Platonism. It construes ideology in the abstract, as the "Other of Science."[29] Rancière:

> The ideology/science opposition can only function by the reestablishment of a space homologous to what the whole metaphysical tradition thought when it opposed science to its other, thus posing the closure of a universe of discourse split [*partagé*] between the domain of true discourse and the domain of false discourse, between the world of science and that of its other (opinion, error, illusion, etc.).[30]

Thinking ideology metaphysically means forcing its different functions, levels, and sites of application to fit a pre-established concept of its essence. Is it not suspect, Rancière asks, to formulate a general theory of ideology without first analyzing its concrete role within class struggle?

Rancière's essay does more than describe the traditional sociological and metaphysical theses implicit in Althusserianism; it charts the political effects generated by these positions. We should note here a key feature of the topographical analysis Rancière conducts. He describes the creation of a division, a *partage*, identifies the logic it employs, follows its effects, and evaluates them in terms of the discourses and practices they give rise to. The *partage* in this case is Althusser's separation of material practices from the theoretical apparatus that discloses their truth. Rancière objects most strenuously to the naïveté Althusser assumes of those engaged in material practices. For Rancière, this division has no other purpose than securing the most traditional of pedagogical arrangements, and the necessity of the philosophical apparatus. Althusserianism is thus diagnosed as the "closure" of a political universe. It is contrasted with some openings to be found in certain quarters of student milieu, so it is important to be clear about the context. Althusserianism asserted itself at a time when higher education in France was subject to an intense debate that ultimately culminated in the liberalization of curricula, the creation of several new universities, and an influx of students from backgrounds traditionally under-represented in French universities. The changes eventually put in place by Gaullist bureaucrats in part grew out of demographic shifts, but largely resulted from the boisterous demands made by students throughout the 1960s. It is in this sense that Althusserianism functioned as a call to "order" addressed to students.[31] During this time, students were questioning the university's position within the capitalist system. They were politicizing forms of instruction, as well as the power relations inherent in traditional pedagogy. Althusserianism attempted to defuse these institutional critiques by shifting the investigation from the forms of power at issue in the teacher-student relationship to a discussion about the content of courses themselves.[32] The science/ideology distinction transformed debates about social functions and procedures into an assessment of whether or not a knowledge was properly materialist. It thereby maintained the fiction that knowledge transmission could be free from the forms of ideology described by student groups, those forms embedded in institutional hierarchies. Althusserianism masked the novelty of student demands, displacing the critique of practices into the realm of ideas. Not only did this gesture forestall a serious reckoning with institutionalized forms of domination, it quietly laid the groundwork for a pedagogical space in which philosophy could be awarded pride of place. Althusserianism is not without a certain amount of rhetorical appeal, allowing its adherents to claim that theory is itself class struggle. By Rancière's estimation, however, this struggle amounts to little more than a shell game in which the revolution continually recedes behind the endless development of science.

After the thoroughgoing break announced by the article on Althusser's conception of ideology, one might think there would be little need for further critique of the master of the rue d'Ulm. Rancière has explained that the book-length publication *La leçon* in 1974 was made pressing by a renaissance of Althusserianism, then attempting to recuperate the lessons of May.[33] It was necessary, Rancière explains, to perform a diagnostic of contemporary Marxist discourse, pinpointing where it had been outstripped by historical events.[34] Throughout, he charts "the effects of this school where a generation of intellectuals learned to frame the relations between Marxist theory and the struggle of the masses," specifically targeting the way Althusseriaism relates theory to political practice.[35] *La leçon* describes how Althusser's "theoreticist" assumptions, predicated upon a sharp divide between those who think and those who act, foreclose possibilities of human emancipation.[36] The text is at points a moving disavowal of Rancière's own Althusserian past. Throughout, we see him rejecting a conception of philosophy premised on the idea that some are capable of thought while others are not.

The work begins as a commentary upon the now infamous lesson in Marxism Althusser provided to John Lewis. Althusser's polemic was a response to a series of critical articles published by the British philosopher in 1972.[37] Contesting Althusser's notion of structural causality, Lewis had affirmed three propositions: it is man who makes history; history is made through "transcendence;" and, man only knows what he himself does. It is not difficult to see in these theses the old humanist enemy, and Althusser was quick to denounce the baleful influence of this trajectory. "This idea of 'man' . . . is the basis of all bourgeois ideology," one which, left uncontested, could defuse the workers' struggles.[38] This disarming mythology, however, functions paradoxically: it sets workers up to fail, by convincing them they have capacities they do not in fact possess. Althusser: "If workers are told, 'it is men who make history,' you do not have to be a great thinker to see that, sooner or later, that helps to disorient or disarm them."[39] To Lewis's vague humanism, Althusser opposed the Marxist-Leninist tradition, uniform in its lessons: when organized by their Party and armed with objective knowledge, it is the masses who make history.[40]

For Althusser, Lewis is representative of the danger *gauchists* and student groups run when they resort to careless rhetoric. Althusserianism thus commits itself, in Rancière's formulation, to a "general policing of theoretical statements [*énoncés*]."[41] Against Lewis, for whom knowledge was a rather straightforward affair, Althusser formulates its difficulties. Revolutionary education must have a rigorously defined object, unfold with a carefully defined methodology, and be officiated over by those possessing specialized training. Althusserian students were themselves renowned for their insistence that the "theoretical formation" was a precondition for political militancy. We have seen already that the science/ideology distinction institutes a tremendous division into the sphere of practices, separating the learned from those who remained enthralled by ideology. In this context, it secures the necessity of scholars in general and university theoreticians in particular. Althusser's elaborate detour through reading achieves little, for Rancière, apart from the creation of a place for philosophy at the top of the division of labor. "History, Althusser teaches, is only knowable and 'makeable' by the mediation of experts [*savants*]."[42] This epistemological proposition justifies, in a single stroke, the exercises of the university and Party elite. Rancière: "The challenge is clear: it is a question of saving philosophy, and 'Marxist philosophy' in particular, as the business of university specialists."[43] *La leçon* thus denounces the "theoreticism" at the heart of the Althusserian endeavor. Like its Platonic forebear, Althusserianism presents itself as indispensable for discerning between true and false ideas, that is, the directives of science and the petit-bourgeois tendencies threatening to take hold of the worker's movement. It is here that philosophy finds its justification, for as long as men and women misjudge the shadows on the cave wall, they will require philosophers to guide their politics.

What is most distressing about Althusserianism, according to Rancière, is that in order to function it requires the masses to wallow in ideology. Althusser's response to John Lewis is exemplary in that it reveals the fundamental hostility of his thought to practices of auto-emancipation. To justify the necessity of the philosophical intervention, Althusser continually transforms, against the letter of Marx's text, the historical and political agency of the proletariat into an indistinct populace requiring edification.[44] This is the central dynamic Rancière analyzes in *The Philosopher*. Philosophy grounds itself by opposing itself to those—"the many, the vulgar many," as Plato expressed it—incapable of arriving at its truths. This is the fundamental point of divergence between Rancière and Althusser: the latter thinker assumes popular movements are hampered by degrees of incapacity, thus requiring the formation of a theoretical avant-garde. For him, the class struggle never unfolds transparently, and therefore relies upon science to clarify its stakes. Rancière, on the other hand, assumes that the meanings of practices are relatively evident to those engaged in them. He even suggests that economic exploitation and political domination require little explanation to those who are its victims. He thus turns his critical efforts against those discourses that profit from announcing these truths in an effort to redistribute the field of capacities.

It is precisely on the relationship between political and theoretical practices that a topographical analysis reveals Althusserianism to be most out of sync with the new forms of politics spawned in May 1968. Emerging, Rancière contends, are practices, discourses, and organizations definable less in terms of doctrinal fidelity than their rejection of authority as such. On the horizon are activists for whom wrangling over terms is secondary to the democratization of the movements themselves. To demonstrate the eclipse of Althusserian Marxism, Rancière places it alongside the experiences of the workers at the LIP watch factory, who, upon learning of plans for the termination of a significant number of their colleagues, forcibly occupied their plant. Rather than simply striking, these workers continued the production and sale of watches under the slogan, "It is possible: we make, we sell, we pay ourselves!" What ensued was an experiment in self-management that gripped the imagination of the French public. In simple economic terms, workers' control produced greater profits than those of management.[45] For its refusal of traditional channels such as labor unions, the event is frequently claimed as part of the political legacy of May 1968. Contemporaneous with the publication of "Reply to John Lewis," these actions signal the obsolescence of the Althusserian perspective. What is most telling are the terms with which these workers articulated their struggle: "The economy is in the service of man, man is not in the service of the economy."[46] The word "man" functions, according to Rancière, not as a lure to lead workers back into the darkness of ideology, but as a means for resisting hierarchy. "Man" is the political name by which workers counter the powers exercised over them, with its extension rebutting directly the division upon which the bosses rely. The question is not whether the name is of bourgeois derivation, but whether it can be made to serve the self-emancipation of a people. The Althusserian equation of "man" and his rights with bourgeois humanism is thus hasty, as a brief history of the workers' movement demonstrates.[47]

In its form, the occupation of the LIP watch factory closely resembles the demonstrations of equality central to Rancière's understanding of politics. We note here how a name of sufficient generality, "man," facilitated the creation of a polemical scene. With it, workers asserted themselves against a distribution in which they had little part. The name allowed for the elaboration of a site of struggle where the goal was to determine who was and was not covered by it. With the use of such names, those engaging in the process of politics alter the relations between what is perceivable, thinkable, and possible. The LIP workers' experiment in self-management asserts in stark terms that a world free of hierarchical divisions is possible. It is on the plane of possibility, Rancière explains, that "the whole ideological struggle between the bourgeoisie and the proletariat is played out."[48] What is at stake is the difference between two worlds. For bosses, state officials, and labor unions, manual production requires supervision; a world of equal relations is thus unimaginable. The LIP affair demonstrates, however, that people have more capacities than they realize. It indicates that the time when intellectuals could instruct workers about what they can and cannot do has passed.

1.3 LESSONS FROM THE ARCHIVES

One of the major political legacies of May was to disrupt the boundaries thought to exist between manual and intellectual labor. Rancière's work of the 1970s should be understood as an attempt to hold open the possibilities created by the dislodgment of the representational mechanisms through which intellectuals attempted to guide political movements. It is this goal that unites, albeit in different fashions, his role in the founding of a journal of social history, *Les Révoltes logiques*, and the book projects that came to fruition in the next decade.[49] This disruption sent Rancière into the archives of the workers' movement, where he would remain for ten years. This experience was essential for the formation of many of his central notions, particularly those pertaining to his understanding of politics as the process of redefining the partitions of the sensible world. Although Rancière is no longer directly immersed in the archives, the insights he gleaned there continue to define the contours of his thought, and its spirit shapes his general approach to philosophical questions. One frequently finds him pitting historical discoveries against the certainties of the philosophers, gestures that, I contend, clear the ground for the implementation of a philosophical practice founded on democratic presuppositions.

The archival labors culminated in the publication, in 1981, of *The Nights of Labor*. These efforts were extended by *The Philosopher* in 1983, a book which, even though it is more explicitly engaged with the history of philosophy, can be viewed as a companion to *Nights*. Whereas the more properly archival text charts the remarkable history of workers who refused to partition their lives according to the dictates of work, and thus their strict identities as workers, *The Philosopher* investigates the means by which philosophy has locked up workers with a discourse on their nature. According to Rancière, philosophy has historically defined itself over and against those engaged in manual labor, championing its powers of discernment against those lacking the time for thought. Both books take exception with the suggestion that thinking is the luxury of a few. The early study follows the steps taken by a few remarkable poets and essayists in defiance of the partitioning supposed to structure their lives as workers, and the latter analyzes the obstacles erected by Plato's argument that each member of the republic should perform only the job for which he is suited by nature.

The archival venture was undertaken during a period in which many intellectuals left behind habitual milieus in order to meet with workers. Many had hoped to recover an authentic working class culture uncontaminated by Marxist theses. *Nights* itself began under the assumption that it was possible to follow a coherent body of discourses from the history of the workers' movement into the present. Rancière has explained that he intended to counterpose this workers' voice to those of its would-be representatives. He was soon forced to abandon the initial outlines of the project for the simple reason that no such culture exists. What he encountered instead was a strange hybrid culture, in which workers refused to behave as workers. Rancière recounts, "I set out to find primitive revolutionary manifestoes, but what I found was texts which demanded in refined language that workers be considered as equals and their arguments responded to with proper arguments."[50] Workers did not simply struggle, as a certain line of thought would expect, nor did they valorize the trades they were compelled to adopt out of economic necessity; they founded journals, composed poetry, and imitated "bourgeois" forms of aesthetic contemplation. Donald Reid explains that this discovery required Rancière to jettison the epistemology of Marxist historiography. One limitation is that histories of class consciousness "mask the contradictions inherent in such entities."[51] Rancière has expressed the methodological insight as follows:

> In many cases, we have a tendency to interpret as collective practice or class "ethos" political statements which are in fact highly individualized. We attach too much importance to the collectivity of workers and not enough to its divisions; we look too much at worker culture and not enough at its encounters with other cultures.[52]

On a political level, the notion of a distinctive workers' culture partakes of what Rancière calls "exclusion by homage." This is typical of the analyses in which "homage to labor, proletarian consciousness, and the spirit of the people" perfect "forms of authority and the discourses of servitude."[53] In contrast to undertakings purporting to know in advance the nature of their objects, *Nights* refuses to categorize the texts composed by these workers. One witnesses Rancière deliberately avoiding the pretense of representing the voices of the archive, allowing workers' texts to circulate in his own, without correcting, classifying, or explicating them.

Nights recounts the lives of individuals who systematically refused their identities as workers. It takes up their story in the aftermath of the July Revolution of 1830 and follows their traces up to the revolt of 1848. It weaves their tale with poems, stories, and essays published in Christian Socialist journals such as *L'Atelier*, and the various publications founded by Fourierites, Saint Simonians, and Icarians, most notably, *La Ruche populaire*. More than a history of utopian socialism, *Nights* describes the subjective importance these associations had for many workers. On Rancière's telling, it was precisely their speculative dimension that was of greatest appeal, for what workers desired were activities in which they could comport themselves as intellectuals. In this sense, *Nights* is a long argument against the discursive-practical form the workers' movement assumed in the second half of the nineteenth century, with Rancière's narrative challenging many leftist shibboleths about the supposed dignity of labor. Rather than finding in manual work a source of pride, his workers describe it as torment. They used their nights, however, not simply to replenish the machines that would report to work the next morning; they engaged in creative and scholarly pursuits. These efforts, Rancière insists, can scarcely be understood as laying the foundations for the European workers' movement. In fact, these nights spinning tales did little besides demonstrate that humanity is not divisible into two distinct sets of capacities. Far from affirming anything like a proletarian identity, these writings, and the activity of writing itself, was a means of refuting what was taken to be natural: that workers work and have little time for anything else. To use a term central to Rancière's later political writings, we can say that their activities were a means of "dis-identification" in that they allowed workers to reject their assigned position in the division of labor through the assumption of capacities they were not thought to possess.

It is crucial for Rancière that these workers embraced modes of expression thought to be foreign to their station. In contrast to the tenets of Althusserian science, these workers sought to establish relationships of equality with owners and managers by deploying humanistic concepts. They asked: Does the category of "man" extend to us, and if so, are we not entitled to equal consideration? They engaged in spirited political discussions, speculations about alternative social conditions, and polemics with their bosses. These workers challenged their economic subordination and exclusion from political life with "the universal language of public argumentation."[54] At the same time, the workers immersed themselves in the creation and appreciation of complicated aesthetic forms. They organized readings, composed poems, commented upon the works of others, and adopted a generalized aesthetic outlook. For Rancière, these interests demonstrate the fallacy of restricting aesthetic pursuits to the leisure classes. These activities were, in a very real sense, a struggle over the delimitation of the economy of pleasures. In them, workers found more than a balm for the daily horrors experienced on the job; they demonstrated that "refined" pleasure is not the reserve of a few.

To achieve this demonstration, workers had to reject the implicit norms about the spaces in which they could appear, as well as ideas about how they should use their time. In this sense, to say that the workers' first victory was aesthetic is not to claim that it was about their having won the right to have their products counted as art. It was about invalidating the distribution of space and time that delimited the capacities they could be seen as possessing. Rancière has since explained how their activities operated upon the distribution of the sensible:

> In order to reframe the space-time of the "occupation," the workers had to invalidate the most common partition of time: the partition according to which workers would work during the day and sleep during the night. . . . That basic overturning involved a whole reconfiguration of the partition of experience. It involved a process of dis-identification, another relation to speech, visibility and so on.[55]

As this discussion indicates, Rancière understands aesthetics in a specialized sense. It pertains here, as it did for Kant, to the *a priori* forms of sensible intuition, that is, the factors—time and space— that occasion the way things appear. Time and space are political because their distributions define forms of subjectivity and political participation. The major obstacle to political participation is the tacit system of distributions that define who can be seen and heard. Rancière's study of nineteenth-century workers' archives taught him that political action begins with the simple act of rejecting the spaces and times one is expected to inhabit. He explains:

> Politics consists of reconfiguring the distribution of the sensible that defines the common of a community, by introducing into it subjects and new objects, in rendering visible those who were not, and of making understood as speakers those who were only understood as noisy animals.[56]

This process is initiated when one contests the spatial-temporal allocations of the dominant order. One can then, under the banner of equality, begin to define new capacities.

Gabriel Gauny in particular embodies the distinct form of aesthetic-political action at issue in *Nights*. Gauny worked days laying floors in bourgeois interiors and spent his off-hours composing a system of principles designed to convert his modest resources into the maximum quotient of freedom.[57] Gauny had a special knack for disassociating his mind from the torments the body endured on the job. By means of his imagination, he would transport himself into a realm of contentment. For Rancière, Gauny's description of a moment of reverie on the job approximates one of the central experiences codified by aesthetics. Gauny explains the laborer's aesthetic attitude thus:

> Believing himself at home, so long as he has not finished laying the floor, he loves the arrangement of a room. If the window opens out onto a garden or commands a view of a picturesque horizon, he stops his arms a moment and glides in imagination [*plane en idée*] toward the spacious view to enjoy it better than the possessors of the neighboring residences.[58]

For Rancière, this instance of disinterested contemplation demonstrates that the aesthetic relationship with the world is not dependent upon material privilege. It is in fact a means of auto-emancipation through which one departs from the dominant meaning that is made of sense. The glance fashioned by aesthetics, as we see in Chapter 3, is as much a new veil that comes to shroud the world in mystery, as it is a means of reshaping oneself through the elaboration of a deliberately decentered point of view. In the case of Gauny, it serves to disturb the distribution of the faculties necessitated by the world of work. The aesthetic attitude allows him to reorient his senses, remove them from the sights and sounds of the jobsite, and thereby insert himself into a sensorium of his own creation. With reference to this passage, Rancière has recently described the politics of these procedures: "The divorce between the labouring arms and the distracted gaze introduces the body of the worker into a new configuration of the sensible; it overthrows the 'right' relationship between what a body 'can' do and what it cannot."[59] The aesthetic, then, is a suspension of the habitual sense of sense wherein new capacities can be discovered.

These instances of systematic detachment from the preordained system of distributions, meanings, and identities formed the first moment in a process that allowed workers to create for themselves new bodies and new worlds. In *Nights*, we see these workers engaged in the constant struggle over the definition and redefinition of their capacities. For Rancière—whose thought is beginning to hit upon the central term of his later reflections on education, politics, and aesthetics—these endeavors can be viewed as attempts to implement and verify equality. The act of writing is a symbolic and practical rupture that effaces the barriers thought to exist between those granted the luxury of thought and those thought to be held captive by the space-time of their employment. It would be wrong to think that these pleasures are a retreat from the work of politics. Rancière: "These hard-won bonuses of time and liberty were not marginal phenomena, they were not diversions from the building of the worker movement and its great ideals. They were a revolution, discreet but radical nonetheless."[60] These everyday revolutions disturb our myths about the nature of work, the beings who carry it out, and the thought of what is possible. It must also be emphasized that, in a very real sense, these tales are a reminder to enjoy what presents itself to the senses, as much as they are about the struggle to assert the rights of the imagination. Gauny himself indicates that it is this capacity, central to the aesthetic tradition, which sets the process in motion.

1.4 LESSONS ON PHILOSOPHER-KINGS

As we have seen, at issue in *Nights* is the practical refutation of the idea that workers should perform only the functions that correspond with their natures. *The Philosopher and His Poor* traces this notion from Plato's argument in the *Republic* that "to do one's own business and not to be a busybody is justice" through to contemporary sociology.[61] It shows how this principle founds a division in which some are thought to be endowed with the capacity for thought, while others are destined only for work. The style and terrain of *The Philosopher* are obviously very different than *Nights*, taking aim at the textual-practical divisions erected when philosophy thinks about the poor. The trajectory, however, is a familiar one. *The Philosopher* rejoins the critique of philosophy announced in *La leçon*, by attempting to show how philosophical thought, in order to mark its difference from other practices of making sense of sense, denies the poor capacities for thought. Indeed, it is not difficult to see the jibes at science throughout as an echo of Rancière's critique of Althusserianism. In the critique of Althusser and with the analysis contained in *The Philosopher*, Rancière describes how a certain mode of thought is detached from the general distribution of practices through a discourse on those who labor with their hands. For Rancière, philosophy locks up the poor because it is interested in preserving its own purity. "It is for the sake of the philosopher, not the city, that one must postulate a radical break between the order of leisure and the order of servile labor."[62] The book traces the form philosophy assumes when it founds itself by partitioning the world on the basis of supposedly distinct natures. Rancière shows how theoretical discourse—which includes Marxism, Sartre's existential-Marxism, and the sociology of Pierre Bourdieu—needs to castigate its others—sophistry, poetry, the confused thought of artisans, and aesthetics—in order to separate itself from the other means by which the sensible is interpreted, distributed, and redistributed.

What is of interest is how Plato's principle that "each ought to perform one social function for which his nature best suits him" justifies a certain separation of theory from other practices.[63] The thread which brings the philosopher-king into being begins with the move from the city of simple pleasures to the luxurious city replete with fine foods, specialized material production, artistic forms, and eventually warfare. Material comforts require someone dedicated to the protection of the republic's wealth, which in turn necessitates specialists dedicated to their education. Someone, it is felt, must preside over imitations, musical melodies, and gymnastic exercises to ensure they are appropriate for the souls who, it is hoped, will be capable of discerning friend from foe. In the *Republic*, philosophy regulates production, determines the auspicious moments for reproduction, decides which spectacles are appropriate, and generally assures that the division of labor remains intact. The philosopher, moreover, promotes or demotes individuals based on judgments about their aptitudes. With carefully designed ordeals, philosophers determine who is best suited for the respective functions of the state. These procedures, Rancière notes, are not so much about constructing a meritocracy as they are about guaranteeing that the orders of the city remain pure. Men of iron and bronze must be prevented from contaminating those of silver. Of course what is most jealously guarded is the gold of philosophy, with Plato's text containing several screeds directed at those who, in spite of their fortunes, insist on pursuing it. For Rancière, philosophy functions as the arbiter of the sensible. The philosopher is charged with ensuring that individuals do not violate their nature and with it the division of labor. Plato's philosopher presides over the distribution of lots and polices them with a discourse on capacities. He adjudicates among different discourses, practices, and imitations to ensure that they do not introduce into the community forms of sense in conflict with the dominant regime of interpretation.

In the republic, social harmony is purchased with a "noble lie" that ascribes the contingencies of social inequality to the dispensations of nature. Indulging in this lie, however, philosophy draws close to its old adversaries, those other ways of making sense that it disparages, sophistry and poetry. How can the science of the true differentiate itself from those bad forms of lying that spell the ruin of the republic, when it itself composes fictions? For accomplishing this, the artisan plays an indispensable role: a discourse on his nature divides discourse in two. Rancière notes how workers are brought forward whenever there is a need to distinguish philosophy from its doubles. This is the significance of the shoemaker, "the generic name for the man who is not where he ought to be if the order of estates is to get on with the order of discourse."[64] In Rancière's study, this figure symbolizes the general disdain philosophy harbors for the laboring classes. The supposed baseness of labor outfits Plato with a weapon for combating those forms of thought said to be of mixed parentage, that is, guilty of bearing too much resemblance to the trades. Comparison with the artisan thus allows one to see the sophist for what he is, a petit-bourgeois intellectual motivated by financial gain, just as it makes it possible to separate those who are truly inspired, the philosophers, from the poets and orators controlled by the power of the purse. Is it not always possible to sniff out the commercial interests lurking in sophistry and poetry? Was it not a major plank in Socrates' defense that he accepted no money for conducting his affairs?

The philosopher is thus distinguishable in that he knows the correct way in which to administer the lie. In fact, he is the one being for whom it is not incompatible with his nature to engage in fictions. The principle of justice again comes to play. It ensures that each person does only one thing, preventing the adoption or imitation of other practices. Philosophers, on the other hand, are those who are capable of imitation. They make of the sensible the meanings they choose, which, it is claimed, serve the community's welfare. As a result of the discourse on laborers, and the divisions they define, "playing, lying, and appearance" are reserved for philosophy.[65] Within the republic's distribution of the sensible, workers are those without rights of imitation, while the sophist, poet, and painter are simply bad workers who "transgress the rule fixing their status."[66]

As Rancière thus presents it, philosophy is a form of thinking that forcefully declaims its birth and obsessively guards its lineage. It is marked by a fundamental and ultimately untenable drive for purity, which compels it to compose paranoid genealogies of origin— distinguishable from critical genealogies—by means of which it attempts to separate itself from other practices. Philosophy, by Rancière's estimation, "can trace the circle of its own autonomy only through an arbitrary discourse on nature and nobility."[67] For this reason, it needs to define itself against other forms of life. The "aristocratic lock-up of philosophy" that Rancière describes refers not to the totalitarian framework Plato is said to have bequeathed; it designates philosophy's reliance upon a hierarchical social order where the negative value of the artisan serves as a point of differentiation.[68] The strange virtue of Plato is that he does not hide this mechanism. He confesses to the manner in which philosophy distinguishes itself from the distribution of the sensible. Rancière:

> The provocative power of Plato lies in the extraordinary frankness with which he expresses what future epistemologies and sociologies will try to obscure: that the order of the true can no more

be grounded in a science of science than the social order can be grounded in the division of labor. The social relation and the order of discourse depend upon one and the same fiction, the fiction that chases the artisan from the realm of fiction. What is excluded is the *lie of art*, the lie that is practiced unwittingly. At the juncture of the philosophical order and the social order only one lie may proceed, the noble lie of nature.[69]

In order to preserve its kingdom, philosophy must justify itself, and it attempts to accomplish this by shuttling between discourse and the social. Philosophy must therefore expel those practices and distributions that would contest its account of the social. At bottom, Rancière contends, the philosopher fears not that "men of iron will get hold of the truth; he is afraid that artists will get hold of appearance."[70] What Platonic philosophy thus forges is a system for chasing away other means of distributing the sensible. In this, philosophy reveals itself as a means of interpreting sense that refuses to acknowledge the fundamental separation of sense from itself, what Rancière terms dissensus. It wants there to be a single meaning assigned to sense, its own, and thus a single direction for the community.

Rancière's topographical analysis follows this aristocratic lockup of philosophy from Greece into the twentieth century. His discussions of Marx and Sartre can be read as the effort to dislodge certain predispositions in leftist thinking, politics, and pedagogy. While there are considerable differences between these thinkers, one can say that both rely upon a conceptualization of the poor as an inert mass, whose passivity is the *sine qua non* of its would-be representatives. This conceptualization is a variation on the Platonic distribution: science flourishes to the extent that workers remain subordinate to the master thinker. The Marxian and Sartrean endeavors each restrict the business of thinking, refuse prospects of auto-emancipation, and come to castigate those mixed beings contaminated by their trades. Workers are those who have no time for the labor of the dialectic; they thus require specialists dedicated to its cause. With such assumptions, ostensibly critical positions reaffirm the most traditional divisions of labor. And, for Rancière, they fail to arrive at what would be a radical alternative: the joining together of the realms of practice, thought, and the affirmation of equality.

For many readers, the real target of *The Philosopher* was not philosophy as such, but one of its descendents in sociology, Pierre Bourdieu.[71]

It should be recalled that *The Philosopher* was written at a time when the socialist government in France was turning to the social sciences for answers about how to alleviate growing disparities in educational results. Kristin Ross contends that Bourdieu produced an analysis "entirely keeping with his time," describing the challenges faced by teachers, students, and administrators, while mourning the lack of any real alternatives.[72] While Bourdieu's *The Inheritors* and *Reproduction* declare themselves as radical critiques of the class system, they also describe its immutability.[73] Rancière's enterprise should thus be viewed as an effort to disturb the fatalism that had accrued around the politics of higher education. This theme comes clearly to the fore in 1987 with the publication of *Schoolmaster*. There, the postulate of equality is raised against the would-be educational reformers whose very discourses are held to reinforce inequality. Before offering a reading of that text (Section 1.5), we should highlight the critique of Bourdieu articulated by *The Philosopher*.

That critique is twofold: first, sociological demystification is too simple; it starts from the premise of inequality, thereby discovering its traces everywhere. Bourdieu maps with exacting detail the educational rituals, cultural games, and symbolic forms through which the rich exercise dominion over other classes. Is it, however, a great secret that the economically dominated are also culturally dominated? In the second instance, Bourdieu's endeavor is problematic because it profits from this denunciation. Sociology, like philosophy, lives on the division of labor, and by presenting itself as an exhaustive science of the social order it attempts to assume the latter's mantle. Once enthroned, it too will police the sensible and ensure that everyone displays the signs corresponding to his nature; however, whereas the philosopher recognized the contingent nature of these distributions, the sociologist leaves us with little hope for changing them. "To ensure his kingship," Rancière explains, the sociologist "absolutized the arbitrary."[74] The reign of "sociocracy" is premised upon treating as illusory the ideal of equality.[75] It seeks to demystify this political value, reproaching those who take seriously its aspirations. In Bourdieu's analysis of the educational apparatus, for example, equality is a suspect term, one which masks the very mechanisms of reproduction. As Rancière isolates the logic of Bourdieu's analysis, the school "eliminates *by making people believe that it does not eliminate.*"[76] That is, it excludes those who do not understand the reasons for their exclusion.[77] To illustrate democracy's failure, sociology posits a fundamental separation between the attitudes of workers and those of the rich. From its vantage point, there is little room for anything besides the performance of a class-based identity, and it will not cease disparaging those who refuse the times and spaces of their class. What Bourdieu's sociology cannot think are the practices and subjectivities, such as those of the worker-poets described in *Nights*, that conflict with its narrow definitions of capacity.

In order to maintain its preserve, sociology, like philosophy, requires the meaning of the sensible to be straightforward, transparent, and univocal. Sociology needs the division of labor, and therefore is compelled to denounce as fraudulent any practices, discourses, and attitudes that would contest the meanings it assigns to the sensible. Sociology cannot abide the separation of the sensible from itself. It is for this reason that Bourdieu declares war on aesthetics, that form of thinking premised on the idea that our sense of sense is never absolute. In *Distinction*, Bourdieu argues that each social group has its own class-specific predilections.[78] Accordingly, taste, in the aesthetic sense, is little more than the extension of material privilege. Rancière has a helpful way of parsing the endeavor when he explains that, for Bourdieu, "taste is *one* where Kant divides it and, conversely, that it is divided in two where Kant makes it common to all."[79] In the first instance, Bourdieu rejects Kant's distinction between the agreeable and the beautiful. For him, the same *habitus* judges both wine and art. Secondly, where Kant postulated a "shared sense," Bourdieu splits the populace into those enjoying the taste of freedom and those who know only necessity.[80] For him, class determines taste, with the symbolic universe rigorously divisible on the basis of income. In order to rule out the kinds of shared experiences of interest to aesthetic theorists, as well as what one might term "aspirational taste," Bourdieu is compelled to investigate more than acts of judgment. Despite the differences between the cognitive and the aesthetic, Bourdieu's surveys attempted to determine whether the surveyed *knew* what they claimed to *like*.[81] The exams he administered under the guise of surveying preferences reveal the true nature of the sociological enterprise: it seeks to contain the possibility of divergent meanings being given to the sensible. "The evil is the community of appearances," as Rancière explains, for it is there that the science of the sociologist is threatened.[82] In order to preserve itself, Bourdieu's sociology must disabuse good-natured aesthetes of the notion that there might be a common humanity detectable in the feelings initiated by nature and art, while depriving the working classes of a means of countering their lot.

Bourdieu's position is not as original as it pretends to be. It reproduces the conventional prejudice according to which aesthetics is simply another name for privilege. We see in Chapter 3 that Rancière's work is developed to counter this premise. We should note here, however, the account of aesthetics that emerges in the critique of Bourdieu, for it is one to which Rancière returns frequently. At the end of *The Philosopher*, Rancière describes aesthetics as a means of dis-identification, opposing to the theses of sociology those of Kant and Schiller. This is how he describes the previously discussed passage from Gabriel Gauny:

> The acquisition of this aesthetic gaze, the paradoxical philosophy of asceticism that this dispossessed worker draws from it, this torsion of the habitus that he imposes upon himself and proposes is also the claim of a human right to happiness that exceeds the rhetoric of proletarian recruiters.[83]

One virtue of the aesthetic, then, is that it conducts us into an indeterminate zone where the destiny of class is thrown off. It neutralizes the properties thought to inhere in a body, transporting it into a world where the distributions of places, times, and capacities are not permanently fixed. It allows sense to be separated from the distribution of the sensible.

As a philosophical discourse, aesthetics contains, in Rancière's estimation, the promise of philosophizing in a fundamental connection with equality. Considered against the backdrop of the history we have been recounting, aesthetics represents both a radical departure and a paradoxical undertaking. It affirms the traditional philosophical vocation of discernment, that is, of drawing distinctions between what is better and worse, while coupling it with a consideration of others. Is this not what Kant demands of us when he describes the pure form of the aesthetic judgment as a reflection upon how everyone might feel when presented with a given representation? Whether or not such a philosophical project is actually tenable is the question with which Rancière leaves his readers at the end of *The Philosopher*. Is it possible, he asks, to simultaneously think the "hierarchy of values and the equality of mixture?"[84] Needless to say, such a thought prohibits philosophy from locking up others in order to secure its hold on the sensible, repudiates the desire to give lessons, and requires that we specify what is meant by equality.

1.5 LESSONS FROM EQUALITY

By any measure *The Ignorant Schoolmaster* is an idiosyncratic book. It recounts the curious fortunes of Joseph Jacotot, an artilleryman in the Republican armies who, when forced into exile by the Bourbon Restoration, devised a system for teaching what he did not know. While in exile, he obtained a position as a lecturer at the University of Louvain, where he encountered a group of students eager to learn from him, but who matched his ignorance of Flemish with a lack of French. Fortune put at his disposal a bilingual edition of *Télémaque*, Fénelon's much-admired portrayal of the wanderings of Telemachus. Jacotot asked his students to learn the French text by comparing it with the Flemish. This "desperate empiricism" yielded unexpected results: after some time, students were not only able to read the French text, but compose essays about its meaning.[85] They were learning without Jacotot's instruction, and he soon employed this method to "teach" other subjects in which he was not proficient. Chance had allowed Jacotot to see what is often obscured in traditional pedagogical relationships: one learns not by internalizing the knowledge of another, but through the exercise of one's own faculties. Simply, what Jacotot had discovered was a way to remove obstacles to students' abilities to make their own discoveries. He and his disciples were not shy about the method's potential to emancipate people from servitude, and in the course of defending it, came to oppose traditional pedagogical practice and most forms of authority. As a result of these experiences, Jacotot was led to formulate a theory of radical intellectual equality. He affirmed that all people are in possession of equal mental capacities.

The idea of equality Rancière finds in Jacotot's writings serves as a touchstone for the analyses he conducts of art and politics. In his telling, Rancière's voice mingles thoroughly with Jacotot's own. In fact, the book, committed to denouncing explication as a form of stultification, works assiduously to avoid the trappings of commentary, and shuns many of the devices—for example, "Jacotot says"—with which authors separate themselves from their subjects. It uses the various documents in which Jacotot propagated his method to create a demonstration of equality. Throughout, Rancière frequently employs the present tense, allowing one to read Jacotot's defense of the equality of intelligences against the presuppositions of Bourdieu's sociology, the Althusserian idea of ideology, and philosophy as it is often practiced. In any context, Rancière contends, the deployment of equality allows previously suppressed capacities to emerge. Its supposition is a destabilizing force which allows those invoking it to assert themselves as political agents. Equality cannot, however, be gradually implemented with measures partaking of inequality, as many political and educational reformers believe. It is either asserted at the outset or is irremediably lost. Combating inequality on behalf of others assumed to be incapable of emancipating themselves simply reproduces the dominant logic of subordination. The assumption of equality provides a different point of departure. With Jacotot, Rancière argues that equality is not a goal to be reached, but a presupposition that gives rise to alternative forms of community, communication, and pedagogy. It is an assumption whose logic must be implemented, and whose functioning must be continually verified.

Few, if any, defenses of this premise will satisfy inequality's advocates. They believe nature has distributed the gifts of the mind unequally. One can speculate that the reason for this commitment is that it justifies their authority. What sustains the positions of educators, to say nothing of the social order, if not the notion that some are incapable of thinking as well as others? Rancière, with Jacotot, admits that the equality of intelligences is a hypothesis in search of proof. In fact, both shift the terms of the debate, contending that while it may be difficult to establish the presupposition definitively, it is a belief that it is legitimate to hold. For Rancière, "our problem isn't proving that all intelligence is equal. It's seeing what can be done under that supposition."[86] In order to maintain this position, all that is required is that inequality not be accepted as an explanation for why some perform certain tasks better than others. Jacotot's defense first separates intelligence from its material effects. It is unquestionable that some succeed in jumping through the hoops of educational institutions more quickly than others; however, this does not mean their performances can be described in terms of intelligence. How, Rancière asks, can one move seamlessly from material facts to the immaterial realm of mind?[87] The second line of defense entails affirming the juncture between thought and expression. This means that, for Jacotot, thought is prior to language, and that all communication is first a will to communicate sentiments and reasoning by means of arbitrary signs.[88] Even if communication is sometimes stilted, it is still possible to contend that the animating intellectual activity is equal. Jacotot thus proffered a different interpretation for why some students appear to learn more quickly: dissimilar results are attributable to different intensities of the will. Intelligence, in all its forms, is the same; the concentration or distraction of the will results in different performances. Rancière: "I will not say that one's faculties are inferior to the other's. I will only suppose that the two faculties haven't been equally exercised."[89] The presupposition of equality, then, is that the world is not divisible into two different types of minds. Intelligence is equal. This is an idea that Jacotot thought accurately summarized his experiences of people learning without having anything explained to them.

Believing that anyone could learn anything, Jacotot dubbed his method "universal teaching." As he understood it, universal teaching approximates the natural method by which one learns through the comparison of two facts. To begin in the universal method, a student must identify a fact, relate it to something else, and recount the connection between the two. For this, no explanation from another is needed. All that is required is the confidence to venture forward into a world of unconnected facts, the will to focus the intelligence, and the courage to find the language for communicating one's adventure. It is true that a master is sometimes required since the will is weak and prone to distraction. The ignorant master, however, is simply someone who verifies our efforts, provides encouragement, and keeps us on track. In this, he is distinguishable from the master who employs explication. This refusal is the key difference between universal teaching and most forms of pedagogy. Explication is the procedure by which a teacher clarifies a text's meaning by revealing what lurks behind its words. It supplements a given text with a commentary designed to make apparent the meaning of the first. As such, it is predicated upon the assumption that the text would not be legible without the professor's intervention. The process thus continually reveals what the student would not have gathered without assistance. As Rancière diagnoses it, explication institutes a relationship between *intelligence and intelligence*, convincing the student of the inferiority of his own. With explication, one learns little more than that one's intelligence relies upon another's. When the student's intelligence is thereby subordinated, the relationship is termed stultification.[90] More than a simple method, explication is the "structuring fiction" of a hierarchical world.[91] "Before being the act of the pedagogue, explication is the myth of pedagogy, the parable of a world divided into knowing minds and ignorant ones, ripe minds and immature ones, the capable and the incapable, the intelligent and the stupid."[92] Universal teaching, on the other hand, is predicated on the assumption that the student possesses equal intellectual capacities. It works to disassociate the master's intelligence from the student's, inaugurating instead a relationship of *will to will*. In universal teaching, a third term is necessary to hollow out the position of the master. The book, in Jacotot's case *Télémaque*, served as a necessary mediation. It allowed Jacotot to distance himself from his intelligence, thereby freeing up the student to discover his own.[93] The master compels the student to make a greater effort, to draw more connections, recognize deeper patterns, and to communicate the results more elegantly. He does not, for all that, tell the student what to think about what he finds. He simply provides the occasion for the student to discover his own capacity.

This sequence whereby the mind realizes its own powers without reliance upon others is what is known as emancipation. For Jacotot and Rancière, emancipation is opposed, point by point, to stultification. Whereas the latter convinces an individual of his dependence upon the intelligence of others, emancipation enables him to discover what he is capable of. The emancipated individual does not doubt his powers, nor does he attempt to subordinate others. He recognizes himself as possessing capacities equal to those of everyone else. Again, the claim is not that all expressions are necessarily of the same quality, but simply that they do not spring from two different natures. Rancière:

> There aren't two sorts of minds. There is inequality in the *manifestations* of intelligence, according to greater or lesser energy communicated to the intelligence by the will for discovering and combining new relations; but there is no hierarchy of *intellectual capacity*. Emancipation is becoming conscious of this equality of *nature*.[94]

Universal teaching's aim was not to form scholars. Its goal was to enable individuals to launch their own intellectual adventures. In this sense, it is opposed to the institutional structures, procedures, and objects of explication. Jacotot disseminated the method widely, helping the illiterate "teach" their children how to read. Anything could serve as a starting point, which is why Jacotot also termed the method "panecastic."[95] The name indicates that the products of human intelligence are not of fundamentally different kinds, that the totality of human experience can be reached from each manifestation, and thus that an adventure can begin anywhere.

Placing thought before language is essential if we are not to subordinate intelligence to the social order or the vagaries of expression. It also serves to transmute knowledge into a creative activity. According to Jacotot, the chief virtue of intelligence is poetry, understood in an expansive sense. We speak as poets when we recount the mind's adventure with imperfect signs. Knowledge consists of drawing connections and inventing the language in which to communicate the findings. Rancière explains, "In the act of speaking, man doesn't transmit his knowledge, he makes poetry; he translates and invites others to do the same. He communicates as an *artisan*: as a person who handles words like tools."[96] Moreover, all communication is creation twice over: it consists of translating into signs one's experience of navigating the world, and the process of counter-translation by means of which one attempts to understand the thoughts of another. In this sense, Jacotot and Rancière contend, artists more readily discover the language of equality than university professors. They renounce the tyranny of the fixed message, creating instead spaces for play, reciprocal engagement, and negotiated meaning. Artistic forms of communication credit their readers and viewers with possessing profound experiences and equal capacities.

For Rancière, the idea of the equality of intelligences is an ever-renewable, untimely presupposition that can disrupt a given distribution of the sensible. In this respect, it plays an essential role in his account of politics. For him, politics is the process of staging the conflict between the world of hierarchy and the one fashioned under the assumption of equality. It should be made explicit that, for Rancière, equality is a supposition in search of confirmation. "Equality is not given, nor is it claimed; it is practiced, it is *verified*."[97] The assumption of radical intellectual equality bolsters capacities previously unrecognized or denied. It allows those deprived of parts within the common world the ability to reconfigure the sensible. Equality does not, however, found new societies, and Jacotot, after some mishaps, was deeply suspicious of all attempts to translate the principles of universal teaching into social arrangements. He strenuously resisted the insertion of universal teaching into organized political frameworks, viewing the latter as bound up with creating distances in order to enjoy suppressing them. For him, the institutionalization of the equality of intelligences was its betrayal. He warned, as Rancière explains, that "individuals are real beings, and society a fiction. It's for real beings that equality has value, not for a fiction."[98] The problem, for Jacotot, was determining how one could become and remain emancipated within the inevitably unequal distributions of the social. In this sense, Rancière retains Jacotot's suspicions regarding institutions claiming to turn men into equals; however, as we see in the following chapter, he argues it is possible to marshal the supposition of equality against unbalanced distributions of bodies, voices, and capacities in order to make life more livable.

CONCLUSION

In this chapter we have explored Rancière's early writings with an eye toward the formation of some of the notions employed in his analyses of politics and aesthetics. We have highlighted the role that a critical engagement with Althusserian Marxism, the archives of the workers' movement, and the history of philosophy play in his understanding of the division of labor and the means by which it is contested. We have likewise witnessed in his presentation of the writings of Joseph Jacotot the articulation of the central element of his own thought: the need to suppose, assert, and verify equality. It remains to indicate how this trajectory relates to his practice of philosophy. Will it permit us to analyze, argue, and invent without contrasting such procedures with those deemed incapable of accomplishing such rigors? Does it allow us to define a form of thinking that would not erect a barrier between philosophy and non-philosophy? Can thought sidestep the positions of mastery from which it has traditionally claimed to give lessons? I contend that Rancière's work does just this, for three interconnected reasons.

Rancière's thought demonstrates itself to be a ruthless enemy of the aristocratic heritage of philosophy. His historical topography exposes the machinations by which philosophy attempts to deny its positioning within the distribution of the sensible. It opposes philosophy's attempts to found itself as an autonomous discourse, removed from the seeable, sayable, and thinkable. Calling attention to a division is to step beyond it. Rancière's thought devotes itself to tracing the terrain on which philosophy has constituted itself through comparison with those unworthy of gathering its fruits. In doing so, it returns philosophical thought to the field of practices from which it attempted to separate itself. It renounces this reliance upon dividing the world on the basis of intelligence, without giving up the ability to draw distinctions. It transfers the act of dividing into a form of analysis that gauges discourses, arrangements, and institutions in terms of their relationship with equality.

Formulating this analysis of the common world in terms of divisions within the sensible deprives philosophy of the means by which, historically, it has monopolized the conversation on the sphere of practices. Philosophy functioned by marginalizing other practices and reserving for itself the right to adjudicate the sensible. Rancière shows how this monopoly is dependent upon a distribution that denies thought to certain practices. Granting credence to the sensible ends philosophy's kingship at the same time as it restores value to other means of distributing and redistributing sense. This displacement of philosophy allows us to discern the ways in which the arts, including philosophy, are spatial and temporal practices that distribute what is perceptible, thinkable, and possible. It also means that the various arts—fine art, literature, politics, and cinema—can relate to one another on an equal footing, with philosophy content to take its place alongside these other arts in a sharing of the sensible.

Whether what emerges is still recognizable as philosophy is a question readers can consider for themselves. It is perhaps important to draw a distinction between philosophy as it is traditionally conceived and the philosophical practice Rancière develops. "Philosophical practice" is not intended in the heroic, Althusserian sense. It indicates instead that philosophy is one exercise among many, with distinctive, historically constituted capacities for clarifying, evaluating, and shifting the terrain of the sensible. Accordingly, philosophical practice is to be distinguished from other practices not by the purity of its genealogy but the modality of its questioning. That form of questioning, as we have seen, is concerned, in the first instance, with diagnosing the presuppositions shaping our present. It sets out the parameters delimiting what can appear to the senses, the logics carrying them forward, and the possibilities to which they give rise or foreclose. It is significant that Rancière's philosophical practice relies upon an alternative point of departure, one outlined by the supposition of equality. This assumption defines the difficult tightrope Rancière walks: he attempts to formulate a critical language for the analysis of the sensible, without presupposing an addressee's incapacity. Said another way, he attempts to create a distance with respect to our present configuration of the sensible, without instantiating differences among the persons sharing in it. In this sense, his practice owes much to strands drawn from the history of aesthetics, that form of philosophy which recognizes the constant separation of the sensible from itself. The significance of aesthetics, for Rancière, consists of thus joining together the act of drawing distinctions with the affirmation of equality. Aesthetics, paradoxically, asks us to evaluate modes of communication, artistic forms, and other arrangements both in terms of our own taste and the thought of others. Whether or not such a reading of aesthetics is sustainable is a question pursued in Chapter 5. It is nevertheless this understanding of the tradition's ambitions which animates Rancière's distinctive style of thinking.[99]

CHAPTER 2

POLITICS BY PROCESS OF ELIMINATION

INTRODUCTION

This chapter introduces Rancière's contributions to political theory by tracing the equation his work builds between politics and democracy. It defends the idea that "politics" should be reserved for democratic forms of organization, communication, practice, and action. This means that politics is distinguishable from other ways of ordering the community by its most basic element, equality. Without equality, distributions, operations, and discourses partake of the opposite of politics, what Rancière calls "the police," which is, as Alain Badiou has noted, a play on the Greek word *polis*.[1] It designates those distributions erected in order to support selective accountings of the city. The police maintains the fiction that no one of any significance has been prevented from taking part in the determination of the common life. For Rancière, politics is the process by which the "part of those without part" counter all such counts based upon their exclusion.[2] To understand Rancière's thought, it is not necessary to insist exclusively upon this formulation, "part of those without part" [*la part des sans-part*], derived from Aristotle's description of the Athenian *dēmos* as that group which "had no part in anything."[3] It occurs alongside other formulations, such as "the count of the uncounted" [*le compte des incomptés*], to express the idea that politics is the process of disrupting the distribution of parts and roles through a claim about the equality of anyone with everyone. With both formulations, what Rancière is describing is the *dēmos*, the very subject of politics. The *dēmos* is a political subject inasmuch as it is capable of exceeding and thereby undermining the police's accounting. Whereas the police defines the *polis* as unified and whole, politics consists of contesting the very definition of the community. The part of those without part is a construction that disturbs the city's logic of counting by inscribing within it an agent not reducible to one of the existing factions. The *dēmos*, in whatever period it finds itself, is that collective subject that comes into being by resisting the attempt of the few to apportion for themselves the rights to direct the community. In order to gain visibility, it contests the assumptions about who belongs, what capacities they possess, and what roles they can occupy. According to Rancière, the means by which the *dēmos* achieves this is equality. In the first instance, this indicates that the *dēmos* comes into being through the paradoxical identification of itself with the whole of the community, that is, by insisting upon the fundamental equality of its members. It also means that politics is not, for Rancière, understandable as a negotiation between the competing interests of already existing parties. Politics is a rupture of this mode of being together that occurs through the assertion of universal equality. With equality, the part of those without part offer another ac/count of the city. Politics is resistance to the domination resulting from the exclusion from "politics."

Rancière's contributions to democratic theory emerge from readings of both ancient and recent history. His return to Greek philosophy serves as a critique of "the politics of philosophers," a label of disparagement referring to philosophy's attempts to end politics. *Disagreement*, his most systematic work on politics to date, shows how, historically, philosophy has been antagonistic to democracy. Rancière contends nevertheless that one can learn much from the texts of Plato and Aristotle regarding the nature of democracy. In this chapter, we attempt to distill a more general conception of Rancière's politics by following his reflections on the meaning of Greek democracy. As one might expect, these analyses are bolstered by references to political struggles native to France, the history of the workers' movement, and the pedagogical practice of Joseph Jacotot. It should also be kept in mind that Rancière's revitalization of democracy in leftist political discourse was contemporaneous with the democratic struggles carried out in Eastern Europe and Latin America. His work can, in part, be seen as attempting to clarify and give sustenance to these movements, as well as offering a more radical alternative to liberalism's theories of democracy. I hope to show how understanding democracy as a disruptive, destabilizing, and generative force can inspire alternatives to the state-sponsored consensus that restricts the possible.

2.1 ON THE TERRAIN OF POLICED CONSENSUS

Rancière attributes the weakness of contemporary politics to the politics of consensus. By his understanding, consensus is the means by which a polity attempts to prevent the emergence of the *dēmos*. Consensus aims to avoid this group's politicization by distributing the various parts of a community without remainder. "The consensus system rests on these solid axioms: the whole is all, nothing is nothing."[4] As the absence of politics, it attempts to render invisible and inaudible those discourses, issues, individuals, and groups that would tear open the self-evidence of the *polis* by giving voice to their exclusion. In a word, consensus posits that a given community has been fairly counted. It is not, obviously, the goal of politics, as it is for liberal theorists; it is the sensible configuration politics must overcome.

Consensus results from and relies upon the police operations that delimit the boundaries of the perceptible, the thinkable, and the possible. "The police," in Rancière's sense, does not refer to the truncheon-wielding cops who crack the skulls of striking workers or unruly students. It is the means by which a society enforces its distribution of the sensible. As we have seen, the distribution of the sensible refers to the general laws distributing lines of sight, forms of speech, and estimations of a body's capacity. For Rancière, the police is a distribution of the sensible that denies the ability of the part without part to supplement the *polis* with a claim of equality.[5] It attempts to contain, manage, co-opt, and undermine the basic "dispute" [*litige*] about the constitution of the community. Some operations include: the selective framing of issues by mainstream news organizations; the management of economic, cultural, and existential insecurity; and the transformation of political names—"the people" or "workers"—into socio-economic identities. All have as their goal the dispersal of the *dēmos* through its equation with the counted parts of the community.

To enforce the status quo, the police attempts to limit political participation. It does this by delimiting in advance the sphere of political appearances, indicating who is capable of speaking, what they are able to say, and what can become a matter of dispute. Sensible operations set the limits of what is conceivable and possible. Rancière:

> The police is thus first an order of bodies that defines the allocation of ways of doing, ways of being, and ways of saying, and sees that those bodies are assigned by name to a particular place and task; it is an order of the visible and the sayable that sees that a particular activity is visible and another is not, that this speech is understood as discourse and another as noise.[6]

The police monopolizes the interpretations of sense in the attempt to create a single direction for the movement of society. It is not, however, a conspiratorial program, and it is certainly not what is commonly described today as "spectacle." The police is primarily a logic of inequality that creates forms of inclusion and exclusion by partitioning the sensible. Police divisions distribute bodies and voices, define what is seen and unseen, and draw boundaries, such as those that exist between the public and the private. It is the police, for example, that tells us that salary disputes are private matters between workers and employers. It can thus be said that "police" refers to the series of assumptions that structure life in common with the aim of avoiding politics. Indeed, it is the interpretation of sense that attempts to strip the sensible of its litigious character.

Rancière describes ours as a "consensual time" to indicate that the logics of de-politicization are becoming more sophisticated and politics itself more difficult.[7] He has set his conception of politics in opposition to a specific variety of consensus prevalent today: the discourses ascendant since the fall of the Berlin Wall that attempt to legitimate the unrestricted reign of the market. This form of consensus employs a particular series of operations to convert democratic struggles into a series of managed conflicts. It frequently exploits the cover of political realism, the doctrine that justifies war, social hierarchies, and economic inequalities by invoking necessity. "Realism is the absorption of all reality and all truth in the category of the only thing possible."[8] It is the ideology that claims to be beyond ideology, one which would have us believe it is now possible to base government on a pragmatic estimation of human nature, the market's laws, and the global situation. We witness a version of realism whenever leaders exploit the imperatives of modernization, economic necessity, or notions such as the "post-9/11 world" to justify unpalatable decisions. Realism gains traction by promoting itself as the efficient alternative to the chimeras of democracy. Our managerial states are its agents and our corporations, its primary beneficiaries. They encourage citizens to be reasonable in their demands and to acknowledge the contingencies of the globalized world, asking us to be content with what we have, and, in lean times, to give back some of our "privileges."

Realism is thus one form that police operations take in their efforts to put an end to politics. It is a discourse that tries to convince us that the existing world is the only one possible. As such, it aims to liquidate the ideas, teleologies, utopian promises, and political names that, in previous epochs, exposed the community to dissensus, or fundamental disputes about its parts and their relations. While realism presents itself as the only rational choice in the management of common life, Rancière makes clear that it too contains its articles of faith. In instances where realism is used to undermine pension funds, lower wages, deny people healthcare, or limit democracy it promises a future in which prosperity and security will offset these short-term inconveniences. What, Rancière asks, is more utopian than a schema whose goal continually recedes into the future?[9]

As we have already argued, Rancière's topographical analysis attempts to make apparent the logic leading to dead-end conclusions, certain closures of the sensible world that restrict the conceivable and the possible. These analyses are animated by the desire to protect the possible as possible, and prevent it from being closed by the police's distribution of capacities. It would be a mistake to think of Rancière as simply battling against ideas, for the positions, logics, and conclusions he charts are not those of a discursive order. They become active in the sphere of practice by circumscribing conversations, delimiting objects, distributing capacities, and defining identities. The various interventions he has carried out in his short yet trenchant essays, as well as his more programmatic reflections on the history and nature of politics, can thus be conceived as operations designed to break apart univocal distributions of the sensible. His analyses circumvent the consensus forced upon thought and practice by discursive-practical constellations such as realism. As such, Rancière encourages us to question the notion that governance is about the management of a shared, if inevitably unequal, prosperity. And, more radically, he opposes the equation of politics with the state.

Against state-supported consensus and its realist theoreticians, Rancière contends it is possible to reinvent politics. He proposes to us that the sensible is never as solid as it claims to be. It can continually be pierced by individuals and groups who marshal the supposition of equality in order to litigate their form of part-taking. Indeed, politics, as dissensus, is the "manifestation of a separation [*écart*] of the sensible from itself."[10] This separation of the sensible takes place when a group moves from invisibility to visibility through the polemical assertion of its equality with the other members of the community. Essential for understanding Rancière's account of politics is a consideration of how these notions emerge through his reading of Greek philosophy. This direction demonstrates a fundamental suspicion regarding political liberalism and theories of deliberative democracy. In fact, he contends we are more likely to find helpful understandings of the process by which people throw off the distributions of the police in some of democracy's most strident critics. It is perhaps a great irony that Plato and Aristotle, two figures who respectively sought to deny and disperse democratic impulses, provide the greatest insights into its powers. As I present it, Rancière's thought attempts to isolate the basic structures of democratic politics, sharpen its self-conception, and bring it to bear more efficaciously on the present. In this respect, Rancière can be viewed as radicalizing the insights of Greek philosophy and turning them against the oligarchy. The past, beheld correctly, opens future possibilities.

2.2 THE AESTHETICS OF COUNTING

Returning to the ancients with Rancière, we learn something essential: politics is about counting. On the way to constructing their ideal states, both Plato and Aristotle begin by asking what a city is, that is, who composes it. They prescribe to each class a specific role or part, with justice held to reside in the apportionment of the whole. These distributions, despite their name, are dramatically unequal. The carefully codified hierarchy of Plato's *Republic* is the prototypical distribution of the sensible. It makes clear that, for the philosophers, justice enforces the distribution of labor. As we saw in Chapter 1, Plato's "one man, one job" principle assigns to each a carefully determined role in the community. Social stability is guaranteed by the virtues specific to each group. Temperance [*sōphrosunē*] or, as it is frequently translated, moderation, is the virtue reserved for the working classes. It guarantees order inasmuch as it encourages a type of contentment with the distribution of lots. One can describe the valorization of moderation as a police operation. It is the original call for workers to mind their roles, moderate their desires, and vacate the spaces and times of politics. It is in this sense that Rancière's call to be "immodest" about democracy should be understood; the first act of politics is to throw off a policed identity.[11]

Politics begins with a rejection of the very sentiments, desires, forms of relation, and expectations imposed by the oligarchs. It is a process of subjectivation [*la subjectivation*], which, as we will see (Section 2.5), signifies for Rancière the movement by which men and women stray from their "natural" allotment of capacities in order to inhabit new bodies in different times and spaces. For Rancière, politics entails the "production . . . of a body and a capacity for enunciation not previously identifiable within a given field of experience, whose identification is thus part of the reconfiguration of the field of experience."[12] It should be indicated here that these instances of creation are not political dandyism, as though politics were merely performance. Politics unfolds by challenging the counts and divisions deemed to be self-evident. Subjectivation operates upon the identities allotted by a dominant culture, locating within them opportunities for the demonstration of new capacities. If politics is able to question the lines between what is heard and unheard, it is because it introduces new voices into the sensible mix.

Not to be confused with Benjamin's thesis about the aestheticization of politics, Rancière describes the aesthetics of politics in order to express the idea that questions of part-taking rely on prior decisions about what will be interpreted as logically formed human speech and what construed as animal noise. Rancière illustrates the aesthetic dimension of politics by making recourse to the double sense of *logos*, which in Greek means both speech and account. Rancière:

> Politics exists because the logos is never simply speech, because it is always indissolubly the *account* that is made of this speech: the account by which a sonorous emission is understood as speech, capable of enunciating what is just, whereas some other emission is merely perceived as a noise signaling pleasure or pain, consent or revolt.[13]

Rancière reminds us that the *logos* is at once speech and a distribution of speech positions; it is through the partitioning of speech that capacities are allocated. Domination, he tells us, follows from the refusal to acknowledge someone's full possession of speech, the basic requirement for political participation.

Consider Aristotle's reflections on natural slavery. The question he pursues in Book I of his *Politics*—Are some slaves by nature?—is not, as is sometimes thought, tangential to the rest of his political thought; it supplies the principle which justifies governance itself. Aristotle argues it is both expedient and just for master to rule slave, for it is only right that superior elements subordinate inferior ones.[14] As is well known, for Aristotle, the *logos* distinguishes the human from other animals, founding its political life. The account of speech he gives, however, also creates a hierarchical partition, with the difference between master and slave, and hence the principle of governance, hinging on different relationships with the *logos*. Whereas the master is in full possession of the *logos*, using it to calculate and command, slaves share in it just enough to carry out orders. Aristotle: "Someone can belong to another, and is therefore a slave by nature, if he participates in reason [*logos*] enough to perceive [*aisthēsis*] it, but not enough to possess [*hexis*] it himself."[15] The *logos*, then, has two primary, political functions: it is the means of social intercourse, and, through its partitioning, a way of ordering the community. The use that is made of the *logos* in accounting for the city's various elements gives rise to an overall sensible given or an *aisthēsis* in which one's political being is determined by one's perceived facility with speech/reason. The aesthetics of politics thus indicates that before being about the negotiation of interests, the community relies upon judgments about what constitutes speech, who is capable of possessing it, what the appropriate places for it are, and what can be addressed as a political issue.

Politics, for Rancière, revolves around the use that is made of this distinction between speech and noise. When a leader, for example, fails to recognize in another nation a "viable partner for peace" or when management refuses to hear workers' demands for better conditions, we witness a variation on Aristotle's distinction between full and partial possession of speech. Politics contests the general aesthetic framework in which these distinctions operate. It consists of forcing an opposing side to acknowledge not only demands for inclusion but also the speech of those making the demands. Politics, therefore, pertains to tacit decisions determining when, where, and how its respective actors appear. It is fundamentally a conflict over voice, between the police interpretations of sense that describe some as braying beasts and the actions undertaken by marginalized groups to demonstrate that what issues from their mouths is human speech. Whereas the police claims that hierarchical divisions of labor are just, politics disrupts such distributions of the sensible with the demonstration of equal facility with the *logos*.

Not every disruption, however, is worthy of the name "politics," and Rancière reserves that term for actions, speech situations, manifestations, practices, arguments, and even works of art and literature that inscribe equality into the policed divisions of inequality. "Nothing is political in itself," he explains, "for the political only happens by means of a principle that does not belong to it: equality."[16] For Rancière, only the supposition of equality allows for speech, action, and organization to break from the police. Without equality, such operations are quickly subsumed by the non-political competition between parts. Politics is opposed to the police in that it employs a fundamentally different logic. Rancière describes this opposition in terms of "worlds" in order to highlight the fact that the police and politics are essentially different orientations toward the community. The police proposes an order founded on the assumption of the inequality of the community's various members. It attempts to naturalize the miscount according to which some are prevented from taking part. Politics, on the other hand, employs an egalitarian logic to break with the subject positions demarcated by the police. The guiding assumption of politics is the equality of anyone with everyone. "Doing politics" consists of placing the two logics in conflict, that is, creating spaces where the two can be opposed and the police hierarchies overturned—however provisionally. The political [*le politique*] is this third space of contestation, an indeterminate and always shifting meeting point of the police and politics [*la politique*].

The process of politics begins with the identification of a wrong [*le tort*], a fundamental dispute over different accountings of the community. It is, Rancière claims, the "original structure of all politics" in that it is the injustice around which the part of those without part is mobilized.[17] Whether it takes place through the oligarch's counting, philosophy's parceling and dispersals of the people, or the distinctions made between human speech and animal noise, the wrong is, in the first instance, an inequality in the allotment of roles. One commentator has noted the sense in which *le tort*—derived from "*tordre*," a verb that recurs in many of Rancière's analyses and which means to wring or to twist—indicates that the wrong is torsion or twisting of the equality underpinning human relationships.[18] Accordingly, social inequality is a wronging or wringing of the more primordial equality on which inequality relies. Politics names such twists of the sensible, bringing them to visibility. It disrupts the supposed naturalness of the initial count with the emergence of a new part, the *dēmos*, which manifests this wrong and carries it against the police order. The presence of the *dēmos* impacts the entire community, for the simple reason that it cannot begin to take part without altering the distribution the sensible constituted at its expense. Its existence transforms the hierarchical city into a political one. Its primary challenge consists of assuming visibility in the policed distribution of the sensible. The part of those without part, then, is the subject of politics in both senses. It is the agent whose emergence turns the consensual community into a litigious one, and its existence as a potential part-taker is the very object of confrontation. The *dēmos* makes explicit the fundamental difference between the wronged order and one based on equality.

The analysis of the Greek experience allows Rancière to describe this encounter between politics and the police as a specialized form of class struggle. This is not to say that politics can be conceived simply as the contest over goods within a society. Politics is the means by which those without part contest the categories, divisions, identifications, and means of social integration that attempt to consign them to nonexistence. The rich attempt to put an end to politics by insisting upon the fundamentally just nature of the distribution. The poor, on the other hand, who embody "nothing other than politics itself," attempt to reconfigure the distribution of the sensible so they can take part.[19] Politics, according to Rancière, is in fact the struggle for the very existence of the *dēmos* as a class. As such, subjectivation is the struggle to create and maintain the *dēmos* against those who threaten it with extinction.

When it came to determining the basis of political participation in Athens, the oligarchs were blind to the poor, claiming they possessed no qualifications to warrant taking part in the city's affairs. While the *aristoi* made recourse to advantages of birth, and the *oligoi* the accumulations of wealth, the poor were said to be without a claim.

This is what Rancière terms the "logic of the *arkhē*." It consists of selecting some element—wealth or birth—and making it the basis for the right to rule. "The principle of this kind of being-together is simple: it gives to each the part that is his due according to the evidence of what he is."[20] Aristotle describes the *arkhē*'s function when he claims that justice in distribution is determined by the proportion of dissimilarity between people.

> If the people involved are not equal, they will not have what is equal; for the origin of quarrels and complaints is equals receiving unequal shares, or unequals equal shares. Moreover, this is also clear from the fact that awards should be "according to worth;" for all agree that the just in distribution must be according to worth.[21]

The logic of the *arkhē* attempts to turn the arbitrariness of the social into a claim on part-taking. Fundamentally, what it means is that the essentially groundless nature of the human community, along with any natural equality that might exist, is covered over by a "geometric equality," claiming that justice awards greater or lesser consideration depending upon the persons at issue. What is always at stake in politics of course is a dispute over what constitutes "worth." Aristotle continues, explaining that different classes themselves lobby for different criteria: ". . . they do not identify worth in the same way, for supporters of democracy say it is free citizenship, while supporters of oligarchy say it is wealth and others noble birth, and supporters of aristocracy say it is virtue."[22]

In addition to outlining the various claims on part-taking, Aristotle also tells us something essential about democracy. It consists of inventing a new title for being counted and taking part, and, moreover, inventing a logic to counter the logic of the *arkhē*. As its etymology indicates, democracy is an-archic, founded in opposition to the activity of determining membership on the basis of principles. It is rather a "manner of prevailing" or "force" [-*cracy*] that undoes the axioms with which the dominant classes distribute the city. Its claim, "free citizenship," creates a polemical claim for part-taking based on the commonality—all are able to make use of their time as they see fit—found among citizens. The *dēmos*, therefore, proposes another, more extensive title for consideration, one based on the claim that all are alike, at least in terms of their freedom. With the claim of equality, therefore, the *dēmos* proposes a different way of relating the various parts of a community.

After a protracted experience of rule by kings, aristocrats, and oligarchs, the *dēmos* constituted itself as a class in order to prevent the few from turning social contingencies into titles for ruling. In its efforts to resist the domination that follows from making birth, wealth, or virtue principles of political rule, the *dēmos* posited another claim, the equality of all. The means by which it constructed the claim of equality was by tying it to the universality of freedom. Freedom is the title of those with no specific qualification, put forward as a way of breaking apart the *arkhē*. As Rancière puts it, "The 'freedom' of the people that constitutes the axiom of democracy has as its real content the rupture of the axiomatic of domination, that is, of the correlation between a capacity to command and a capacity to be commanded."[23] In the Greek context, this freedom was itself achieved by means of the class struggle that culminated in Solon's reforms. In order to quell widespread exploitation and social instability in the early sixth century BCE, Solon instituted a type of class compromise, liberating a class of indentured peasants, while refusing, as some had done, to redistribute property. The primary result of his shaking-off of burdens [*seisachtheia*] was that men could no longer fall into slavery for debt. And while Solon prevented the lower classes from holding office by making property ownership a precondition of political participation, he drew up a system of laws that applied equally to all. The most significant legacy of this was freedom [*eleutheria*], both in the sense that Athenian-born males were able to conduct themselves as they saw fit, and guaranteed basic political rights such as freedom of speech [*parrhēsia*]. Once freed, workers and farmers gained an essential tool in their arsenal against the oligarchs, with these reforms serving later proponents of democracy as a constant reference point.[24] The resulting freedom grounded the claim of equality, as Rancière explains:

> The people are nothing more than the undifferentiated mass of those who have no positive qualification—no wealth, no virtue— but who are nevertheless acknowledged to enjoy the same freedom as those who do. The people who make up the people are in fact simply free *like* the rest. Now it is this simple identity with those

who are otherwise superior to them in all things that gives them a specific qualification. The demos attributes to itself as its proper lot the equality that belongs to all citizens.[25]

The essential contribution of the *dēmos* consists of inventing a new claim on political power. Rancière thus cautions that democracy should not be understood as one regime among others. Indeed, the logic of equality is so distinct from the logic of the *arkhē* that one can claim that it defines an entirely different *aisthēsis*. Rancière describes it as a power that liquidates all attempts to found politics on first principles. Democracy activates the gap separating the contingencies of birth from the right to rule. It demonstrates the essential groundlessness of any political title. It is for this reason that democracy elicits the hatred of the philosophers.[26] More positively, one can understand democracy as a force with which to counter the distribution of roles and capacities. It is the activity that allows the *dēmos* to define another means for assuming a part, to indeed begin to take part. Democracy derives this power from nothing else than the supposed equality of anyone and everyone. By positing, asserting, and staging equality, the *dēmos* alters the very fabric of the community, shifting the sensible parameters and drawing new relationships between its members. And while the concept of equality upon which it relies is continually in need of verification, it is, as Rancière says, not nothing.

2.3 SUPPOSING, VERIFYING, AND DEMONSTRATING EQUALITY

Equality is a necessary component of any discourse or practice claiming to be political. For Rancière, equality is what prevents these forms of engagement from replicating the police order. It is this understanding of equality—its scope, function, and generative capacities—that remains to be developed.

Todd May has proposed understanding Rancière's conception of active equality as a critique of liberalism's distributive paradigm. For May, distribution itself is of the police order, for to receive equality is always to be less than equal.[27] Truly democratic politics, May contends, exists when equality is a presupposition for speech, organization, and action. I am essentially in agreement with this analysis, in particular the sense of normativity May derives from

Rancière's notion of equality; however, here I want to offer a different account of equality, one focused more on the status of this concept within Rancière's thought and politics. I propose to examine the nature of equality, described by Rancière at various points as a supposition, an inscription, a signifier, and as artifice. Essential to my account of equality are the procedures of verification that are the means of creating its universality. This approach enables us to give greater specificity to the confrontation between the hierarchies of the police and the counter-assumptions of politics.

Rancière makes two important claims about equality. The first is that it is an irreducible fact of social existence, which, try as they may, the proponents of inequality can never entirely efface. The second is that equality relies upon its demonstration. These two claims are related, for it is often the attempt to justify inequality that results in equality's demonstration. As we saw in Chapter 1 with Rancière's discovery of the educational theories of Joseph Jacotot, the equality of intelligences can never be proven to the satisfaction of skeptics. Fortunately, however, emancipation consists only of working to verify this postulate. For this possibility to remain open, it is necessary to prevent inequality from naturalizing itself. To achieve this, Rancière shows how, at some point, inequality inevitably presupposes equality. He argues that it is only with recourse to the latter that we can make sense of social life in general, and the efforts on behalf of inequality in particular. This observation allows Rancière to invert one of the central problems of modern political philosophy, that of establishing the equality of a political community's members. He does not argue that humans are essentially equal, but that all attempts to justify inequality are incoherent. The reason is simple: in order for authority to be more than arbitrary force, it must inevitably give reasons. This process of supplying reasons undermines the claims advanced on behalf of inequality, for when it attempts to explain the hierarchies it would erect, inequality presupposes equality.[28]

To illustrate this point, Rancière frequently makes recourse to the account of the plebeian revolt given by Livy in his *History of Rome*.[29] The events revolve around Menenius Agrippa, who served as the patrician ambassador to the plebs occupying Aventine Hill. In an attempt to restore order to the city, Menenius resorted to the familiar fable of the body politic with its hierarchical division of labor. He explained that everyone has a place, and without patrician command the plebeian body would soon starve. The problem with his explanation was that it had to be spoken, thereby positing a group of addressees capable of understanding it. As Rancière summarizes, "The principle of superiority is ruined if it has to be explained to inferiors why they are inferior."[30] A command presupposes that it can be understood, cutting across the relationship of dissimilarity from which it is articulated. Rancière: "There is no service that is carried out, no knowledge that is imparted, no authority that is established without the master having, however little, to speak 'equal to equal' with the one he commands or instructs."[31] Hierarchical locutions, therefore, sketch communities markedly different from the ones they attempt to explain, and it is only with recourse to this second community of equals that we can understand the anxious efforts to divide the world into unequal parts. This, then, is Rancière's response to Aristotle's partitioning of the *logos*: there is no meaningful distinction between perceiving and possessing reason. Understanding an account of inequality requires one to continually translate it, that is, rewrite it in one's own words. Thus, in a situation where domination relies upon denying someone's full possession of the *logos*, the simple act of understanding a command can become an occasion for staging a counterdemonstration of equality.

As we have seen, there is in Rancière's thought a disjuncture issuing from Jacotot's work between intellectual equality and social equality. For Jacotot, it was foolhardy to attempt to implement the latter on the basis of the former, for society is nothing if not a system of ranked and ordered contingencies. In fact, Jacotot warned the emancipated to keep their distance from social engineers, claiming that social equality is a *contradictio in adjecto*. For Rancière, "A community of equals is an insubstantial community of individuals engaged in the ongoing creation of equality. Anything else paraded under this banner is either a trick, a school, or a military unit."[32] Equality defines a community that "has no substance," one that "takes place without having a place" [*a lieu sans avoir place*].[33] The supposition of the community of equals shadows the social order, indicating another way of being together. It can be used to disrupt social arrangements sanctioning the unequal distributions of capacities; however, the community defined by equality must be continually reactivated and placed in a polemical relationship with the existing distributions of community.

The process of politics consists of bringing the logic of this insubstantial community of the emancipated to bear upon the social. It is always possible, Rancière contends, to discover the traces of equality within inequality and to play the former against the latter. With parables such as the one derived from Livy, Rancière shows that inequality is never separable from equality, even though they are thought to be terms of the furthest remove. Inequality depends upon equality in order to gain meaning, relying upon it when it tries to give an account of itself. Critical political thought calls attention to instances where inequality has been abstracted from the equality that forms its basis. It exposes the former as unstable, requiring as it does the assumption of equality in order to explain its functioning. With this idea of equality, politics draws connections between individuals at different locations in the police order. It uses the postulate of the community of equals to facilitate social transformation by placing the two definitions of community in conflict with one another.

Given that the community of equals is insubstantial, one could say that, for Rancière, equality is virtual, provided one does not conclude that it is unreal or without the ability to generate effects. "Equality is not a fiction," Rancière proclaims, indicating that it has a specific topology and distinct form of causality.[34] Regrettably, "There is no constant body of the demos that would support democratic pronouncements."[35] Equality is not a timeless value to which we can appeal, or even something to be taken for granted once it has been inscribed within the trajectory of Western political thought. We cannot be content with lumping contemporary struggles under a ready-made concept, but must continually work to verify equality. This is not to say that equality's inscription, within history, culture, and institutions, does not facilitate other struggles. It is a force that, once deployed, can build momentum, much in the way that the Greek experience provides an example of how the part of those without part might be reinvented within the context of a struggle against the contemporary transnational oligarchy.

This idea that equality relies upon its demonstration gives to Rancière's politics both an activist flavor as well as a type of modesty. For Rancière, politics is more normative than the defenders of a politics based upon the rejection of the Enlightenment customarily assume. For him, it is not simply about affirming differences or disrupting the power dynamics at work in a given group. It is about generating obligations to recognize the existence of a shared world through the creation of polemical sites where equality can be verified. Claiming that equality is the *only* universal, however, means that this universality is not derived from other concepts, such as Humanity or Reason.[36] Equality follows from a demonstration, both in the logical and performative sense, but it does not reside in the terms used for staging those demonstrations. While equality is a universal, it is not an *a priori*. This means that the creation of cases of equality is more active, local, and reserved than typically assumed by both the opponents and proponents of universality. Rancière explains:

> The mode of effectivity of Truth or Universality in politics is the discursive and practical construction of a polemical verification, a case, a demonstration. The place of truth is not the place of a ground or an ideal; it is always a *topos*, the place of a subjectivization in an argumentative plot.[37]

The insight is twofold. First, Rancière believes we deprive politics of important resources if we discount its normative content. We should attend, at the level of practices, to the specific forms of universality political actions are capable of creating. This entails, in the second instance, rejecting traditional approaches to universality, many of which, aside from being difficult to defend philosophically, are so abstract as to be meaningless. The question Rancière provides us with is, given that many theories of universality also require demonstrations of their applicability to specific cases, why not reverse direction and make the universal follow from the demonstration, that is, from the practice of politics itself? Accordingly, politics should be understood as a fashioning and testing of equality, a norm that emerges from a local context and which has only as wide an application as a group is able to claim for it. This position, Rancière contends, may allow us to "break out of the desperate debate between universality and identity."[38] It enables us to describe how in politics something contingent, insubstantial, and without foundation—like equality—can nevertheless function as a source of obligation.[39] Rancière thus describes equality as partaking of an always-provisional universality. The "polemical universal," understood in contrast with abstract universals, asks whether or not there is a shared capacity running counter to a community's hierarchical arrangements which would provide for a different logic of part-taking.

As such, it is always already engaged with the particular. Indeed, it emerges only from the work of the particular.

Actual demonstrations are often necessary to create the conditions in which others recognize the import of equality. These actions create a shared world where previously one was denied. Demonstrations are significant, despite much conventional wisdom, for they overturn exclusionary partitions of the sensible. Rancière:

> The logical schema of social protest . . . may be summed up as follows: do we not belong to the category of men or citizens or human beings, and what follows from this? The universality is not enclosed in *citizen* or *human being*; it is involved in the "what follows," in its discursive and practical enactment.[40]

Demonstrations create possibilities for the part of those without part to begin to take part. They do this by first imposing a sensible obligation upon others to recognize the rationality of others. The tailors' strike of 1833, to which Rancière refers frequently, is the perfect example of the logic of the "what follows." He describes the conflict not in terms of demands for higher wages, but as a process of giving proofs. In order to be considered partners in dialogue, the tailors had to confront their bosses with their existence as human beings. Strikers invoked the equality inscribed in the Charter of 1830 that pronounced all French people equal before the law. How, they asked, if they are equals can their demands be summarily dismissed? The workers' actions thus attempted to stage the contradiction between two premises, the major one contained in the Charter and the minor one implicit in their treatment. By striking, the tailors attempted to enforce their right to consideration. We can view the claim for equality as following from the exacerbation of the contradiction between the Charter and the tailors' treatment—not the Charter's empty principle. It was their ability to construct arguments, to engage with those of their opponents, and to define alternative modes of being that sustained the demonstrative case. It is significant that the tailors spent a good deal of time refuting the statements issued by their bosses. In altering their supposed relationship with the *logos*, they demonstrated their claim upon equality. It is this polemical space, prior to what is customarily thought of as the political, where politics takes place. It is here that the universality of equality succeeds or fails.

Of course the essential insight carried over from Jacotot's pedagogical theory is that equality must serve as a starting point, not simply a goal to be achieved. Without the assumption of equality, even well-intentioned people working to reduce inequalities tend to reproduce them. You get what you start with. It is for this reason that Rancière has no patience for those forms of political and sociological theory intent on proving that inequality is the truth of our democracies. The intellectual-political task instead, as Rancière sees it, is to reinvent the scandal of democracy. This consists of contesting hierarchies where they are to be found, and constructing demonstrations of equality. Equality, as Jacotot taught, is an assumption that multiplies itself by producing proofs. To concede with Jacotot that the equality of intelligences can never found a society is not to claim that the latter is immune from critique or transformation. It forces us, however, to reject the utopian conception of politics that echoes the police's wish to end politics. This refusal is not the occasion for mourning or a reinvigorated political realism. It indicates that there is, and will be, much to do to make inequality attempt to justify itself. Making inequality speak, equal to equal, causes the insubstantial community of equals to grow.

2.4 DISPUTING SUBJECTS AND LITIGIOUS OBJECTS: POLITICS AS DISSENSUS

As we have seen, police operations marginalize certain voices, while activating others; they distribute competencies, carve out relationships of command, and prescribe the times and places in which certain bodies can appear. They attempt to unify the city and neutralize politics by preventing the emergence of the part of those without part, the agent that, in disclosing the wrong of the city's accounting, undoes consensus. Politics opposes consensus by means of dissensus. Dissensus, whether the straightforward political variety or the type employed by art, is the means by which the sensible is deprived of its self-evidence, punctuated, and subjected to dispute. Dissensus is the process of politics itself in that it is the activity of countering the police distribution of the sensible with the egalitarian supplement. Through polemics, demonstrations, strikes, speech scenes, poetic activities, and the definition of new capacities dissensus breaks open an interpretation of sense thought to be incontestable. As Rancière explains, the sensible is always once removed from itself, meaning that it never assumes a stable configuration or a single direction. Dissensus, in its essence, is the activity of exposing and activating this breach within the sensible.

The police opposes politics by claiming that there is no part of those without part. Dissensus fragments the community by making visible what previously went unseen. It operates, first and foremost, on the aesthetics of the community, those implicit decisions about who is included and in what way, as well as those judgments about what counts as voice or noise. It thus has two primary operations at its disposal: it questions who counts as a subject worthy of taking part, and what constitutes an object, that is, possible topic of politics. Dissensus multiplies "litigious objects and disputing subjects" in the midst of the supposed tranquility of consensus.[41] It thereby questions a society's definitions of competence, forms of relation, and divisions of labor. Dissensus also operates to bring together domains previously thought separate. It challenges, for instance, the division between the public and the private, by asking, for example, whether schools, factories, offices, homes, and hospitals are political spaces. It turns such locales into locations of dispute, questioning the sense they are given by the police order. Likewise, dissensus asks whether or not things such as wages, space, infrastructure, and transportation are not matters of public concern. In short, dissensus is the process of rejecting the meanings the police makes of the sensible.

If consensus promotes the obviousness of the status quo, dissensus opposes it with postulates of another world. It operates on space and time in order to create a new terrain for the confrontation between the police and the part of those without part. Rancière describes dissensus as the action of creating the stage upon which one can appear as the equal of one's adversary. This shifting of the overall *aisthēsis* is necessary to allow for the emergence and recognition of new political subjects. Practices, such as strikes and demonstrations, sketch the outlines of a different world, which they force us to consider alongside of our own. Politics is the activity of holding in conflict the world of the police and the one defined under the assumption of equality. It was, for example, a dissensual relationship that took place in the self-management of the LIP watch factory. In a place where previously there was little besides hierarchy, the workers' actions gave birth to a distribution founded on equality. Dissensus consists of making apparent these fundamentally heterogeneous ways of parceling out capacities and parts.

It is for this reason that Rancière speaks of politics as "made up of relationships between worlds" and not simply as conflicts over power.[42] The object of this critique is not Foucault, whose genealogical presentations of disciplinary, pastoral, and bio powers served as a propaedeutic to political activism. It is rather some of the uses made of his thought by the "*nouveaux philosophes*," a group of former *gauchistes* who traded in the legacy of May 1968 for positions of media power. Peter Dews has analyzed the interpretative violence to which this group—Lévy, Glucksmann, et al.—subjected Foucault's genealogical critiques of rationalities in order to equate reason itself with the totalitarian projects carried out under the names of Hegel and Marx. For Dews, the *nouveaux philosophes* eviscerated the political and its distinctions between left and right with the vague vocabulary of "power" and "resistance."[43] It is significant that Rancière refuses to pose his analysis in these terms. For him, the concept of power has outlived its usefulness. It was formerly an instrument for problematizing aspects of existence erroneously believed to be apolitical. It provided resources for critiquing phenomena as diverse as education, urbanism, the framing of life in the media, and the ability of class, race, gender, and heteronormative privileges to perpetuate themselves. It sustained, in short, the thesis that "everything is political."[44]

It is sometimes said, perhaps with too much satisfaction, that for Rancière politics is rare. His thought is not intended to deny the multifarious forms of domination that exist within our societies, nor the many projects designed to counter them. It attempts instead to reinvestigate the specificity of politics. It holds to what is most radical in its various endeavors, seeking to convert them from minor struggles for recognition, goods, and power into full-fledged projects of emancipation. Rancière:

> What makes an action political is not its object or the place where it is carried out, but solely its form, the form in which the confirmation of equality is inscribed in the setting up of a dispute, of a community existing solely through being divided.[45]

The political is born only by confronting the police with what is foreign to it. This is of course equality. "Political" thus properly applies to discourses and practices forged under its assumption. Describing this relationship in terms of "worlds," instead of conflicts over power, allows us to highlight the breach that politics introduces into the sensible.

This notion of opposing worlds itself recalls the phenomenological tradition's discussions of the world-disclosing power of literary texts. Works of literature, as many contend, open up a counterworld by diverting the resources of this one. The world of the text thus serves as a vantage point from which to measure and critique the composition of our own. From a Marxist perspective, Herbert Marcuse theorized the potential of literary texts to serve as the refuge of lost values, describing what he saw lurking in them as a utopian potential. For him, literary texts counter this world, rife with alienation and exploitation, with one in which humankind is reconciled with the historical development of its productive forces.[46] Absent from Rancière of course is the utopian teleology inspiring Marcuse's reflections. Nevertheless, it is worth noting the structural affinities, especially given Rancière's discussions of politics' aesthetic dimension. Dissensus rejects the apportionments of the already ordained community in which some are held not to exist by creating a new common world wherein one demonstrates his ability to understand, speak, and critique the oppressor's language. For Rancière, politics consists of creating the spaces and times in which those ordinarily thought to be unequal demonstrate their equality. It then allows us to contrast this political world with the everyday world of the police.

This theory of politics as dissensus undercuts the Habermasian models of communicative action that aim at consensus. In contrast with this perspective, Rancière contends that the objects of politics and the status of its actors are never pre-constituted. It is precisely the nature, standing, and relationship between these elements that politics puts in question. This means that at the heart of any community there is conflict over what constitutes reason, what is a legitimate object of political discussion, and what it means to be a political subject. Moreover, whereas Habermas relies upon the rationality that should obtain between participants able to adopt first- and second-person points of view, Rancière contends politics is composed by subjects employing expanded political names. The perspective opened by equality, and the identifications it sustains, is not reducible therefore to the competition or negotiation between pre-existing parts. Politics is the process of connecting individual subjectivities with the whole of humanity, such as when an individual announces, "We, the workers of the world." Politics, then, is not about the reciprocal exchange of perspectives or the negotiation of competing interests; it is about creating and maintaining a class.[47]

For Rancière, political speech relies upon poetic, world-opening devices, such as the one above, whose enunciations fashion collective subjects. These subjects do not exist prior to the process of politics. As we have seen, one of the chief political struggles of the part of those without part is to create and maintain its existence. Expansive political names and the logic of equality are the basis for these instances of creation. They forge impossible subjects that shift individuals away from their locations in a distribution of the sensible. The poetic moments of politics are the creative linguistic actions that challenge the divisions between capacity and incapacity, between rulers and ruled, between those with and those without part. To this world of inequality, they oppose one founded on the assumption of equality. The first moment of this process involves contesting the divisions upon which hierarchical societies depend. For this, politics relies upon locutions, manifestations, and the demonstration of capacities thought not to exist. These actions, in the second instance, design a rival conception of the world in conflict with the existing one. The activities of the worker-poets analyzed in *Nights* can be viewed as having this form. Their activities were dissensual in that they disrupted the identities of those destined simply for work. In order to achieve this they had to question the partitioning of their lives, along with the assumptions about what it should be used for. Writing, for them, was part of a politics of world opening. It was not simply a vehicle for giving voice to their grievances; the activity itself was a means of removing themselves from a sensible order in which they had little part. It enabled them to create new capacities, and therewith the new space-time configuration in which to attest to their equality.

Dissensus means, then, that the police distribution of the sensible is never secure. It is continually opened by those who, as subjects questioning their capacities, question its objects, parameters, and partitions. The distribution of the sensible is that which is put in question by the activity of subjectivation.

2.5 THE SUBJECTIVE PROCESS OF POLITICS

This section analyzes the process by which individuals stray from their supposedly natural places within the police order through the creation of new capacities. It is the process that Rancière refers to as subjectivation. If dissensus creates the stage of politics, one can claim that subjectivation establishes its players, provided we do not separate the two processes. The relationship is an intimate one, for as we have already seen, the questioning of capacities that individuals and groups engage in functions as the motor of dissensus. Subjective processes, such as writing and adopting aesthetic outlooks, alter the meanings customarily assigned to the common, sensible world. By focusing here on the process of subject creation, we are simply taking another angle on democracy, which for Rancière relies on sustaining a specific type of subject under the assumption of equality. In this sense, the goal is to create political subjects of sufficient universality capable of altering the sensible configuration of the community.

The notion that the subject is not something given, but produced, has a long and varied history within French philosophy, and it will be helpful to indicate two of the most proximate references to better gauge Rancière's contributions.[48] In his late writings, Althusser analyzed the process by which ideology transformed the individual into a subject. Central to his account was the act of interpellation, the moment in which ideology hails an individual, thereby compelling him to recognize its applicability to his being. The subject, rather than the individual, is thus for Althusser always an ideological production. It is a form of consciousness produced by institutions to constrain the individual's capacities for thought and action, thereby ensuring the preservation of the capitalist relations of production.[49] Likewise, for Foucault, subjectivation is the process by which the human being recognizes, internalizes, and constructs himself according to scientific discourses or norms of behavior. The subject, for the early Foucault, was the result of any number of discourses and disciplines imposed upon the individual. In his later genealogies of the subject, the picture is more complex, with subjectivation understood as the result of the techniques by which human beings are constituted *and* constitute themselves as subjects.[50] Subjectivation here begins to assume some positive significance, with Foucault's researches into the "care of the self" and the "aesthetics of existence" disrupting the process of unreflective subjectivation and restoring transparency to the process of self-formation.

In contrast to these figures, Rancière describes subjectivation in positive terms. Rather than the imposition of an ideological state apparatus or the functioning of a power/knowledge, the creation of subjectivity is, for him, an integral part of politics. This requires of course that we distinguish between the *identities* forced upon people in the midst of the police order, and the political *subjects* they create in breaking these allocations. Indeed, for Rancière, it is only through the elaboration of bodies and voices not identified in the distribution of the sensible that politics takes place. For him, the "overblown promises of identity" must be overcome through the creation of a class that belongs to no one in particular and thus potentially to everyone.[51] Failing this, politics remains trapped in the consensual logic of negotiating interests, which is always a zero-sum game. Politics relies upon a unique agent, the *dēmos*. Its creation allows for new forms of part-taking to emerge. Subjectivation, then, is the process by which the part of those without part struggle, in spite of their differences, to constitute themselves as a subject. The assumption of equality is the vehicle, both of this transformation and its identification with the whole of the community.

The process of subjectivation contains two closely related moments. In the first instance there is the movement of dis-identification whereby the eventual subject of politics tears itself away from the identities, capacities, desires, and interests defined by the police. Any time an individual actively challenges the naturalness of his position within the dominant order, the process begins. When workers, for example, assume aesthetic attitudes, writing poetry or stopping labor in order to contemplate the view from an open window, forces are set in motion that move them away from their habitual identities. This first moment is negative and critical. It rejects the identities that have been stamped on bodies, the assumptions made about their capacities, and the spatio-temporal locales to which they have been relegated. The second moment entails the creation of new subjectivities in excess of the parts already identifiable in the community. These political subjectivities revolve around "impossible identifications," names belonging to no one in particular because they are not simply the reiteration of policed identities.[52] Strictly speaking, these subjectivities cannot be inhabited by the person or group making the identification; however, they provide the means for escaping the policed identities that limit individuals. The impossible identification allows the subject to extend beyond itself. In doing so, it redefines its capacities and insists upon its commonality with others. These identifications create beings that are together inasmuch as they are between identities. Equality is thus generative in that its assumption allows for the active work of subjective creation. Impossible identifications rely upon tactical, world-opening devices such as: "We the people," "proletariat," and one which was formative for Rancière, the May 1968 slogan, "We are all German Jews."[53] These declarations create subjectivities that are capable of lifting individuals out of their positions in the police order. Political names are at once poetic and polemical; they outline a shared world, and relate its inhabitants in a manner different from the one to which they are accustomed. Announcements such as "workers of the world" and "wretched of the earth" create political subjects and redraw sensible parameters. They work against the police claim that there is no part of those without part, inscribing it into the count of the community. It is important that these names be of sufficient generality, and not exclusive to any one of the city's parts. This can rightly be interpreted as a critique of the identity-based forms of politics that reject in advance possibilities of universality. Rancière explains that "the current dead end of political reflection and action is due to the identification of politics with the *self* of a community."[54] Such identifications replicate the police logic of counting.

If change is to be more than the substitution of one police order with another, actions, speeches, and identifications must themselves rupture its very logic. Politics combats the nonpolitical competition between parts by inaugurating a polemical space in which to contest the logic of counting. We witnessed this, for example, in the audacious claim made by the *dēmos* to be equal to the rest of the Greek *polis*. In its struggle with the oligarchs, it used freedom as a transitive property to create an identification with the rest of the community. By means of this operation, it claimed to be equal to those customarily thought to be superior. The *dēmos*, in Rancière's thought, is the structure of subjectivation. As we know, it is more than simply a historical name or relic of the past; it is a power reactivated whenever someone excluded from the reckoning of the community begins to take part by making recourse to an identification with the whole of the community. The *dēmos* sustains the logic of testing whereby individuals and groups litigate their particular cases in order to test the universal's reach. The *dēmos* is an excessive subject, and must remain so if it is to retain its political force. At its best, it prevents individuals and groups from lapsing into the narcissism of their differences.

According to Rancière, contemporary political practices would do well to call into question the identities that have been assigned, coded, and classified, along with the mechanisms that lead to the equation of the political with these policed identities. The vehicle for doing so is equality. Its introduction ensures that subjectivation is a process of drawing connections between people formerly thought dissimilar. "Politics is the art of warped deductions and mixed identities," Rancière reminds us, not because it is founded on lies, faulty logic, and compromises, but because it is an inventive process that blurs traditional boundaries to create new forms of being-together.[55] It does not, for all that, efface the very real differences between people, for it does not assume an abstract conception of human nature. The commonality upon which politics relies is that of the polemical in-between. It creates paradoxical spaces, times, and names that belong to no one in particular and everyone in general.[56]

To echo Foucault's famous claim, one might say that the political task is not to discover who we are, but to refuse who we are.[57] Doing so is the first step in the process of creating who we might become. While Foucault turns to the study of Greek ethics in order to re-appropriate different forms of self-relation as resistance to contemporary biopolitical imperatives, Rancière examines nineteenth-century labor movements and Greek politics in an effort to describe the ways in which individuals and communities, through their rejection of what is given, redefine the *polis*. Subjectivation is a type of unselfing that replaces the police's definition of the self with a conception of the self as other. "The logic of emancipation is a heterology."[58] This means that politics is about the other, both in the sense that it is addressed to others, and about verifying equality with others. The place of this demonstration is not identity, but the virtual community of intelligences that asserts itself whenever inequality attempts to naturalize itself.

With this perspective in mind, we can understand why Rancière contends that a lack of politics is at the root of many of the so-called social problems facing Western societies. Racism and xenophobia, for example, stem from our failures to forge identities different from those of the police. Objectively, we know that the number of immigrants has not greatly increased in recent years. Yet, their presence is everywhere deemed a subjective threat. Is the scapegoating of immigrants in the United States and Europe attributable to a lack of politics? It certainly serves to put off reckoning with issues of social justice, but is it itself the result of consensus? With respect to French society, Rancière has rejected "ethics" as a possibility for dealing with xenophobia. Too often in ethics, others are either conceived from the vantage point of the same or remain completely other. Even if the self is said to be implicated by the other, or on some accounts, discovers its indebtedness to the other, these terms remain in force. For Rancière, politics was formerly the means by which immigrants shed police identities in favor of ones that allowed for participation in the common life.[59] From the vantage point of human emancipation, immigrants might once again become workers, students, or citizens. Politics is thus the means of overturning police identities—in both directions. It provides the occasion for recent arrivals to cast off the labels with which bureaucracies burden them, and it allows the native born to stray from limiting national identities. The subjective practice of politics calls notions of self and other into question. It refuses to treat sameness and otherness as problems for social workers or fodder for theorists of clashing civilizations.

This emphasis on subjectivation helps us to understand what commonly goes by the name of solidarity. World-opening names provide not only the means by which an excluded group assumes a part, they open a space for those already allotted a part to work on behalf of equality. The scope and manner in which this concept can be verified is broad, extending both obligation and invitation. This is not to say that all is easy and tranquil. Dissensual politics prefers polemics, discord, and confusion to the identities, places, and capacities owned by the police. It is an arduous task to identify wrongs, give them a name, and maintain a federation in opposition to them. The struggle of politics is subjective, in the sense that it consists of building up and maintaining these groups in visibility against the forces that would return them to the shadows. This work, however, is not without its seductions—it offers the same pleasure one takes in any creative activity.

CONCLUSION

Animating Rancière's writings is a desperate call to reinvent politics. He characterizes our time as "post-democracy," indicating that many ways of dealing with the problems of living together are not at all political. Strategies of social management are dedicated to preventing the part of those without part from establishing itself in its excessiveness. They support a form of legitimation described as "democracy *after* the demos."[60] This consensual form of legitimation strives to reduce the many parts struggling to question the means of inclusion and exclusion in today's globalized *polis* to conflicting yet manageable partialities. Post-democracy treats those parts that would throw off the logic of counting as nothing more than competing interests. Exhaustive polling, for example, deprives "opinions" of their litigious character, just as ever more intractable identities pit against one another individuals who should find common cause in opposition to economic elites. Both consensual mechanisms equate politics with the state, reinforcing the latter as the arbiter of a whole that is nothing more than the sum of its parts. Politics requires not only a critique of the mechanisms by which the people are divided and conquered; it requires the creation of an actor not reducible to one part among others. It necessitates the elaboration of an agent exceeding the state's counting.

Despite its ancient derivation, Rancière's account of the part of those without part can be used to understand and bolster contemporary political movements. It brings to light the collective power that can be assumed by those without voice in this world. It unites those thought to be dissimilar in a fundamental rejection of identitarian police logic and the affirmation of a world in common. The part without part is that class, be it the Athenian *dēmos*, the people of the revolutionary era, the industrialized proletariat, the victims of colonization, the *sans-papiers* of Europe, the economic refugees of North America, ethnic minorities, and lesbian and gay people, who expose the community as constituted through their exclusion. Their appearance exceeds the mechanisms of negotiation and integration provided that, as a class, its members do not seek merely recognition, but assert equality to break open distributions in which they have no part. Thinking and practicing contemporary struggles in terms of equality can allow for more than a simple shuffling of the sensible. It can set in motion a disruption of the distribution that employs the practice of counting.

After following Rancière's presentation of politics' basic structures it might be tempting to conclude that there is something inevitable about democracy's eruption. This would be a self-defeating conclusion, for it would deny the difficult work entailed in constituting the *dēmos* and preventing its dispersal. Subjectivation is the struggle to preserve what is most radical about politics, the improbable identification of a group with the whole of the community. It must combat the ever more sophisticated logics of de-politicization prevalent today by insisting upon the assumptions, names, discourses, and practices that escape the policed and counted parts. Rancière's perspective, however, allows us to take comfort in the difficulties existing powers have in sanctifying that which "is" as "good." All hierarchies stumble when compelled to give an account of themselves. We must, therefore, continually place our governments, institutions, relationships, practices, and discourses in question. Countering them with the affirmation of equality remains, as Rancière explains, the most "untimely/excessive" [*intempestive*] of exercises.[61]

CHAPTER 3

RETRIEVING THE POLITICS OF AESTHETICS

INTRODUCTION

Readers expecting to find in Rancière's recent writings on art a new "aesthetic theory," understood as a philosophical reflection on the nature of art or a criterion for taste, will be disappointed. His writings are not intended as a program for artists to follow, or a system of concepts for critics and curators to exploit. This is not to say that a direction for art and criticism cannot be gleaned from his work, but that if one emerges, it does so by means of a genealogical exposition of neglected aspects of the aesthetic tradition. A preference for works that somehow insist on the capacity of viewers is nevertheless evident in the places where Rancière analyzes specific instances of contemporary production. The ability of art to posit the equal capacities of its viewers follows from the "aesthetic revolution," the wholesale cultural transformation that fundamentally altered the identity of art at the end of the eighteenth and beginning of the nineteenth centuries. As we will see, the art of the "aesthetic regime" does two essential things: it engenders a form of equality in its production and reception, and it carries the promise of life reconfigured. What Rancière does offer, then, is an account of art's political capacities. He achieves this by describing the way art alters the distribution of the sensible through the creation of experiences that are opposed to it.

Perhaps what is most remarkable about the art world's recent embrace of Rancière's work is that it has done so despite his insistence upon voices as unfashionable as Kant, Schiller, and Hegel. This backward glance has the effect of disrupting certitudes about the present, specifically those propositions about the history, nature, and capacities of art. In this sense, his position is a marked departure from many of today's dominant discourses, such as those which tell us that art is far removed from most people's lives or the reminder of collective or personal trauma. As I argue in this chapter, this retrieval of eighteenth- and nineteenth-century texts, and the displacement they achieve with respect to standard theories of art, creates the space wherein art can rediscover a capacity for dissensus. To permit art this form of intervention, it is necessary to describe the postulates accompanying the birth of aesthetics. Central to this endeavor is an account of the break aesthetics proper articulates with respect to Platonic and Aristotelian understandings of art. This project also entails rejecting the dominant picture of twentieth-century art historiography—its categories of modernism and postmodernism—and the implicit teleology to which it subscribes. This is the place to stress, however, that while Rancière's understanding of art is deeply historical, it is not so in the sense that many may expect. Rancière is not offering an account of stylistic movements or forms that have allegedly superseded one another, just as he is not offering a reflection on the timeless grandeur of art. The three regimes which he describes—the ethical regime of images, the representative regime of art, and the aesthetic regime of art—do not correspond strictly to temporal periods, even though there are certain historical moments central to the formation of each. A regime is not a time frame, but a series of axioms that arrange art and position it in relation to other practices.

3.1 ANALYZING THE PART OF ART

It should be kept in mind that the analysis of the distribution of the sensible provides the context for Rancière's discussions of art and the history of aesthetic theory. The recent interest in art should be viewed as a continuation of this larger project of forging a topographical analysis of the means by which the sensible is constructed, parceled out, and contested. As we have seen, aesthetic concerns, taken in the expanded sense, have been present in Rancière's work since the beginning. *Nights* examined the ways in which the partitioning of night from day, along with its assumptions about worker identity, could be overturned by refusing to appear in prescribed times and places. If this analysis can be termed "aesthetic," it is not simply because workers found solace in writing poetry by candlelight, but because their actions altered the sphere of appearances according to which workers inhabit a specific space and time. *The Philosopher* tracked this partitioning of the sensible from Plato's strict division of labor through to contemporary sociology's assumptions about the capacities of different economic classes. It showed how at the heart of these endeavors to delimit the philosophical apparatus were several presuppositions about how its other, the poor, could be present within the sphere of appearances. Chapter 2 explained how Rancière's writings on politics are notable for their isolation of the role sense plays in the formation of community, and indicated how attending to this dimension might revitalize our understanding and practice of politics. Equality too, it can be argued, has sensible properties, in that it is the means by which the sensible becomes unstuck, revealing its contingent and transitory character. As a starting point for politics, it gives rise to a different overall *aisthēsis*. These considerations lead us to reject the idea that there are major breaks between Rancière's archival, political, and aesthetic works.

Any account of the relationships between art and politics must examine the ways in which art is thought to be separated from or joined to the larger distribution of the sensible. The distribution of the sensible is the system of divisions that assigns parts, supplies meanings, and defines the relationships between things in the common world. One such part belongs to art, with the larger distribution prescribing how the arts relate to other ways of doing and making. As such, the distribution of the sensible defines the nature of art, along with what it is capable of. The notion of the regime of art allows Rancière to reconstruct the practical and conceptual networks that have defined art and situated it with respect to the more general sphere of appearances. One can think of a regime as the system of principles that allows certain practices to be recognized as art. The identification supplied by the regime in turn determines the form of efficacy that art can have vis-à-vis other practices. To analyze a regime of art is to at once examine the identity ascribed to art by the distribution and how art corroborates or contests that distribution.

Needless to say, this analysis is premised upon rejecting standard conceptions of art's fundamental remove from other practices. The point of Rancière's analyses is in fact to see how different understandings of sense allow or prevent art from distributing and redistributing the sensible. Just as for Rancière there is no pure politics, there is, for him, no pure art or aesthetics either. What he analyzes are the different ways in which art's capacity to reconfigure the sensible is denied, affirmed, or mishandled. If Rancière questions art's supposed autonomy, however, it is not because he views art as bearing directly, or always in the same manner, upon the political. Despite the political capacities he unearths, Rancière is not interested in the art customarily designated "political." To understand his position, we must therefore resist instrumentalizing art and treating his writings on its various manifestations as simply politics by other means. He describes instead how modest, sensible interventions can be seen as harboring propositions regarding human emancipation, while insisting upon the distinctiveness of these practices as artistic practices. In this sense, what is most exciting about these analyses is the indication they provide that the arts, even those thought far-removed from the political concerns of the day, can play a role in transforming the world. Art challenges what is sensible, thinkable, and hence possible, on the condition that it not surrender its identity as art.

The challenges involved in charting these exchanges where art and politics meet, as well as the separations that define art and non-art, are innumerable. This is why Rancière recounts, in historical terms, the various overlappings, borrowings, and points of distinction existing between the domains of art and life. For him, the question of art's relationship with or separation from life is itself determined by various distributions of the sensible. His writings on literature, art, and the aesthetic tradition proper thus recount the general conditions that allow or prevent art from taking part in the distribution and redistribution of the sensible. From his literary studies to his recent treatments of visual art, Rancière has advanced an account of three heterogeneous manners of conceiving, practicing, and arranging the arts: the ethical regime of images, the representative regime of art, and the aesthetic regime of art. Each regime structures a specific relationship between words, vision, and affect, indicating how art becomes active or not within the order of appearances more generally.

Rancière has compared his research into art's historical conditions of possibility with Foucault's archaeological method. Both are historical-transcendental projects that describe the conditions that must exist for a discourse, be it literary, philosophical, historical, or artistic, to be recognized as such. As developed by Foucault, archaeology is a form of historical analysis designed to place in sharp relief two periods of discursive and visual practice. Its chief aim is to describe the *episteme*, or general space of knowledge within a given period. For Foucault, archaeology recounts the tacit system of rules governing the production of statements, visual arrangements, as well as their forms of interaction.[1] It can be helpful to think of a regime as similar to the *episteme*, provided we take care to distinguish their respective formulations. Rancière himself has noted their affinity, while stressing their differences. He describes his methodology as "something like an archaeology more open to the event than Foucault's, but without any Benjaminian messianism."[2] This is a way of saying that, for Rancière, regimes are not mutually exclusive historical thresholds: they transmit models for ordering the sensible, but they also intermingle with one another and are subject to exceptions. Rancière again:

> I differ from Foucault insofar as his archaeology seems to me to follow a schema of historical necessity according to which, beyond a certain chasm, something is no longer thinkable. . . . I thus try . . . to historicize the transcendental and to de-historicize these systems of conditions of possibility.[3]

Following from this methodological commitment, Rancière avoids reducing regimes to precise styles or periods. While he points to specific texts, authors, and movements as being indicative of the differences between regimes, they lack the hard-edged historical specificity of Foucault's *episteme*. This means that the boundaries separating regimes are less distinct and the sense of historical transmission more fluid. What unites these notions, however, is the attempt to subject conditions of possibility to historical analysis. When Foucault speaks of the archaeological level and Rancière the regime, each is attempting to isolate the system of historical positivities which structures the field of possible experience and expression.

A regime is thus a particular way of assigning meaning to the forms of sense created by artistic practices. It is designed to allow the politics of a particular practice and conception of art to come to light. It allows us to describe how art relates to and departs from the broader distribution of bodies, capacities, and practices.

3.2 THREE REGIMES OF ART

Rancière has described three major regimes of framing the forms of sense composed by art, the first of which he calls the "ethical regime of images." Within his discussions of art, it is employed the least for the simple reason that, within the ethical regime of images, art as such does not exist. This regime finds its footing in Plato's critique of imitation. In Chapter 1 we saw that these restrictions spring from the principle according to which one man must perform one and only one job. Indeed, as Rancière presents Platonism's motivations, it is to create a distribution in which only the philosopher has the right to construct fictions. Poetry, understood as *poiēsis*, or bringing something into being, is judged by Plato as subversive to the division of labor and allotment of capacities outlined in the *Republic*. When justice resides in a harmony among the various parts of the city, and when this order is guaranteed by a fiction, new narratives, images, and rhythms harbor the potential to unbind established communities. "Images," whether plastic, literary, or auditory, must therefore be contained. Plato achieves this by evaluating two things: an image's faithfulness to an Idea, and its effects upon a community. The two criteria are related, for with recourse to Ideas Plato forges the distinction between the true arts that preserve the integrity of the community and the malicious simulacra that undermine it. The latter category of images must have their ethical effects, the way they insert themselves into a people's habits, controlled. The problem is not simply that Plato places art under the watchful eye of politics; it is that he recognized no such distinction. His position prevents art as a distinctive form of making and knowing from emerging from the policed divisions of the community. For Plato, there exist only practices that support or undermine the hierarchies of soul and *polis*. There is an ethical relationship with images whenever a discourse, practice, or arrangement subordinates art's ways of doing [*technai*] to the *arkhē* of community. One can witness it in the various efforts to sacralize the museum space, the converse attempts to demystify the work of creation, and the Heideggerian contrast between our destitute age and a time before the gods fled.[4] Far from being obsolete, art is subsumed under the presuppositions of the ethical regime whenever the "sacred service" of founding and preserving a community defines the production, display, and discourse on objects.[5]

The representative regime was developed from the principles found in Aristotle's *Poetics*. That text is the first thoroughgoing effort to individuate art and grant it some freedom with respect to the community and the rituals of religion. Aristotle's distinctions inaugurate a certain relationship between the sayable and the visible that defines not only Greek tragedy, but also the system of distributions operative throughout the Classical Age, that period of European history customarily dated as beginning in the middle of the seventeenth century and extending to the end of the eighteenth century. Its axioms define the systems of the *belles-lettres* and the *beaux-arts*. These forms of arranging the internal elements of art, as well as defining its relationship with life, contrast sharply with the aesthetic revolution that sundered Classicism's distributions with the birth of literature and so-called modern painting.

Aristotle's conception of *mimēsis* responds directly to Plato's suspicion regarding *technai* freed from the bonds of an *arkhē*. In the *Poetics*, Aristotle attempts to define a form of fiction that would grant art some autonomy from the community's distributions, while making concessions to the ethical concerns voiced by Plato. Aristotle affirms that under certain conditions the representation of action is different from the creation of simulacra. While art is to some degree individuated, Aristotle restricts the practice of imitation, limiting it to serious actions performed by subjects worthy of consideration. He provides this as the essential definition of tragedy:

> A tragedy, then, is the imitation of an action that is serious and complete, as having magnitude; in language with pleasurable accessories, each kind belonging separately to different parts of the work. It imitates actions in a dramatic not a narrative form; with incidents arousing pity and fear, wherewith to accomplish the catharsis of such emotions.[6]

Of the six components of tragedy—fable [*muthos*], characters, diction, thought, spectacle, and melody—Aristotle accords priority to the fable. For him, the recounting of a causal order of events by the fable or plot should inform the internal structure of the poetic work, and subordinate its other elements. The priority on action shifts the site of art's connection with life. In theoretical terms, the ethical effect, the catharsis of harmful emotions, is said to follow from the unfolding of dramatic action, itself subject to certain strictures. Provided it adheres to a system of norms regarding the creation of the cathartic effect, art can be viewed as having a positive ethical and social function. Aristotle argues that inferior compositions produce their effects by means of the accessory elements so reviled by Plato. Centering artistic production on the representation of action, however, allows for these effects to be controlled, and for the fable to be put to work in the service of community.

The result of these commitments is that the visibility of the theatre, and indeed the other arts of the representative regime, is reserved for the transmission of speech [*logos*]. This relatively straightforward speech, requiring only time for its meaning to become apparent, is one that Rancière contrasts with the aesthetic age's more complicated picture of thought [*logos*] as shot through with *pathos*. The representative regime's axioms of *mimēsis* define a strict relationship between *poiēsis*, a manner of making, and its *aisthēsis*, the effects it produces. The relationship between these three terms was cemented by an underlying conception of human nature, which was simultaneously the thought of who should be represented and in what way, as well as how artistic arrangements would be received.[7] Concretely, what this means is that there are very precise rules for performing artistic labors, themselves thought to produce very definite affective responses. The center of the work is the fable, which recounts a series of well-ordered actions. This means that within the representative regime, character development, description, and language itself are distributed around the axiom of action and, by and large, left underdeveloped. From a critical perspective, it is relatively easy to evaluate a given work; one need simply determine whether it successfully conveys a story.

The picture of human nature upon which the representative regime relies corresponds to a theory of social nature. Rancière is quick to describe the political significance of these poetics: "The representative primacy of action over character or of narration over description, the hierarchy of genres according to the dignity of their subject matter . . . these elements figure into an analogy with a fully hierarchical vision of the community."[8] The restrictions on subject matter—tragedy should concern itself with persons of decent character, worthy of our attention—rank the subjects of art according to a hierarchical vision of community. The representative regime is thus a distribution of the sensible that determines what can be the subject of art, into what genre it should be placed, and how it is to be depicted, with reference to the more general distribution of capacities. It is in general a system that outlines the conditions according to which imitation can be recognized as distinct from other ways of doing and making, and the source of a normativity that defines the forms appropriate for the representation of specific subjects.

This distribution, and the priority it places upon the conveyance of speech, determines the visibility of classical painting. The axioms of representation indicate, for example, what is a "high" or "low" subject, as well as the manner in which it should be treated. This poetics also accounts for the priority accorded to mythological, religious, and historical scenes over genre painting. Following the logic spelled out by Aristotle, the former deal with actions, while the latter presents the viewer with curiosities barely worthy of being represented. This distribution of the sensible also supports the well-known differences of scope and size in paintings throughout the Classical Age: large canvases were reserved for the representation of events, while scenes from the lives of common people were handled on a diminutive scale. Secondly—and this is a related point—the imperatives of representation, primarily the relationship between painting and discursivity, are what, for a large part of painting's history, compel it to attempt to pull three dimensions out of two. Painting's rediscovery of illusionary space in the fifteenth century must be understood as stemming from the privilege accorded to speech and action, not merely the outgrowth of technical developments or the humanist worldview. For Rancière, "Classical poetics established a relationship of correspondence . . . between speech and painting, between the sayable and the visible, which gave 'imitation' its own specific space."[9] Abstraction, on the other hand, becomes possible only through an invalidation of the idea that painting is a vehicle for the transmission of speech. To concern itself with itself, the subject of painting must first become a matter of indifference or, in Rancière's terms, equality, the major innovation of the aesthetic regime.

For Rancière, the aesthetic regime encompasses a broad selection of artistic currents as diverse as realism, romanticism, abstraction in painting, the supposed intransitivity of modern literature, and even the development of the social sciences. What unites these disparate endeavors is their elimination of the representative regime's rules for pairing a given subject with a specific mode of presentation. The aesthetic regime of the arts is thus, at the most fundamental level, the abolition of the representative regime's normativity. *Poiēsis* and *aisthēsis* remain linked in the sense that interventions and arrangements continue to produce effects in viewers; however, they are no longer guaranteed by the principles of *mimēsis*.[10] Henceforth, their relationship is indeterminate, and must be established on a case-by-case basis through analysis or reflection. Aesthetics, here understood as the form of thinking that takes art as its object, emerges with the recognition that there are no preexisting rules for presenting the objects, situations, and peoples of everyday life within the context of art, or indeed for rigorously distinguishing between the two spheres. Aesthetics, one might say with Rancière, is the discourse that announces the rupturing of the theories of human and social nature that underpinned the representative regime.[11] The practices and theories of aesthetic art are the breaking down of determinate connections between artistic causes and spectatorial effects. The aesthetic regime is itself the rupture of the "concordance of sense and sense" formerly supplied by the framework of the representative regime.[12] Rancière: "'Aesthetics' above all means that very collapse; in the first instance, it means the rupture of the harmony that enabled correspondence between the texture of the work and its efficacy."[13]

The aesthetic revolution was inaugurated when artists, designers, writers, and critics attempted to "reinterpret what makes art or what art makes."[14] In thus questioning the representative regime's definition of art, these practices overturned the boundary which had defined art as separate from life. Revoking the principle of *mimēsis*, the arts of the aesthetic age find fodder in the material of everyday life. Its artists contend that the lives of common people, the interiors of bourgeois homes, the markets of Paris, and the commodity form can all become the subject matter of art. By being incorporated into art, these materials are endowed, simultaneously, with meaning and an intransigent presence that resists complete comprehension. These practices create a "sensorium" wherein anything framed can become the raw material of art. For example, Stendhal's transfiguration of utilitarian objects into symbolic charges loaded with significance confirms for Rancière "the ruin of the ancient canons that separate the objects of art from those of ordinary life," testifying to new relationships between "the conscious productions of art, and the involuntary forms of sensible experience."[15] For Rancière, the aesthetic sensorium's indifference to subject matter is important, for it is the basis for his contention that, in the break with the edifice of representation, a form of equality can be found.

The aesthetic identification of the arts is thus more than simply the rupturing of the representative division between art and life; it gives rise to promises for a future made over under the influence of artistic values. For the idea of human nature, the aesthetic regime substitutes the conception of a humanity to come. Its texts speak to us of human beings liberated from habitual forms of thought and the divisions of the past, from the domination of other men and self-imposed alienation. It should be borne in mind that the most proximate political event for the aesthetic regime is the French Revolution, a tremendous overturning of classifications that corresponds to the blurring of boundaries undertaken by the arts. As Rancière indicates, the revolution simultaneously liberates works of art from their representative functions—service to religion and illustration of the aristocracy—while endowing them with the future-directed temporalities of revolutionary fervor. In the first instance, the effacement of these representative functions is a precondition for the appreciation of these objects in terms of their purely sensible qualities.[16] In the second, the hopes of the age and its belief in progress become tied up with the work of art. As is known, revolutionary aspirations provided the justifications for the public museum projects undertaken throughout Europe, most notably the establishment of the Louvre in 1793. Many of these institutions were framed by the discourses of the aesthetic regime and outfitted with the logic of historical development codified by Hegel's *Lectures on Aesthetics*. Together, they give rise to the idea of the "story of art" as that which carries itself and humanity into the future.

The aesthetic revolution is not, however, reducible to political upheaval, and indeed sustains a deeper, more all-encompassing conception of revolution. It aims, as Rancière explains, not simply at a change of political regimes, but to change the meaning of life. In philosophical terms, the aesthetic sensorium is recognizable by its fundamental difference from everyday experience. It suspends the activity of reason on passive sensibility, thereby inaugurating a new relationship between the human faculties. Freed from the domination implicit in the habitual functioning of the mind, the goal instead becomes the harmonious unification of these two aspects of human existence, as in Kant's description of the "free play" of the faculties. It is an ideal quickly given political significance with Schiller's calls for an aesthetic education that would free humankind from intellectual dependency. For Rancière, this more profound vision of revolution provides a critique of the limited form taken by the French Revolution. In short, it extends to humanity the promise contained within works of art.

The aesthetic regime thus creates the terrain wherein art is reinvigorated by being brought into contact with life, while life, it is thought, can be re-formed under the influence of aesthetic values. This relationship between art and life, however, is not as simple as many assume. The relationship is marked by a fundamental paradox that makes art the harbinger of a new life, only to the extent that it is defined as distinct from life. Indeed, it is art's heterogeneity with respect to the everyday that allows it to carry the promise of a new life. The paradox, moreover, is redoubled. In order for art to be art, it must be more than art, that is, carry this promise of impacting life. The fundamental tension of the aesthetic regime is that art is art only in that it carries the promise of being more than art, and it carries this promise only to the extent that it distinguishes itself from life. In other words, autonomy and heteronomy are intricately bound up with one another. This is the central paradox of the aesthetic regime that defines art's role within the distribution of the sensible. Rancière:

> The politics of art in the aesthetic regime of art, or rather, its metapolitcs, is determined by this foundational paradox: in this regime, art is art inasmuch as it is also non-art, something other than art. . . . There is an originary and unceasing contradiction at work. The solitude of the work carries a promise of emancipation, but the accomplishment of the promise is the suppression of art as a separate reality, its transformation into a form of life.[17]

In defining itself as different from life, art impacts life, or promises to do so. In fact, only in doing so is it art.

This ambiguous identity where art's autonomy and heteronomy function as two sides of the same coin means that aesthetic art has a unique form of efficacy. What Rancière stresses is that any political agency on the part of art stems from its refusal to be part of the everyday system of meanings assigned to sense. The aesthetic identification of art is a repudiation of the logic that defines, most immediately, the ethical and representative regimes, as well as the everyday distribution of the sensible. Aesthetic art is a neutralization of the set of relations between bodies and capacities, between what is seen and what can be said of it. It overcomes not only the hierarchies implicit in the practices of the representative regime, but also our expectation that the meaning of a form is readily identifiable.

In this respect, aesthetic art distances itself from that logic that attempted to determine the effects that a work would have on its spectators. Art creates a gap between sense and the meanings made from it. For this reason, Rancière has recently described the "heterotopia" as occupying the "heart" of the aesthetic experience.[18] Art's spaces—be they those of separation, tranquility, abstraction, subtraction, or contestation—work by invalidating the meanings customarily given to perceptions, affects, gestures, and bodies. The aesthetic cancels the logic binding bodies to specific places and times, and it is through these operations that new capacities can be discovered or invented. What the aesthetic form of art thus entails is a way of making and doing that cannot but question the relationships between different objects, subjects, forms of presentation, as well as the estimations placed upon people and things. Aesthetics is political because it introduces dissensus into the world of shared appearances and meanings.

It is this terrain that has given rise to the various movements, theoretical reflections, and misunderstandings we have witnessed over the past two hundred years. Rancière's historical eye takes aim at the various positions which have attempted to claim for art an essential identity, either under the banner of autonomy or by completely effacing the boundary between art and life. Rancière's work is critical of the theories of art that obscure its politics by diverting it into any number of discourses on art's autonomy or sunder it by equating it immediately with life. He seeks to defuse the discourses of mourning that take root by tending too far in either direction, showing how their responses to and expectations for this paradox are limited. He attempts to hold open this zone of exchange where art bears the promise of a new life by keeping itself at a distance. Before critiquing some of the historic-theoretical apparatuses that block this politics of the aesthetic regime, we must spell out more fully what this promise entails.

3.3 EQUALITY IN ART

The aesthetic identification of the arts rejects the representative regime's system of hierarchical distributions. The cumulative effect of this rupture is the positing of new forms of relation between the arts themselves, the subjects they depict, and the manner in which they relate to their audiences. At the most fundamental level, the aesthetic age questions the strict pairing of content and form that, for the representative regime, made it incumbent upon artists and authors to represent certain subjects in specific ways. As we have seen, this distribution in turn sustained the subsequent privileging of certain genres over others. Outside of the Aristotelian framework, the principle that there is a form of discourse appropriate to a given subject matter, or a single form of visibility for a given subject, collapses. This also means that the distribution in which certain arts were said to take precedence over others is dissolved. In the aesthetic regime there are no longer any rules prescribing how the subjects of art should be handled or for rigorously determining in advance what can be the subject of art. As Rancière explains, the subject matter of art has become a matter of indifference, with anything now capable of being framed and presented for contemplation. This, then, is the first form of equality one can point to in the aesthetic regime of the arts. The aesthetic regime contends that there is no longer any meaningful distinction between the potential subjects of art. In the aesthetic regime, equality first manifests itself as indifference, in that anything and anyone can become the subject of art.

As a result of the breakup of the representative regime, the experience of art is likewise altered. The second source of equality is thus to be found in what is now rightfully termed the aesthetic experience. No longer does the consideration of art entail simply absorbing the speech imparted by the fable; it involves reflecting upon whether or not the subject matter and the means of expression are adequate to one another. Aesthetics, in the restricted sense, attempts to think through this new situation in which the traditional codes are no longer applicable. Its investigations of feeling are paradigmatic, for they respond to the recognition that it is no longer possible to provide a rule-based account of how and why certain presentations are appropriate and others not. On Rancière's reading, aesthetics is the form of thinking that simultaneously reflects and implements this newly fashioned equality. He explains, "Aesthetic experience eludes the sensible distribution of roles and competences which structure the hierarchical order."[19] In doing so, it articulates a radically heterogeneous distribution of the sensible that questions the relationship between speech and visibility sustained throughout the representative regime. What it implements is a new rapport between sense and reason.

Aesthetic art achieves this suspension of the hierarchical distribution of the sensible by challenging the cognitive forms upon which they are predicated. Whereas the representative regime conceives of art as the activity of the concept on the passivity of matter, aesthetic art elicits their free and harmonious interaction. Rancière here describes the ideal of the aesthetic experience: "The fabricating activity and the sensible emotion [*l'émotion sensible*] meet each other 'freely,' like two pieces of nature which no longer testify to any hierarchy of the active intelligence on the sensible passivity [*la passivité sensible*]."[20] And he continues, arguing that the aesthetic experience is itself the inscription of equality into distributions founded upon the supremacy of reason. "This separating of nature from itself is the place of a new equality. And this equality inscribes itself in a story that bears . . . a new promise."[21] The aesthetic form of relating to the world, one occasioned equally by art and nature, is thus the creation of a world at odds with the one we customarily inhabit. The picture it sketches of the mind so engaged serves as an indication that there exist other possible ways of ordering sense.

Rancière's work in this area has largely consisted of clarifying the promise of equality announced by the texts of the aesthetic age. By his account, the experiences they supply provide resources for invalidating the division of the world into unequal parts. They allow us to subject the sensible to a process of fictionalization that runs counter to the order of domination. On a certain reading, this is what is at stake when Kant asks us to evaluate the mere presentation of a palace, independently of our thoughts about the extravagances of the rich.[22] The palace is not treated as the expression of luxury, but as a disassociated representation that invalidates the meanings customarily found in the sensible. In this sense, adopting an aesthetic attitude is a means of subjectivation that allows spectators to contest the estimation of their capacities. Doing so generates a counter-worldly experience in which those without a share in the wealth of the world take part in its pleasures. As we saw in Chapter 1, Rancière contends that it is only nostalgia for the old order of firm identities and incontestable boundaries that leads sociology to attempt to discredit these forms of experience. Rancière's defense of aesthetics thus involves combating the anti-aesthetic discourses claiming that such experiences are simply the privilege of a few.[23] Returning to these historical sources, Rancière sheds light on the capacities of current art practices to shift and reconfigure the sensible. The isolation of this "meta-political" dimension of art counters the central tendency of cultural criticism which conceives of art as little more than a mirror of the capitalist order. On the contrary, Rancière contends, its ways of doing and making supply alternatives to the dominant configuration of sense. Its postulation of equality provides a vantage point from which to gauge other ways of doing and making.

The third and final level of equality is detectable in the form of spectatorship announced by the aesthetic regime. Rancière's presentation of it makes recourse to the writings of Joseph Jacotot, who, long before the German artist Joseph Beuys declared everyone an artist, extended his method of universal teaching to the arts. Indeed, Jacotot's pedagogical theory, and the conception of communication upon which it is premised, is integral to the rehabilitation of spectatorship Rancière proposes. As we have seen, Jacotot defended the idea that thought precedes language. Such a position is necessary if we are to avoid equating thought with its expression. With this commitment, we can explain disparities of expression as the result of a will that is wanting, while still maintaining that the intellectual substance from which they spring is equal. By this account, writing and speaking are poetic processes that involve attempting to find expressions for the experiences, feelings, and thoughts one is having. In the first instance, communication is an activity of translating immaterial thoughts into material signs. One gains facility with this process through the repeated and strenuous exercise of the will. The resulting products in turn require a counter-translation on the part of another in order for them to become meaningful. Understanding is the result of applying one's will to the traces left by another in the effort to translate them back into the immaterial realm of thought. These thoughts can then serve as the spark for another instance of creation, and so on indefinitely. Communication, for Jacotot and Rancière, does not transmit the contents of knowledge; it fictionalizes the experience of one's thoughts and emotions, while inviting others to do the same. At bottom, communication is premised upon a desire to be understood that posits an equality between those so engaged. One might even claim that communication is a process of co-creation in that its messages would be meaningless without the activity of those to whom they are addressed.[24]

Poetic forms credit their audiences with possessing this ability to re-create the words of the poet or work of the artist into their own terms. In this sense, the poet's lesson is opposed to that of the stultifying master's. The address of the latter reproduces inequality in the very act of attempting to abolish ignorance. Explication, as we have seen, posits a dissymmetry between two intelligences, making the student dependent upon the master for advancement. The poet, on the other hand, creates a community of equals when he speaks. What he offers is simply one translation of the experience-poem everyone shares. Jacotot and Rancière credit the seventeenth-century dramatist Jean Racine with having hit upon this insight. "Like all creators, Racine instinctively applied the method . . . of universal teaching. He knew that there are no men of *great thoughts*, only men of *great expressions*."[25] Racine, it can be supposed, sensed the danger in assuming anything besides equality: that of condemning oneself to a world in which one is never understood. He made the contrary assumption. Believing his audiences already capable of great thoughts and emotions, he channeled his energies into finding expressions to solicit greater works of co-creation. He was under no illusion that one could become an artist through anything besides the exercise of the will and the supposition of equality.

For Jacotot and Rancière, the equality of persons is not a goal to be advanced by educational and political reform or through the lobbying of art. It is a principle that is either verified or denied by our educational, political, or cultural practices. Aesthetic works affirm this principle when they treat those to whom they are addressed as capable of understanding their messages. Rancière explains:

> The artist's emancipatory lesson, opposed on every count to the professor's stultifying lesson, is this: each one of us is an artist to the extent that he carries out a double process; he is not content to be a mere journeyman but wants to make all work a means of expression, and he is not content to feel something but tries to impart it to others. The artist needs equality as the explicator needs inequality.[26]

If there is anything in Rancière's writings approximating a principle with which to judge contemporary forms of production, it stems from this idea that art and the experiences it occasions can be the proving grounds for the equality of intelligences. As indicated at the outset of this chapter, Rancière favors works that posit the intelligence and agency of their viewers. This requires that we challenge the idea that literary, visual, and material arrangements carry in their wake responses following directly from the artist's intentions. Suspending this logic of cause and effect thus creates a gap between sense and meaning that allows for viewers to become active in the process of counter-translation. Rancière has thus formulated a theory of the capacities to be found in the experience of spectatorship. As he explains, "The problem is to define a way of looking that doesn't preempt the gaze of the spectator. . . . Emancipation is the possibility of a spectator's gaze other than the one that was programmed."[27] Aesthetic works inaugurate a more indeterminate space-time, where the meanings of sensible productions are not immediately apparent. They are the occasion for a breakdown of the meanings and directions habitually given to sense. This suspension of the logic of cause and effect found within the aesthetic regime follows from the collapse of the representative regime's strict pairing of content and form, as well as its supposition that it can determine the effects of a presentation on its audience.

In this respect, critical comments directed at contemporary art are attempts to hold it to the promise of the world without hierarchy announced in the sensorium of the aesthetic regime. This entails describing what Rancière views as the logic of stultification found in many quarters of contemporary art. For example, Paul McCarthy and Jason Rhoades' *Shit Plug* (2002), an installation of glass bottles containing the excrement of visitors to *Documenta 11*, was diagnosed as one of the many "stereotypes that critique stereotypes," while the German artist Josephine Meckseper's photographs of the waste carelessly discarded by anti-war protestors were described as profiting from the inversion of the critical procedure of juxtaposing clashing images by which art once spurred insight.[28] These gestures, while perhaps correct in their political consciousness, reproduce the model of explication, setting up the artist as the one with insight into the nature of art tourism or commodity culture, and viewers as those to whom it must be transmitted.

Artistic stultification is thus discernable in those arrangements that want to transmit directly from artist to viewer certain sentiments or forms of knowledge. They are, one might say, attempts to short-circuit the poetic processes of translation and counter-translation that Jacotot posited as the essence of communication. One of the central challenges for art aspiring to be critical is to refuse didactic means of expression. It is in this sense that one sees the import of

Jacotot's crucial distinction between intelligence exercised on intelligence and will exercised upon will. The former position produces stultification, while the latter compels one to venture forth, translating an artist's work into one's own terms. Art that attempts to make viewers understand at any cost subordinates their consciousness to art, thereby confirming the policed estimation of capacities. The break between sense and meaning achieved by the aesthetic regime means that artists cannot in good faith insist upon the univocal nature of their forms without reinstating the hierarchical logic of the representative order. Practitioners can take comfort in Rancière's suggestion, however, that it is not a lack of understanding that sustains the status quo, but rather a "lack of confidence" in our capacities for changing it.[29] Art is capable of bolstering this confidence on the condition that it adopt more subtle means of communication, rather than attempting to digest in advance its messages.

The Emancipated Spectator, in particular the essay that carries that name, is an important extension of this line of thought, serving for the time being as a bookend to the reflections contained within *Schoolmaster*. The essay critiques those well-intentioned forms of art and theory that desperately want to liberate us, but end up reproducing the logic of stultification. It is directed at those positions that construe spectatorship as fundamentally passive and thus something to be overcome. While Rancière's remarks deal primarily with theatre, his analysis could equally apply to certain tendencies within contemporary visual art. Influenced by Guy Debord's hypothesis of a society of the spectacle, we have witnessed the proliferation of a great number of artistic strategies designed to liberate viewers from their supposed passivity. Whether through a *détournement* of the consumer society's refuse, the administration of shocks intended to stir viewers to wakefulness, or the creation of scenarios, such as one finds in so-called relational art, the aim is to turn viewers into participants. These approaches share the same assumptions as the forms of theatre Rancière diagnoses as having been created in opposition to spectatorship. Whether Brecht's learning plays [*Lehrstücke*] or Artaud's theatre of cruelty, the aim is to convert individuals to a new way of life by first liberating them from their positions as spectators.[30] The premise of course is that being a spectator is necessarily pernicious, and intractable to such a degree that it requires the intervention of art. Many forms of theatre and art thus offer themselves as vehicles for viewers to become active. This procedure of suppressing differences is well known. It belongs to the distribution in which only the schoolmaster knows how the student is to proceed in the acquisition of knowledge. It is the very logic of stultification.[31]

Rancière has been critical of these practices and the vaguely Situationist discourses upon which they depend. He detects in them an uncharitable conception of the art audience's capacities. For him, the reformers of theatre, art's would-be liberators, and the theorists of the spectacle each perpetuate the image of a passive humanity incapable of overcoming its alienation. In response, he questions chiefly the assumption that spectatorship is opposed to action, tracing this position to the concept of the image upon which it is based. Despite the fact that it is often presented to us as the freshest of theoretical perspectives, Rancière shows how the discourse of the spectacle is in essence one of the oldest. At bottom, the voice that denounces the all-consuming power of the consumer society is the same as that which warned us of the images on the cave wall. Through the influences of Feuerbach and Marx, a type of Platonism creeps into Debord's formulations. It is this perspective on the image that forces the equation of looking with passivity. Rancière asks, "Why identify the look [*regard*] and passivity, unless on the presupposition that looking [*regarder*] means delighting in images and appearances while ignoring the truth behind the image?"[32] The identification of spectatorship with passivity thus belongs to a distribution of the sensible in which there is a strict division between activity and passivity, itself founded upon the distinction between images and real being. These oppositions, Rancière contends, are "embodied allegories of inequality."[33] Together, they define a distribution of positions and capacities in which to be a spectator is to be inferior to those playwrights, actors, and artists who are active.

Jacotot's remarks about the essentially poetic nature of communication provide the resources for opposing this conception of viewership. The spectator is already active, argues Rancière, in that a work necessitates counter-translation. "This is a crucial point: spectators see, feel and understand something in as much as they compose their own poem, as, in their way, do actors or playwrights, directors, dancers or performers."[34] The viewer constantly interprets, selects, and navigates his way through a given arrangement, in a sense recreating it each time. This position will allow us to dismiss distributions in which there are inevitably those who are active and those who remain passive. "Emancipation," Rancière explains, "begins when we challenge the opposition between viewing and acting. . . . It begins when we understand that viewing is also an action that confirms or transforms this distribution of positions."[35] Spectatorship is a form of inhabiting the world that follows traces, draws connections, and offers interpretations. It is essentially the activity of establishing new relationships between seeing, doing, and thinking. Spectators need not be emancipated, for indeed spectatorship already disrupts the consensus that tells us there is only one way to interpret reality.

This theory of emancipation leads us to be suspicious of those forms of art that would have us see and feel exactly as the artist or director would have us see and feel. In order to escape from this logic of cause and effect, the mediation of a third term is required.[36] Just as Jacotot's *Télémaque* disassociated the master's intelligence from the pupil's own, aesthetic arrangements are needed to uncouple the artist's from the viewer's. Creating an image, object, installation, action, or phenomenon that belongs to no one in particular, and thus potentially to everyone, serves to break the logic of stultification. This is why it is self-defeating to speak of an art directly equated with existence or one which would be a means for gallery visitors to act out the forms of conviviality lacking in other aspects of life. Without distance, without a space for translation and counter-translation, there is little to distinguish art from other attempts to divide the world into two. Emancipated art, therefore, does not compel viewers to become active, for of course dictating the terms of participation only makes viewers dependent upon others for their liberation. It requires only that we identify the ways in which they are already active. It requires that we insist upon the postulates of equality implied by the aesthetic identification of art.

3.4 IN PLACE OF MODERNITY

Rancière frames the aesthetic regime as a grid of historical intelligibility to take distance from some of the familiar historico-theoretical concepts that mishandle or block the politics of aesthetics. As a chronological marker, the aesthetic regime carries us from the end of the eighteenth century into the contemporary period. It demonstrates how two periods, modernity and postmodernity, customarily thought to be separated by a rupture are in fact united by a shared network of presuppositions regarding how art relates to itself and the larger distribution of the sensible. By modernism, Rancière understands the familiar thesis that the arts have engaged in practices of self-purification in order to rid themselves of elements borrowed from other arts. For critics like Clement Greenberg, the spirit of modernity is encapsulated in the Kantian project of the first *Critique*, which he understands as the process of subjecting reason to a tribunal of its own making. For Greenberg, the arts undertake an analogous endeavor, using their respective forms to establish the limits of their media.[37] Postmodernism rejects the formalism inherent in this agenda. Its strategies for combating modernism include: introducing "low" elements derived from popular culture, the development of new practices, such as performance, and, in theoretical terms, attempting to challenge art's remove from life. Both paradigms, according to Rancière, define forms, histories, and theories of art that obfuscate the politics of the aesthetic regime. With respect to modernism, he contends that it is a limited perspective on the much broader transformations that start at the end of the eighteenth century. In the second instance, he views contemporary rallying cries such as those of postmodernism as only a partial recognition of what was lost with the invention of modernism. By my account, Rancière's interventions into these historiographic debates are the attempt to separate artistic production and reception from discourses that obscure what is emancipatory about aesthetic art.

Rancière traces the various "emplotments," or meanings that are made of the "original scene" of aesthetics contained in Schiller's *Letters on the Aesthetic Education of Mankind*.[38] He argues that preserving the politics of aesthetics relies on maintaining the ambiguous connections between art's autonomy and heteronomy. With Schiller, Rancière is interested in how art is charged with the twofold task of creating both a new world of art *and* a new life. Rancière:

> Schiller says that aesthetic experience will bear the edifice of the art of the beautiful *and* the art of living. The entire question of the "politics of aesthetics"—in other words, of the aesthetic regime of art—turns on this short conjunction. The aesthetic experience is effective inasmuch as it is the experience of that *and*.[39]

What is at stake, for Rancière, is the difference between the aesthetic point of view and the various configurations made from Schiller's account by other theories and histories of art. Both modernism and postmodernism make questionable uses of Schiller's sensorium. They fail to grapple with the connections between art and life to be found therein and thus mishandle its politics. For Rancière, art produces intimations of a new world premised upon the cancellation of hierarchies. Aesthetics allows us to describe this promise and indicate how it is dissensual.

To understand this politics it is necessary to note the manner in which Schiller links art and life in his descriptions of the aesthetic experience. To illustrate this intertwining, Rancière calls our attention to the end of the "Fifteenth Letter," where Schiller describes the *Juno Ludovici*. Schiller:

> It is neither charm, nor is it dignity, that speaks to us from the superb countenance of a Juno Ludovici; it is neither of them, because it is both at once. While the womanly god demands veneration, the godlike woman kindles our love; but while we allow ourselves to melt in the celestial loveliness, the celestial self-sufficiency holds us back in awe. The whole form reposes and dwells within itself, a completely closed creation, and—as though it were beyond space—without yielding, without resistance; there is no force to contend with force, no unprotected part where temporality might break in. Irresistibly seized and attracted by one quality, and held at a distance by the other, we find ourselves at the same time in the condition of utter rest and extreme movement, and the result is that wonderful emotion for which reason has no conception and language no name.[40]

Rancière cautions that any claims regarding autonomy apply to the experience Schiller describes, and not the work of art. In Schiller's presentation, the work is itself loaded with that unusual causality in which its removal from the everyday meaning of sense allows it to impact life. Schiller's *Juno* is an example of the very intermingling of autonomy and heteronomy at the heart of the aesthetic regime. The sculpture initiates a fundamentally altered perspective, giving rise to a promise for a reconfiguration of life more generally. For Schiller, the aesthetic state is opened by the goddess' difference from everyday sense. This is why Rancière claims, "The whole motto of the politics of the aesthetic regime . . . can be spelled out as follows: let us save the 'heterogeneous sensible.'"[41] Art contains this promise of founding a new form of life because it belongs to a sensorium foreign to the everyday. The sculpture is this difference, and hence provides the occasion for an "education," inasmuch as the experience of it achieves what is impossible from the perspective of everyday cognition. The aesthetic experience unites directions—attraction and retreat, rest and movement—thought to be contradictory.

To have a greater sense of the paradox and promise operative in Schiller's text, it is important to be clear about the historical context for the *Letters*, as well as the immediate location of the paean to *Juno*. With respect to the former, it is generally well known that the *Letters* are in part a response to the French Revolution. Schiller can be understood as framing aesthetic education as a solution to the possibilities opened up by the monarchy's fall, as well as the excesses of the revolutionaries. The question, as Schiller sees it, is what should humanity do with its newly won freedom? He explains that, "if we are to solve that political problem in practice, [we must] follow the path of aesthetics, since it is through Beauty that we arrive at Freedom."[42] Schiller thus attempts to outfit humanity for its unique historical-political condition, and he undertakes this by synthesizing the duality inherent in human nature. This latter project is at stake in the key sequence capped by the description of the goddess. For Schiller, a play impulse, whose object is beauty, mediates between the sense impulse, whose aim is life, and the form-giving impulse, whose end is morality. Operative in the creation or contemplation of beauty, the play impulse allows man to synthesize the sensuous and rational aspects of his nature. Schiller's famous maxim is of course, "Man plays only when he is in the full sense of the word a man, and *he is only wholly Man when he is playing*."[43] Play does not indicate that, for Schiller, art is merely sport, but that it is a place where we learn to take up necessity with freedom. Through beauty's "living shapes," the individual becomes conscious of sensible and rational existence, both of which, for Schiller, compel the individual in conflicting directions. Beauty's living shapes, at once sensible and intellectual, annul these two compulsions. Beauty breaks from the physical realm of pure sense, while resisting complete capture by consciousness. Its existence thereby allows us "to play at once with our affection and with our respect."[44] This is the sense in which beauty founds the "still more difficult art of living."[45] It instructs mankind in the process of reconciling the dictates handed to it by life and reason.

This analysis is indicative of the identification art assumes within the aesthetic regime, as well as the relationship it maintains to the larger distribution of the sensible. What play and beauty signify, for Rancière, is a departure from dominant meanings of sense. Here, it is helpful to make explicit the Kantian framework informing Schiller's position. What aesthetic art achieves is a suspension of the activity of the understanding upon a passive sensibility, or the everyday status of the mind known as cognition. Rancière interprets Schiller's suspension of the dominance of the rational faculty as the sensible refutation of a world divisible into two. "What the aesthetic free appearance and free play challenge is the distribution of the sensible that identifies the order of domination with the differences between two humanities."[46] Play is, accordingly, the subversion of the logic in which everything must be doing something, and through which one faculty subordinates another. The aesthetic state thus "manifests a liberty and an equality of sensing," legible as a political promise.[47]

What Rancière's presentation of aesthetics thus offers is an account of how art maintains a paradoxical form of politics. Aesthetic art is the inscription in sense of a form of sense that disrupts and disqualifies the everyday hierarchical distributions of sense. This is premised on the idea that art is a self-secluding form, *and* a form of life. The paradox is clearly spelled out by Schiller when he explains that "the Beautiful is not to be mere life, nor mere shape, but living shape—that is, Beauty."[48] The aesthetic regime thus gives birth to a form of art that intermingles with non-art. For Rancière, successful theories of art hold to this ambiguous and complicated political space where art makes promises that it cannot keep. They are mindful of that fact that insisting exclusively upon art's autonomy turns it into mere art, while denying the differences between artistic practices and the practices of life turns them into mere life. Both options simultaneously end art and the politics of aesthetics.

"Modernity" has proven to be one of the most confused and abiding ways of handling this paradox. It averts the challenges posed by the aesthetic age's intermingling of art and non-art by attempting to construct narratives of art's autonomy. An essential aspect of this endeavor is construing the breakup of the representative regime as a ban on resemblance. With this premise, modernism attempts to preserve a form of *mimēsis*, as when Greenberg, for example, describes modern painting as the "imitation of imitating."[49] As Rancière explains, however, the aesthetic regime's repudiation of *mimēsis* is not simply an iconoclasm waged against figuration; it is the destruction of the network that made images function as hierarchical estimations of community.⁵⁰ The breakdown of the representative regime, moreover, is the collapse of a distribution that rigorously separated art from life. Stepping beyond *mimēsis* founds not only art's autonomy, as the narrative of modernism would have it; it is also the historical pre-condition for strategies associated with art's heteronomy, such as the admixture of "high" and "low" forms, the blurring of the distinction between art and life, and the exchanges between the arts themselves.

Several of Rancière's studies directly challenge the legacy of modernism by charting the connections between the arts themselves, and with social reality more generally. Two literary studies, *La parole muette* and *Mallarmé, La politique de la sirène* are exemplary in this regard. The former book analyzed the emergence of literature through a displacement of the *belles-lettres*, with its hierarchy of genres and strict, representative foundations. The "silent speech" [*parole muette*] born in the aesthetic age is simultaneously the creation of a world in which writing reposes upon itself and one where everything speaks. This poetics sustains both the ideal of a pure literature concerned only with form, and a writing that would express and shape life in general.⁵¹ The text on Mallarmé challenges the idea that modern writers deal exclusively with problems of language, arguing against conventional wisdom that Mallarmé's practice embraces choreography, music, and design.⁵² In *The Future of the Image*, Rancière uses the similarities between the supposedly pure poetry of Mallarmé and the eminently practical industrial design of Peter Behrens as a case in point in his critique of the idea that modernity is a period in which the arts set about their respective efforts of self-purification. Poet and designer are examples of the de-specialization characteristic of the aesthetic regime, for Mallarmé and Behrens both undertake to generate the "types" that will usher in new modes of collective life.⁵³

Modernism is thus a limited understanding of the rupture inaugurated by the aesthetic regime. It is a way of thinking that avoids the confusion of the heterogeneous sensible. This is the flawed starting point of the many art historical narratives that it is now commonplace to critique. In taking only part of the aesthetic formula, they fail to provide a full account of the past two hundred years of art, and ultimately leave wanting a discussion of how art relates to the greater distribution of practices. In formulating the aesthetic regime, Rancière is thus calling for a reinvestigation of the history of art. Aesthetics is that indisciplinary knowledge that investigates the condition in which it is no longer possible to exploit pre-established principles in order to define the differences between the arts themselves or the separation between art and life. The approach it defines is at odds with those notions of modernity that attempt to isolate the arts from one another and the sensible more generally. As an alternative to modernism, the aesthetic regime can allow for fuller explanations of the cultural transformations that parallel the political upheaval of the French Revolution and permit us to describe the politics of a given art by highlighting its exchanges with, and separations from, life. This situation, as Rancière explains, is fundamentally one of "disorder."[54] It is that which the notion of artistic modernity would like to sweep aside. It is necessary to reactivate this disorder if we are to recover the political capacities of art.

3.5 AGAINST POSTMODERNITY

In large part, Rancière is dismissive of the idea that postmodernity is a new paradigm within art, literature, and culture more generally. He argues, "Postmodernism . . . was simply the name under whose guise certain artists and thinkers realized what modernism had been: a desperate attempt to establish a 'distinctive feature of art' by linking it to a simple teleology of historical evolution and rupture."[55] As we have seen, modernism attempts to found the autonomy of art, concealing a fundamental antinomy at the heart of the aesthetic regime. When the contradictions between art's practices and this narrative became evident, theorists posited a new paradigm; however, this new understanding of art does not, for Rancière, adequately recapture the emancipatory promise of the aesthetic regime. In fact, in place of the aesthetic regime's co-mingling of art and politics it substitutes the art-ethics dyad. What Rancière describes as the "ethical turn" of aesthetics and politics is in essence one way of defusing art's political capacities. What is at stake in this substitution is the difference between the possible and the impossible, for when aesthetics becomes ethical, viewers learn only that the sensible is immutable.

Rancière's opposition has been directed primarily at Jean-François Lyotard's appropriation of the Kantian sublime. Lyotard's writings continue to exercise a tremendous influence on discussions of art and aesthetics, especially in the French context, and his work was significant for the formulation of the idea of postmodernity. For Lyotard, postmodernity is a rupture that has irrevocably altered the field of knowledge. He describes it as an incredulity directed against all-encompassing systems of meaning, such as Christianity, Marxism, Enlightenment notions of progress, and even the sciences themselves. For Lyotard, the postmodern condition is the decline of these meta-narratives to the advantage of linguistic and epistemological plurality.[56] This epistemological diagnosis is inseparable from the program of activating and testifying to differences that Lyotard assigns to art. His contribution could thus be seen as twofold: first, he shaped conversations regarding postmodernism in terms of rupture, framing the postmodern as a skeptical break with modernity's chief epistemological categories; and secondly, he attempted to outline a new direction for the avant-garde, by distinguishing between modern and postmodern forms of production.

According to Lyotard, both modern and postmodern art are cut from the Kantian sublime. In the "Analytic of the Sublime," Kant articulated the sense of disharmony the subject feels before a presentation that simultaneously repels and attracts. In experiences of either great magnitude or might, there is an inability on the part of the imagination to satisfy the demands made by reason for a form with which to totalize experience. The accompanying cognitive dissonance eventually gives way to a type of self-awareness, which is an awakening of the mind to its supersensible vocation. What reason learns, and what the subject deems sublime, is that found within itself is a preeminence over nature, even when the latter is considered in its most awe-inspiring forms. The sublime is, for Kant, anything that convinces the mind that it possesses "*a power surpassing any standard of sense.*"[57] In short, the feeling of sublimity provides the subject with a recognition of its freedom from the phenomenal realm, and thus its capacity for morality.

For Lyotard, sublime experience extends beyond the exceptional scenes described by Kant. It is discernable in the practices of modern and postmodern art, both of which testify to the existence of the unpresentable and the subsequent sundering of the mind's capacities for representation. The key difference is that the modern is "nostalgic" for joining together the ideas of reason with their material presentation. "It allows the unrepresentable to be put forward only as . . . missing contents; but the form, because of its recognizable consistency, continues to offer to the reader or viewer matter for solace and pleasure."[58] Postmodern art, on the other hand, denies viewers "the solace of good forms."[59] It devotes itself instead to imparting a stronger sense of the unpresentable. These art works, according to Lyotard, destabilize the nostalgia for order, totality, and closure. Lyotard's thinking is of course inflected by the horrors of the twentieth century, first and foremost the Shoah. It is with reference to this event that Lyotard gives to art the ethical responsibility of witnessing to reason's undoing. Art, for Lyotard, can attest to such atrocities, but only obliquely. He explains:

> It is important, very important, to remember that no one can—by writing, by painting, by anything—pretend to be witness and truthful reporter of, be "equal" to the sublime affection, without being rendered guilty of falsification and imposture through this very pretension.[60]

The reworked Kantian sublime is the key concept with which Lyotard endows art with an ethical-memorial task. He explains that it is the task of postmodern art to activate the difference between the ideas of reason and their sensuous manifestation, and in this way indirectly grow our awareness of that which thought is incapable of thinking. By this logic, art must renounce representation, and devote itself instead to finding new ways of revealing that representation as such is condemned to forgetting. Art, for Lyotard, represents the impossibility of representation.[61]

In response to Lyotard's position, Rancière advances two primary criticisms. In the first place, he argues that questions regarding the possibility or impossibility of representation partake of a historical error. Mourning the impossibility of art to fulfill its task of representation, above all with respect to the limit case of the Nazi death camps, relies upon an understanding of art that is no longer our own. It is only when one insists that it is art's role to faithfully represent experience that one can lament its failure. Rancière uses the distinction between the representative and aesthetic regimes to argue that the issue is poorly posed. "The argument of the 'unrepresentable' does not fit the experience of artistic practice. Rather, it fulfils the desire that there be something unrepresentable . . . in order to inscribe in the practice of art the necessity of the ethical detour."[62] This detour blocks in advance any connection between art and politics, making the affirmation of anything besides the existence of the unpresentable a form of idolatry. As Rancière explains, "The avant-garde is endowed with the paradoxical duty of bearing witness to an immemorial dependency of human thought that makes any promise of emancipation a deception."[63]

In the second instance, Rancière follows Lyotard's re-reading of Kant in order to indicate how it annuls the capacities contained in sublime experiences. Lyotard's sublime is an undoing of the dynamic of supersensible discovery developed by Kant. Whereas for Kant sublime presentations allow reason to discover its ability to surpass sense, for Lyotard the sublime is an indication of the mind's dependence. The aesthetic shocks he ascribes to art are the reminder of the mind's inability to surpass the sensible. Lyotard's position is, for Rancière, the latest in the line of thought that attempts to radicalize the shock of art in order to insulate it from commercial kitsch. It too is part of the lineage that views the aesthetic experience as fundamentally different from ordinary experience. Lyotard maintains the aesthetic's radical difference from the everyday; the problem is that he no longer construes it as emancipatory. On the contrary, art's otherness is the reminder of the complicity between thought and the order of domination. Rancière describes the position thus, "Aesthetic experience is that of a subjugated mind, subjugated to the sensible, but also and above all, through this sensible dependence, to the law of the Other."[64] Rather than promising a new sensible configuration, the aesthetic, for Lyotard, indicates thought's fundamental incapacity to imagine it otherwise. This is of course the key difference between Lyotard and Rancière. Whereas Rancière, following Schiller, interprets the heterogeneous sensible as sustaining capacities for sensation and thought, Lyotard construes the aesthetic as an affliction to be undergone. The otherness of art that was once the promise of emancipation becomes, with Lyotard, a reminder of thought's capture. By his account, art no longer promises; it testifies only to the fact that it cannot testify.

The deployment of the sublime within discussions of art, against Kant's warnings, ultimately deprives art of its political potential. Despite Lyotard's many engagements with works of contemporary visual art, his reflections subordinate its practices to the dominant sensible order. His discussions confirm instead the distribution of bodies, minds, and capacities, as well as the meanings that are made of them. One might argue that Lyotard's is a police reading of Kant inasmuch as it suppresses the politics at the heart of aesthetics. Such a position is a flawed response to the ambiguous identity of aesthetic art. Like modernism, it renounces the connections between self-secluding forms and dreams of emancipation. In a sense, Lyotard's account of art is even more problematic than those of modernism, for it inscribes art within a sensible no longer conceivable as subject to transformation. What Lyotard thus threatens to cancel is the possibility of art and aesthetics functioning as dissensus.

3.6 ART AS DISSENSUS

Freed from these problematic conceptions of art, we are in a position to describe art in terms of dissensus. Dissensus is the process of transforming the sensible by placing it in conflict with a rival conception of the world. As one might expect, the arts are uniquely suited for this task. They can be viewed as containing rival configurations of sense, and are frequently the means of introducing a breach into the sensible. When thinking about dissensus in the artistic context, care must be taken not to efface the fact that aesthetic art contains its own politics, one that prevents art from being directly equated with politics as such. Art is never political in the same way that, for example, a strike is, as it is invested in the distinctiveness of its forms. This politics of art follows directly from the central tension of aesthetic regime: that of holding in close relation art's autonomy and heteronomy. Indeed, the will to hold itself in a new and ambiguous relationship with life is what allows art to advance the promise of life reconfigured. Here, we follow Rancière's various uses of dissensus in his discussions of art in order to offer a more general account of art's political import. For him, dissensus functions on a number of levels, which it is the task of this section to synthesize.

To clarify the various aspects of dissensus, I propose treating aesthetic dissensus as containing three levels, which are all discernable in Rancière's writings. Aesthetic dissensus means that works of art fashion and sustain new subjects; they create new objects and new forms of perception; and, finally, they offer experiences fundamentally dissimilar from the everyday ordering of sense. This presentation is not intended to indicate that these elements of dissensus are separate from one another, but to rejoin the discussion of political dissensus from the previous chapter. There we saw that politics consists of reconfiguring the sensible by means of a supposition foreign to it. This inaugurates a movement which allows that which was previously invisible to become visible. This movement is not simply the negation of an existing state of affairs; it entails constructing a counterworld, and placing it in a polemical relationship with the existing world, so to challenge and possibly overturn the customary distribution of the sensible. The means of creating this world include fashioning new subjects, introducing new objects, and offering a new estimation of the capacities of those inhabiting the distribution. Dissensus is intimately related to the capacities of aesthetic art, which performs these functions.

In the first instance, we know that art is one of the ways in which marginalized voices manifest themselves. Provided that they do not appear in scripted ways, art allows the part of those without part to manifest a voice they were thought not to possess. These activities counter domination, which is usually an admixture of two forms of sensible exclusion: it consists of denying that the sounds issuing from someone's mouth are human speech and/or it involves preventing them from inhabiting the space-time of politics. Plato's *Republic*, for example, defines a sensible configuration in which the absence of artisans from politics is supported by a strict estimation placed on their capacities, and the refusal to allow them to engage in practices of imitation. For Rancière, the workers' activities analyzed in *Nights* serves as a counterpoint to such distributions. The primary means by which workers convinced themselves and others of their equality was through writing. This practice was dissensual inasmuch as it allowed for the emergence of capacities and thus forms of subjectivity not previously identifiable within the police order. Importantly, this means that dissensus is not simply the affirmation of the names and identities prescribed by the police; it entails the elaboration of capacities thought not to exist. Aesthetic acts are interventions that form points for a broader resistance by first opening up worlds where subjects can constitute themselves as political subjects. Art, in this first instance, is one means of assuming the subjectivity required for politics. It enables those denied it the ability to demonstrate their facility with the *logos*.

Second, artistic practices disrupt the sense of self-evidence with which we treat the sensible. Even the narrow world of galleries, biennials, and museums contribute to problematizing the general space-time of communal life. At its best, its objects and forms of display question the partitions sustaining the general *aisthēsis*. Dissensus at the level of the art object, image, installation, or action means that art alters the parameters of the sensible world. Rancière here invites us to think works in a much more active sense than is generally permitted by traditional theories of art. For him, its products operate on the sensible aspects of the *polis*, serving to question its elements and redefine its boundaries. This does not mean, however, that the products of art are equivalent to the forms of shock dear to postmodernists, although this is no doubt one strategy available to the arts; dissensus means developing the unexpected, the unscripted, and the dis-identified. It means pursuing small openings, "discreet affects," and affirmations of capacity.[65] This position regarding the operationality of art means that dissensus is not a question of mere perspective; it does not simply allow us to *see* the world differently, it actually *modifies* the sensible world. This restoration of existence to art follows from the breakdown of the representative regime, a partitioning that insulated the art work by defining it in opposition to life. Art operates upon the objects, distinctions, and boundaries of the sensible, serving to expand what can be seen and heard. In the second instance, then, dissensus contests the parameters of the sensible world. Provided one does not reinstate the old logic of cause and effect, one can view art as containing concrete proposals for the transformation of life. It offers viewers alternative temporalities and spacings, and calls upon them to question the way in which the sensible configuration of the world is presented as given.

We have already seen how such proposals for a new life were fashioned with the expectations Schiller placed upon the *Juno Ludovici*. It remains for us, however, to indicate why this promise is dissensual. This is the third form of aesthetic dissensus: the art of the aesthetic regime fashions a sensorium antagonistic to the dominant order. Art achieves this by providing us with a dramatically different form of experience, thereby sketching a counterworld that can be placed in a polemical rapport with our own. Artistic works occasion dissensus when they prompt a suspension of the everyday vocation of the mind, in particular those forms founded upon the subordination of the sensuous to the rational. They thereby enable viewers to depart from the more generalized distributions of sense that condition the subjective arrangement of the faculties. Aesthetic experiences can be seen as invalidating customary forms of relation, most immediately our experiences of space and time. Indeed, with respect to the *Juno*, Schiller describes a time of rest and repose in which the demands of the world fall away, and a space beyond space where force is neutralized. Such objects hold individuals in what is referred to as reflection. This state is distinguishable from cognition, a relation of the subjective faculties marked by the structuring of sense by reason. Aesthetic art, by virtue of its heterogeneity, founds this new arrangement of the faculties. In reflection, sense is freed from its subordination to reason. This freedom of the faculties is prompted by the strangeness of the work's presentation. As a sensible form, the work of art holds open the relationship between sense and reason. It disrupts reason's ability to think and dispense with sensible material. The ensuing investigation of each faculty in their depths creates a feeling of satisfaction. It allows the human being to feel free of the demands made upon his faculties by the habitual distribution of the sensible.

As we saw in Chapter 2, an essential aspect of dissensus is equality. This, according to Rancière, is what we find in Kant's description of the free play of the faculties and Schiller's discussion of the play impulse. Rancière: "Aesthetic free play—or neutralization—defines a new mode of experience that carries a new form of sensible universality and equality."[66] In allowing the faculties to find a new relationship with one another, aesthetic art inscribes equality into the field of experience. This equality exists first among the cognitive faculties, which are described as entering into an unprecedented and harmonious relationship with one another. It is fair to say that, on Rancière's reading, this equality is more than simply symbolic. It is a tangible inscription of equality that the viewing subject experiences in a domain customarily subjected to a hierarchical arrangement. In the second instance, this inscription is the allegory of a world no longer divisible into two. For Rancière, even the most self-secluding of arts harbors this political promise. They create sensible-mental arrangements that are a reproach to inequality itself. The arts, one might say, open up a world within the existing world by placing the relationships they arouse among the faculties in opposition to the common world.

In Rancière's estimation, this counterworld is what Schiller advances under the guise of the aesthetic state. His aesthetic revolution is a more radical and wide-ranging transfiguration of humanity than the political one that preceded it. The problem with the French Revolution, according to this reading, was that it treated the people simply as passive matter to be formed by a new system of laws. Its very goals, forms of organization, and processes kept in place the old logic of form imposing itself on matter. Rancière explains, "For Schiller, the Revolution turned to terror because it still obeyed the model of the active intellectual faculty restricting the passive sensible materiality."[67] In simply seizing and transforming state power, the revolutionary process maintained the central means of domination: the idea of two distinct levels of humanity—those who command and give form, and those who obey and are molded.

In contrast, aesthetic experience defines, in cognitive and social terms, an experience that points to the inherent conservatism of even ostensibly radical forms of political action. It contends that anything short of equality will inevitably become the property of the police. Real revolutions abolish the distinctions between activity and passivity, between those who form and those who are formed. This is why, for Schiller, the revolutionary project needs to be completed by an aesthetic education. Its experiences would simultaneously revolutionize humanity and defuse state power. It posits that sense and reason can be related to one another equally, thereby challenging the conception of politics according to which the goal is to obtain power and impose social reforms or a news system of laws. Equality sees these strategies for what they are: police operations that reproduce the dominant distribution of the sensible. Aesthetic experience instead outlines a world of dissensus in which the various parts of mind and community are related on the basis of equality. While the aesthetic world is no doubt only a promise, this does not prevent it from becoming active in the undoing and remaking of our own.[68]

Dissensus is possible because the sensible is never beyond contestation. It is subject to an ongoing battle between different forces, premised upon different assumptions, and following different logics. This means that those seeking to control the sensible in order to profit from a hierarchical distribution can never close it with a thorough justification. The practices of art are one of the most direct ways in which the coordinates of the sensible are contested. Its practices intervene in the sensible in order to question the allotment of parts, the objects of dispute, and the parameters of thought. Even though art, according to Rancière's position, cannot and should not tell us expressly what we should think and do, it has a truly political function, one that is independent of the explicit commitments of its artists. Art touches upon the aesthetic dimension of the political and, even when it seeks most to depart from it, can inspire its transformation.

CONCLUSION

The aesthetic regime is an identification of art that links artistic practices to the larger distribution of the sensible, thus endowing them with unprecedented critical powers. Art's capacity for dissensus springs from the tension at the heart of this regime, which creates a form of art that makes promises for individual and communal emancipation that it cannot keep. This paradox makes art's efficacy follow from its difference from life, and therewith renders it unable to directly impact life upon pain of sundering its powers. This is the tension, according to Rancière, that artists, theorists, critics, literary scholars, and art historians have been interpreting differently for over two hundred years. To fully grasp its force, it was necessary to rid ourselves of two problematic responses to it, those of modernism and postmodernism. Any accounting of the sins of the histories carried out under the auspices of either must inevitably mention that both concepts rather arbitrarily consign to the dustbin of history those practices and products that do not fit, respectively, with a strict formalist agenda or the strategies that allegedly overtake it. With Rancière, we have indicated a conceptual opening for reinvestigating and reinvigorating the arts by describing their multifarious relationships with life. Much historical work, however, remains. Accordingly, histories and theories of the arts that insist upon their essential separation from one another or from life must be re-immersed in the complicated field of the aesthetic regime from which they were subtracted. The aesthetic regime, and the recovery of the politics of aesthetics, means that we must think the encounters between art, literature, philosophical reflection, and the re-valuations of life they contain, in an ever more indisciplinary fashion.

With the aesthetic regime, one can rediscover how the ideal of a new humanity was born simultaneously with the idea of a new art. According to the framework of this regime, art and humanity would both be free from hierarchy, with the practices of the former serving as the sensible promise of the latter. Aesthetics seizes upon these experiences, seeking to clarify them and make sure they are not lost. The critical practice of dissensus brings them into conflict with the efforts to police the sensible. Rancière, for his part, draws what he thinks is the obvious conclusion regarding these states of repose and reflection opened up by works of art. He interprets them as a sensible manifestation of the equality that we have been attempting to verify. According to him, when we assume equality in our creative practices or when we are treated to it in our roles as spectators, we witness its promise of emancipation. And while one would be hard pressed to claim that the equal relationship between the faculties occasioned by works of art carries us very far towards real political equality, its inscription in sense is significant. It means that equality is possible, and that the sensible can be made to yield to its supposition.

CHAPTER 4

REGIMES OF CINEMA

INTRODUCTION

Our consideration of Rancière's writings on film in a separate chapter does not indicate that it is a more recent intellectual development, or that his reflections on the moving image are separate from his larger discussions of art. At a personal level, cinema has been a source of inspiration to Rancière since his student days, and his interest in it reflects the cinephilia that gripped Paris in the 1950s and 1960s.[1] He has recently explained how this culture was a form of dissensus, inasmuch as its alliances questioned the notion that art had to adhere to certain forms or occupy specific times and places in order to be legitimate.[2] Rancière has published in the pages of *Cahiers du cinéma* since the late 1970s when the journal was attempting to expand beyond its rather limited Althusserian perspective, and has contributed a number of essays to *Trafic*, the French cinema journal founded by the critic and theorist Serge Daney after his tenure at *Cahiers*. Writing on film forms an increasingly large part of Rancière's output, only a portion of which has been collected in *Film Fables*, his most extensive and systematic reflections on the art to date. Suffice it to say, Rancière's interest in cinema is deep, abiding, and necessary for any understanding of his more general intellectual project.

In terms of his scholarly work, the reflection on film is integral to an understanding of the poetics of the different regimes of art, and in some instances enables Rancière to describe with greater precision the visuality that results from the different regimes. This discussion of Rancière's theoretical contributions as well as some of his particular analyses of individual films builds upon our understanding of his various regimes of art, in particular the directions outlined by the representative and aesthetic regimes. This means that, for Rancière, the cinema has a unique historicity, one too often neglected by histories of stylistic development or philosophical reflections on the ontological status of its images. Cinema is, Rancière explains, the "art of the twentieth century thought up by the nineteenth century," in the sense that its aspirations, strategies, and games were "predetermined by the categories of aesthetic thought."[3] The cinema is heralded by the aesthetic age's investment of the sensible world with the powers of thought and speech. This poetics of the sensible that speaks is, for Rancière, the primary contribution of romanticism. As an example of speech having been carried to matter, one could cite the short text jointly authored by Hölderlin, Schelling, and Hegel, "Oldest Programme for a System of German Idealism." There, it is argued that if humanity is to make any moral progress, ideas must become sensible. "The philosopher must possess as much aesthetic power as the poet."[4] As we will see, this sensorium of the aesthetic age, which endows mute matter with the capacity for thought and speech, supplies art with a new conception of creative labors. It displaces the Aristotelian schema in which artistic work was conceived as the activity of bringing form to matter. It develops instead the idea that creation results from an admixture of conscious and unconscious processes. For the aesthetic regime, especially in its more romantic dimensions, the task of art becomes that of passively recording the magic of the sensible world. Because of the camera's passivity, the cinema is thought to most fully realize the dream of a purely passive art. Its "technique" would be the cancellation of the artist's technique, which allows the world to express itself directly.

This aesthetic inheritance of passivity, however, is only one half of the equation. The cinema is also the place of the representative regime's restoration. As we saw in the previous chapter, Aristotle's model of poetics subordinated the visual elements [*opsis*] of dramatic productions to its fable or plot [*muthos*]. His poetics made it the task of art to create a space for the coming-to-presence of speech [*logos*]. From an artistic point of view, the work was conceived as a series of events that were to be arranged into a meaningful whole. For various reasons, the cinema is compelled to adopt aspects of this poetics. Its primary task will be the composition and illustration of fables according to the Aristotelian model. Moreover, the cinema rehabilitates many of the expressive codes found within Classical theatre, and distributes its fictions according to genres. It is thus the unlikely embodiment of two competing conceptions of art. Cinema, for Rancière, is a mixed art in that it continually negotiates between these two poetics.

For Rancière, individual films are the result of a strange logic in which the film's fable—its stories, scripts, and chronological arrangement of events—is repeatedly "thwarted" [*contrariée*] by shots, scenes, images, sounds, moments of narrative suspension, and instances of translation from literary to cinematic fable that interrupt the linkage of actions. These poetic strategies, or, as Rancière terms them, "games," borrow from the aesthetic regime its ideal of a purely passive art. The cinematic art is a unique mélange of the arrangement of actions into a meaningful whole according to the model bequeathed by Aristotle and the aesthetic scenes that counter its progression. The interlacing of these two poetics defines the specificity of cinema. The medium functions, paradoxically, as the expression of both regimes, coming into being at the intersection of these two poetics. This chapter follows some of the cinematic games analyzed by Rancière, attempting to situate them in terms of the logics defined by each regime. It places his thought in dialogue with other currents in film theory and defends the modest approach to film analysis that he offers. This chapter concludes with a reflection on the politics of cinema, where it is claimed that the cinema is uniquely suited for inscribing equality into spaces reserved for hierarchy.

4.1 A HISTORICAL POETICS OF CINEMA

It is difficult to categorize Rancière's writings on cinema, and indeed they seem deliberately fashioned to overturn customary classifications. His analyses might at first glance appear to be a type of cinematic formalism, concerned as they are with the combination of a film's constitutive elements—montage, the framing of shots, and editing. One quickly notes, however, that these analyses are inseparable from an analysis of the film's plot. More than a mere narratology, however, these discussions chart the deep intertwining of film's two logics. For Rancière, cinema can testify to its powers only by countering the representative logic of action with strategies of thwarting borrowed from romantic poetics. While cinema is made possible by these two inheritances, it is also constrained by them, being part of an industry that for a large part insists upon the representative logic of well-ordered actions. Therefore, to distinguish themselves in the task of representation, directors must manipulate a film's formal devices. They incorporate touches, shots, and even scenes that exceed the demands of the plot. It is this thwarting of the fable which allows cinema to give evidence of its distinctive artistic merits. The crossed logics of historical forces and personal decisions are what make films compelling, and that to which Rancière directs our attention. His texts are in a sense a film lover's account of these procedures. They highlight the unique gestures by which films make their own creations of the stories upon which they are based.

In an important essay "*L'historicité du cinéma*," Rancière explains that with film he is primarily interested in three elements. On the one hand, there is the *aesthetic* logic of romanticism that has accompanied cinema since its birth. This is the idea that the passivity of the camera and the energy of its images introduce a new form of "writing" that overcomes the opposition between sense and thought. This logic is coupled with the *representative* idea of art inherited from Aristotle, which makes fiction the arrangement of actions into a unified whole. Against the grain of much film theory, Rancière insists that this element, the story to be illustrated, is essential. Finally, there is the *artistic* logic according to which these two poetics are joined. An individual film is thus the specific meeting of the aesthetic and representative logics. As Rancière describes it:

> A cinematographic fiction is in effect the specific linking [*enchaînement*] of two types of sequences: sequences finalized according to the Aristotelian representative logic, that of assemblages of actions, and of non-finalized sequences, lyrical sequences that suspend action and escape the imperative of meaning to allow one to simply see "life" in its "stupidity," in its raw existence, without reason.[5]

In truth, the image of existence opened up by the camera will be more complicated than this quotation indicates (Section 4.2). The point here, however, is a methodological one. Rancière's analyses of individual films are centered on the combination and rivalry of these two poetic inheritances. They are bolstered by a sense of the theories, technologies, and techniques by which films come to be. For this reason, it is appropriate to describe Rancière's approach as a "historical poetics" of cinema. He recounts how, by means of the constraints placed upon it and capacities at its disposal, filmmaking realizes new configurations. Its final products always bear the marks of this double and conflicting inheritance. They are the combination of fables that advance a causal order of events and the images that undo it.

Film Fables is itself a linking-together of texts published at different times and given a deceptively simple arrangement: it begins with canonical works from the silent era and German expressionism, passes by way of two *auteurs* dear to the *Cahiers* crowd and the *Nouvelle Vague*, Anthony Mann and Nicholas Ray, and concludes by looking at two highly self-reflexive works of video-age montage, Chris Marker's *Le tombeau d'Alexandre* and Jean-Luc Godard's *Histoire(s) du cinéma*. Along the way, it engages Deleuze's landmark cinema books and takes exception with Godard's recounting of the twentieth century and its relationship with cinema. These last two operations (Sections 4.4 and 4.5) are premised upon an understanding of the historical poetic analysis Rancière proposes in place of these histories, and clear the ground for describing the political capacities of cinema.

Although it is arranged chronologically, *Film Fables* is not a film history, nor even, claims Rancière, a counter-history.[6] This means that the text is not intended to present an alternative telling of the history of cinema, even though it places in question many customary divides, such as the notion of a cinematic modernity and the division between the silent era and the development of the talkie. The effect of his text is to displace many of the divisions and categories upon which film histories rely. His investigations are in this sense an effort to create a new space for viewing and the attempt to head off the discourses that have in recent years proclaimed the exhaustion of the medium. Rancière:

> I wanted to call into question a conception of history in terms of progress or decadence: the paradigms of origin, of evolution or rupture, and in the first place this divide [*partage*] between a representative *ancien régime* and an anti-representative modernity which serves cinema, as elsewhere, as a dominant scheme.[7]

If Rancière's book is not a simple history, neither can it be equated easily with film theory. It is a scrupulously nominalist work that offers few general reflections on the medium, except to indicate how it is pulled between two poetics. Its descriptions serve only to defend the modest thesis that "Cinema can only make the games it plays with its own means intelligible to itself through the games of exchange and inversion it plays with the literary fable, the plastic form, and the theatrical voice."[8] The work celebrates these games and challenges the strands of film theory that would rather not acknowledge the medium's literary and theatrical heritage. Rancière's historical poetics, I contend, is thus best understood as bridging the divide between film history and theory. Rancière is not attempting to construct the ontology of its images or restore certain directors to their rightful place in history. He follows closely the movements of certain films with the aim of "making them resonate differently."[9]

4.2 CINEMA, THE DREAM OF THE AESTHETIC AGE

To illustrate how cinema is in part the realization of the demands placed on art by the aesthetic regime, Rancière makes recourse to the film theory of the 1920s, drawing out its connections with the ideals of art espoused by figures like Kant, Schelling, Hegel, and Novalis.[10] The film theory of the 1920s is indeed startling in its reactivation of the artistic ideas of that earlier era, even if—and this is a point that needs to be stressed—Rancière ultimately diagnoses it as disingenuous with respect to the actual functioning of cinema. *Film Fables* opens with a long quotation from one of early film's most ardent theorists, Jean Epstein. The quote is from Epstein's *Bonjour Cinema*, the most significant work of film theory from that period. This text attempts to break with the representative poetics of the theatre by praising the camera's powers of perception, its capacity for transfiguring matter, and its immediate links with the human nervous system. Epstein concludes, "The cinema is true; a story is false."[11] For Epstein, cinema is true because it is the art most devoid of artistry and technical manipulation. Indeed, as one commentator puts it, "Epstein wrote as if the camera itself functioned like an analogous metal brain, independent of human agency."[12] Rancière's citation of Epstein has given rise to confusion, so let it be clear that for Rancière, "Epstein only arrives at this pure essence of the cinema by extracting a work of 'pure' cinema from the filmed melodrama."[13] Rancière places *Film Fables* under the quotation from Epstein in order to indicate how this perspective is limited when compared with the actual poetics of cinema.

Denying the camera's agency was one part of a strategy for advancing cinema's claims of arthood. It allowed its early theorists to distinguish film from the novels, theatrical productions, and scenarios that formed its starting point. By insisting upon the effects generated by the passive activity of the camera, theorists could describe its distinctive mode of visual presence. For Rancière, this equation of activity with passivity, said to be at the center of the creative process in the aesthetic regime, is at work in cinema. He explains that "the cinema, with its unconscious eye, has the instrument which enacts the romantic concept of the work as the identity [*égalité*] of a conscious process and an unconscious process."[14] For Rancière, this aesthetic identification of art replaces the Aristotelian schema in which making a work consists of bringing an intelligible form to sensible matter. He explains that, on the contrary, for the aesthetic regime, "art is . . . the identity of a conscious process [*démarche*] and an unconscious production, of a willed action and an involuntary process [*processus*], in brief, the identity of *logos* and *pathos*."[15] This intermingling of activity and passivity makes aesthetic art the overcoming of a certain number of oppositions operative within the Aristotelian framework: thought and matter, knowledge and non-knowledge, and *logos* and *pathos*. In a sense, we witnessed a form of it in Schiller's paean to the *Juno*, where the aesthetic experience was said to be the neutralization of a number of competing forces, such as rest and movement. Rancière provides something of a genealogy of this aesthetic theme, tracing the introduction of *pathos* into *logos* from Vico's search for the "true Homer" and the novel form of hermeneutics employed by this undertaking, through to Schopenhauerian and Nietzschean aesthetics.[16] In various places, he indicates how literature shares this dream of passivity, attempting to divest writing of the author's conscious intentions to the advantage of sensible life. This unification of willed and unintended processes, of an "absolute doing" and an "absolute passivity," is one which finds itself developed in Schelling's *System of Transcendental Idealism*, Hegel's lectures on aesthetics, and the romantic conception of creativity.[17] It is perhaps best articulated in Kant's account of genius. According to Kant, only a small portion of artistic production is deliberate, with the end results ultimately unexplainable in terms of rules. For him, fine art worthy of the title *genius* ultimately stems from a force arriving from outside of the subject. This is what Kant, and later the Romantics, call nature.[18]

Even though it is now customary to snicker at such notions of creativity, it is not recognized frequently enough that they are in fact subordinate to a corresponding form of signification that still underpins many contemporary strategies. It should thus be made apparent that the goal of artistic passivity is intimately bound to a dual conception of signification at the center of the aesthetic regime. If artistic labor now involves blankly reflecting the world back to itself, it is because the world itself has been re-evaluated and endowed with significance. A "silent speech" [*parole muette*] thought to reside in material things forces the authorial voice to yield to the task of collecting and organizing its traces. Creativity becomes, accordingly, hermeneutic, with the artist's task that of reading the material world and reconstituting its meaning. "Everything speaks," as Novalis exclaimed, and the artist is the one who gives voice to the traces of *logos* scattered throughout the world. Rancière describes this new figure thus:

> He travels in the labyrinths or substratum of the social world. He recovers the vestiges and transcribes the hieroglyphs painted in the configuration of obscure or ordinary things. He gives back to the insignificant details of the prose of the world their double poetic and signifying power.[19]

The romantic age carries speech to things, treating the sensible world as a series of signs to be deciphered. As Rancière explains, for it, "Everything is trace, vestige, or fossil."[20]

At the same time, however, as the romantic age finds meaning in material things, it also posits their resistance to full capture. This "everything speaks" is countered by the obstinacy of sensible things. In them, it is thought, something resides which is dark, obscure, and resistant to the web of meanings in which the aesthetic age attempts to shroud the world. A "deaf speech" [*parole sourde*] thus testifies to the sensible world's resistance to complete capture by thought.[21]

Cinema, as well as photography, inherits this double poetics where, on the one hand, everything speaks and where, on the other, there is a silent, unobtainable presence of sensible things resistant to economies of meaning. A number of works explore the consequences of this silent speech, with *The Aesthetic Unconscious* providing a general sense of the consequences for Western thought, and *Film Fables* and *The Future of the Image* extending the problematic of writing as the admixture of *logos* and *pathos* to explain the new "image-value" created by the breakup of the representative regime.[22] Aesthetic images trade on this double power, being at once "the inscription of the signs of history and the affective power of sheer presence."[23] They oscillate between signification and force, meaning and that which resists it, and between the hieroglyph and raw presence.

Rancière has analyzed the different configurations struck from this dual poetics, indicating its usefulness for critiquing contemporary exhibition strategies.[24] He has also—significantly for our purposes—stated its importance for understanding cinema. "The cinema is . . . the most 'immediately' romantic art. It spontaneously applies the principle of this double resource which loads up every sign with the splendor of its insignificance and the infinity of its implications."[25] The cinema has as its very precondition this transfigured sensible world endowed with meaning. This silent speech is to be distinguished from the order of the fable, for what the camera recounts is an adventure of perception-thought culled from the dynamism of the world. Epstein explains his ideal, distinguishing it from the fable: "I want films in which not so much nothing as nothing very much happens. . . . The humblest detail sounds the note of a drama that is latent."[26] "*Photogénie*" is the term early film theorists used to describe the alchemy of the medium. It encapsulates the camera's ability to immerse spectators in a world of microperceptions, to defamiliarize everyday objects, and to endow ordinary places with extraordinary significance. The cinema's images are thus at once manifestations of speech and silent power, for when we look beyond its fables, the cinema allows us to discover the silent drama that escapes the human eye.

When cinema and its theorists assume romanticism's form of signification, they thereby take on the ideal of a passive art. The movements of matter and light can be framed and deemed significant, for they belong to the world made over in the image of its double poetics. The cinema theory of the 1920s is the place where this case for the unity of thought and the sensible is made most forcefully. As Rancière explains, for a figure like Epstein, "The matter seen and transcribed by the mechanic eye . . . is equivalent to mind: a sensible immaterial matter composed of waves and corpuscles that abolishes all opposition between deceitful appearance and substantial reality."[27] The writing of sensible-intelligible light that Epstein champions is at once sensible and cognitive, for it inherits the mélange of thought and non-thought inhabiting the sensible. The implication, then, of the aesthetic regime's identification of *logos* with *pathos* is that it is quite simple to create something of significance and power. One can passively record the silent speech continually forming around oneself, while removing the traces of one's interventions. The cinema is held to be the best realization of this process: with the camera's inherent passivity, one need only set it rolling in order for the magic to begin.

Cinema, however, maintains a complicated relationship with this activity-passivity schema. While other arts like the novel insinuate scenes of passivity into representative sequences, that is, thwart the arrangement of events ordained by the logic of representation, the cinema moves in the opposite direction. It begins with the camera's passivity, constructing its art according to the conscious selections of its operator. Far from being the purely unconscious art that would immerse us in the immediacy of sensible things, the cinema is a mixture of the camera's unconscious eye and the director's conscious regard. The camera is already passive, thereby requiring its artists to assert a type of mastery in order to make apparent this initial passivity. Cinema thus in part restores the representative regime's poetics, according to which creation is the directed imposition of form on matter. Cinema will also make recourse to the distributions of that regime, rehabilitating divisions of genre, character types, and the fable itself. Rancière explains:

> Cinema literalizes a secular idea of art in the same stroke that it actualizes the refutation of that idea: it is both the art of the afterwards that emerges from the Romantic de-figuration of stories, and the art that returns the work of de-figuration to classical imitation.[28]

There is thus, for Rancière, an antinomy at the heart of cinema resulting from the place it occupies in the history of ideas and artistic practices. Whether because of its technical means, theatrical forebears, the nature of the film industry, or the impossibility of a purely passive art, cinema develops at the intersection of two logics. It strives to remain true to the romantic ideal of creating images where nothing very much takes place except the tension between signification and mute presence, and in order to make this passivity evident it insinuates these images into a fable. These fables are in turn what help to build into these images their double force. The film is a thwarted fable in the sense that it is the meeting point of these two logics, whose encounter is explored more closely in the following section. And its images, according to Rancière, have the dual function of advancing and suspending the order of events.

With respect to early film theory, however, what we witness are the dreams of the aesthetic age being reignited by the emergence of a new technology. These discourses created an ideal that has not ceased to inhabit theoretical reflections on film, but are problematic, according to Rancière, because they capture only part of the cinematic experience. Epstein's text, for example, interpretively selects, de-figures, and recomposes cinema in tandem with the anti-narrative poetics of the age. In truth, Epstein ". . . hailed an art that existed only in his head, an art that was just an idea in people's heads."[29] Epstein and others such as Élie Faure argued for a cinema of pure plastic forms that did not exist, one that was dramatically at odds with the cinema of the day, particularly in France where the industry was engaged largely with theatrical adaptations. Epstein erected this ideal by twisting the medium's expressive elements from the narratives to which they belonged, an operation familiar to Rancière's readers as a "defigurative description."[30] As Rancière describes them, defigurative descriptions are the theoretical-linguistic activation of a medium's latent possibilities according to the dictates of a new idea of art. They are discourses that emphasize previously neglected aspects of a medium, such as when critics discuss the expressionistic touches of representative art, thereby transforming the understanding and practice of a given art. Such gestures are common to both nineteenth-century art criticism and early cinema theory. They are repeated by Deleuze and Godard, as we will see, to different ends. It is in vain, however, to attempt to efface cinema's fable. The poignant images Epstein cites—faces, the door-latch, the drop of ink at the tip of the fountain pen, the cigar in the ashtray—are meaningful because of the narrative to which they belong. Detaching a few key scenes from the surrounding action, we might say that Epstein composes a fable of anti-representative cinema.

All such analyses are ultimately limited by the fact that they fail to take account of the dual function of cinematic images. On this point, the lesson of Rancière is that the image is always a more complex function than was previously thought. On the one hand, these images are fraught because they are omens of an impending action within the narrative sequence. On the other hand, they slow down, disrupt, and complicate the causal order to which they belong by introducing moments at odds with a sequence of well-ordered actions. The cinema's images, despite the protests of much film theory, have thus a quasi-discursive element that operates simultaneously with its role as plastic form. Their value needs always to be determined by the other images that surround them as well as the relationships that they sustain or suspend. Any image, then, contains conflicting relations of sense and meaning that cannot be thought under the idea of a "pure cinema."

Rancière rejects two possible responses to the lost dream of a pure cinema: nostalgia and condescension.[31] The former would have us mourn an ideal that never was, while the latter would lead us to castigate those enthusiastic critics who have, in a sense, constructed their own films with the films at their disposal. This analysis of the ideals and expectations built up around the art of the moving image is intended instead to liberate us from the faulty notions we may carry to the screen. While these expectations were themselves generated by the culture of cinephilia, they can only leave us disappointed when measured against the actual state of the medium. Rancière's topographical analysis is, as we have seen, particularly attuned to oppositions, obstacles, contradictions, and their subsequent overcoming. In this instance, the topographical analysis of cinema allows him to follow the procedures by which artists grapple with the forms of thought, technical means, and commercial possibilities at their disposal. If any conclusion can be drawn from these discussions—especially in what is a dark time for the culture of cinema—it is a hopeful one: ". . . the art and thought of images have always been nourished by all that thwarts them."[32]

4.3 THE LOGIC OF THE THWARTED FABLE

By now it should be apparent that, for Rancière, there is no general nature or essence of the image. For him, there are different practices, strategies, and logics of "imageness" [*imagéité*].[33] Even though historical frameworks and established poetic practices play a role in structuring an image, its final form is always the outcome of a process that is in each instance unique. Frequently, the images in question contain more than one direction and can be analyzed from multiple points of view. Rancière is fond of describing cinematic images as "functions," because doing so enables him to explain, on the one hand, how a particular image serves to advance the causal order of the fable, and, on the other hand, how the same images introduce discontinuities that complicate its unfolding. Cinema's images must, therefore, be thought according to the discursive networks to which they belong, the forms of visual presence they employ, and the combinations with other images exploited in their making.

This section describes a few of the thwarts Rancière isolates in *Film Fables* in order to illustrate the richness and complexity of the encounter between representative and aesthetic poetics. Part of the appeal of Rancière's thought is that it frees analysis from many of the orthodoxies that hobble contemporary artistic discourse, such as the will to cling to the purity of the image and its supposed separation from language. While film theory has largely insisted upon the uniqueness, that is, the predominantly visual nature of its medium, attending to the thwarted fables resulting from these encounters allows us to overcome the visual essentialism that hampers many analyses. For Rancière, language is not a mode of expression that has no place in cinema, even the cinema of the silent era, but is selectively inserted at various points and in different ways to hollow out images, breathe new life into them, or carry them into other contexts. The fable itself is a certain form of speech that requires analysis. It is precisely these connections between speech and visibility that the notion of the film fable allows us to describe.

On this score, it is interesting that Rancière makes recourse to devices from classical rhetoric, such as syllepsis and synecdoche, in order to describe the logic of cinema's thwarted fables. This is not an instance of forcing the visual into linguistic categories; the film is itself the process by which these devices are transformed and placed into new systems of significance. Discussions of Rancière's cinema book tend to overlook this level of thwarting in favor of the more spectacular scenes, sounds, and gestures that interrupt the logic of well-ordered actions. It is correct that these latter strategies counter the representative arrangement of images. Rancière frequently points to a director's use of fragmentation, the counter-intuitive presentation of actions, discrepancies between a scene's visibility and narrative meaning, the use of voiceover, moments of play or violence that do not advance the plot, as well as the unexpected and excessive gestures that break up the straightforward Aristotelian dramaturgy. These examples of "counter-effect" and "counter-movement" are perhaps the most obvious examples of thwarting.[34] They are, strictly speaking, the useless moments that suspend, disturb, and even contradict the fable's causality. The point is not, however, that film simply recounts a story composed of two types of images, one aesthetic and the other representative, but that in the cinema these two elements are so interdependent that they need to be analyzed simultaneously. Overemphasizing the role of the more spectacular thwarts, therefore, runs the risk of masking the deeper field of exchanges between the logic of actions and the sensible passivity strived for by the camera. For my part, I find the thwarting logic between the two poetics to be much more intimate than a simple cataloguing of games between two types of images. The thwart is not merely something added onto the representative ordering of events. It is the very process by which the fable becomes a film fable. The aim of Rancière's analysis, then, is to describe not only the logic of well-ordered actions and the procedures by which they are undermined, but also the distinctive forms that result from their meeting. It is telling that in order to illustrate this encounter, Rancière frequently analyzes the scenes directors have added to the literary fable in order to change or complicate its visibility/meaning. This means that the film fable is at times a rejoinder to a literary fable.

One of Rancière's primary concerns is to determine how a film transforms a literary text into its own medium. This is the broadest form of the thwarting logic in question: the transposition of the theatrical or novelistic fable into the film fable. Rancière's essay on F.W. Murnau's *Tartuffe*, for example, considers the operations that the play must be subjected to in order for it to yield distinctly cinematic images. The problem of transposition is especially acute with respect to a hypocrite who, in the theatrical version, trades upon the double meaning of words in order to intimate to the audience his true nature. No such recourse is available to Murnau, who scrupulously follows the constraints of silent film. Early on, Tartuffe's covetous gaze signals to viewers that our man is a fraud; however, for Rancière, this device is insufficient for accomplishing the work of Molière's words. The film fable requires a more radical visible solution. Murnau thus shifts the action from the treachery of the eponymous lead to the domestic drama brewing between Orgon, the husband who has temporarily fallen under the false prophet's spell, and his wife Elmire who must break him of it. "Murnau's film," Rancière explains, "is about Elmire's machinations to win back her husband, about the operation she must perform to excise from Orgon's heart the intruder who has made her invisible to him."[35] Tartuffe is thus figuratively, and by cinematic means, transformed into a shadow who separates Elmire from Orgon, thus disturbing the aesthetic distributions of the household. The cinema deals with hypocrites with the means at its disposal: it configures the lines of visibility and invisibility in order to indicate the disorder that they create. Rancière explains the principle: "Cinema . . . doesn't lead hypocrites to confess, but tells the stories of substantial and beguiling shadows that have to be destroyed."[36]

It is of course difficult for the medium that creates such shadows to also dispel them. Murnau's solution, while particularly ingenious, requires yet another thwart, one borrowed from the representative regime's partitioning of genres. In the final sequences of the film, Elmire lures Tartuffe into a visible field where his incongruity with the household becomes manifest. Rancière notes the contrast between the luxurious interiors of the aristocratic home, and the bedroom, reminiscent of Dutch genre painting, where a seduction is to take place. In this space, the shadow is given body, one whose very coarseness makes it impossible to "hide the identifying traits of its origin."[37] With this visual contrast, it becomes apparent to all, including Orgon, that this man is out of his element. Rancière concludes: "Tartuffe is visually expelled . . . well before he is physically thrown out by Orgon."[38] This second thwart is borrowed from a distribution of painting in which visibilities are linked with corresponding estimations of social class. Its inclusion means, for Rancière, the film could not achieve what it needed to by its own means. It thus rehabilitated the representative regime's partitioning of images into genres. "Murnau's film fictionally eliminates Tartuffe at the very high price of having aesthetically to eliminate with him all of cinematographic expressionism. Hence the film's grayness of tone."[39] The resulting product is thus a tangled web of different poetic inheritances pulled from theatre, the age of aesthetics, and representative painting. Its thwarts are the places where these different influences counter one another. The purpose of Rancière's historical poetic analysis is to recount how they are fitted together, and to impart a sense of how the film comes into existence through the intersection of these different poetics.

A similar filmic transposition is at work in Nicholas Ray's classic of the film noir genre, *They Live by Night*. The film adapts Edward

Anderson's novel *Thieves Like Us*, the story of two star-crossed lovers on the run from the law. Rancière's essay, along with the companion piece on the Westerns of Anthony Mann, can be read as testing the thesis about cinema being a mixed art, with two limit cases: both the Western and the crime drama are heavily scripted Hollywood productions that employ readily predictable scenarios and easily recognizable expressive codes. The discussions of each point to the ways in which both Mann and Ray are, to a greater or lesser extent, conscious of their place within this system, and make their art by insinuating scenes of aesthetic poesy into a predetermined order of events. This is indicated by the distinction Rancière adopts from Mann, that of the difference between "doing" and "having to do." While the having to do is dictated by the plot's broad outlines and the conventions of the genre, the doing is left to the director's discretion. Mann, for example, complicates his films by composing scenes of excessive violence and unexpected tranquility, neither of which fit squarely with the demands of narrative. Indeed, Mann is exemplary because he is at once a classical artist who fulfills his bargain with the audience by delivering a well-organized story, and the one who carries the genre to its limits, commenting upon its characters and mocking its conventions. His fables are thus knit with the tensions between the Western genre and a meta-commentary about its history.[40]

For his part, Nicholas Ray reworks the realist poetics of Anderson's novel so that it will yield a particularly rich cinematic affect. Ray composes his fable by means of a fragmentation of and subtraction from the novel's telling of events. These procedures imbue his images with the poignant sadness of two children already defeated by forces larger than themselves. His film is thus the meeting point of two different poetics. As Rancière explains, "Romanticism against Classicism is not the outpouring of feelings against cold rigor, but one beauty against another: the beauty of a perfectly crafted Aristotelian plot . . . against . . . the original loss of what 'can never be found again— never!'"[41] In order to build the nostalgia upon which these latter images rely, Ray must first compose a moment of perfect happiness that will haunt the remainder of the film—the meeting of the young couple soon to be up against the world. This initial happiness circulates throughout the film, giving poignancy to the couple's desperate flights. Rancière explains this principle: "an image is made from the mourning of another image."[42]

Everything hinges on the way in which we are introduced to Keechie, the love interest, and Bowie, a young and decidedly unhardened escaped convict. Whereas the novel introduces Bowie and the reader to a relatively banal object of desire—the female form beneath some clothes a bit too tight—the film separates Keechie's body from easy identification. She can appear before Bowie, and the viewer, in the garage as an "apparition," only as a result of "numerous appearances and disappearances, additions and subtractions."[43] There are two distinct operations at work, both designed to break up the novel's narrative continuum. In the first place, their initial meeting is visually understated in order to heighten our anticipation of Keechie's appearance. In the car that retrieves Bowie from his hiding place, we are allowed only a few fragmentary glances of Keechie who appears as "two cheeks lit up by a glare of light, two hands clasped around the steering wheel, and a white voice."[44] This scene, according to Rancière, "swallows" the form through which the realist novel communicated their relationship to readers.[45] It replaces the novel's uncomplicated visibility with one that is abstract and fragmentary. In the novel, Keechie was easily assimilated to Bowie's vision, consciousness, and desire; in the film, she resists them all. "Cinema has to frustrate the natural realism of mechanical reproduction. Indeed, it is through a very specific operation of subtraction that the film distances itself most sharply from the novel it adapts."[46] This thwarting of realist poetics is put to good use, setting the stage for the garage scene where all is won and lost. It is here that Bowie and the viewer first observe Keechie, outfitted in coveralls and ready to help with the repair work facing the escapees. The first procedure of abstraction gives way to a second, that of isolation. Ray's task is to show the sparks of young love catch fire in the midst of a hostile world, and in this sense the scene is a synecdoche for the larger film. But how does one create intimacy between two characters contending with repair work and a crowd of onlookers who allow no privacy? Anderson makes recourse to Bowie's inner thoughts, describing the sensations associated with budding love. Ray, however, shifts the drama to Keechie, whose attentions fall, however fleetingly, upon Bowie. The camera provides a few frames of Keechie and Bowie together, separating the pair from the world of the fugitives. Ray thus cuts up the garage into two incompatible spaces to indicate the conflicting allegiances. Indeed, these competing spaces are carried, in one form or another, throughout the film, with Keechie and Bowie isolated from the world to which they were "never properly introduced," as the title shot indicates. This garage scene culminates with a moment of utopia that simultaneously suspends and advances the film's plot. Rancière:

> With the repair work done and their sentiments clear, Keechie emerges from the depths of the garage like a dream, takes one of the handles of the jack, and helps Bowie drag it back to where it belongs. This pure moment of happiness around a jack surpasses every image of idling under the shade of a coconut tree.[47]

The happiness is marred, however, by the onslaught of a world that will not wait, and it is in fact this contrast between the moment around the jack and the ensuing events that endow these images with such beauty. Rancière describes this dynamic as a romantic poetics of original defeat: as viewers, we know that as soon as Keechie consents to become part of Bowie's world she too will be lost.

The logic of these combinations means that we are led to reject any theory of the cinematic image that would insist upon its essential purity. One cannot have access to these moments with recourse to phenomenology or any other methodology that treats these forms as isolated visual phenomena. Indeed, as the analysis of *They Live by Night* indicates, our thinking of cinema must become ever more attuned to the relationships and historical positions that give these images their force, and indeed to the very procedures by which they are constituted as images. The cinema's images are created at the intersection of the classical poetics of narrative and the strategies of abstraction, fragmentation, and counter-movement valorized by the age of aesthetics. While the beautiful moments of cinema are often created as moments of respite, idleness, or reverie within the film's temporal sequencing of events, they cannot be separated from the direction supplied by representative poetics. Even when scenes of tremendous visual power appear to completely cast off the order of the plot, the camera remains parasitic upon it in order to endow its images with significance. The cinema's forms of visibility are created between arts, by making and unmaking connections with literary language, theatre, painting, and the unique perceptual powers of the camera. Indeed, the camera's passivity opens up a space and time fundamentally at odds with those of well-ordered actions. It would be a mistake, however, not to analyze how such temporal and spatial shifts are recognizable only because of the narrative contexts to which they belong. The logic of thwarting means that Rancière is reluctant to advance any theories about the essence of cinema. In fact, he insists that one should not attempt to equate these thwarts with the nature of the medium, as they are procedures borrowed from other arts. His cinematic writings are not intended as an exhaustive inventory of the art form, but designed to place in question some of the theories, methodologies, and histories that constrain its possibilities. Throughout these writings, we see Rancière working to activate the gaps between different poetic inheritances, existing technologies, and the practices of cinema. To open up spaces where invention might take place, he takes exception with some of the dominant, and in his estimation, limiting ways of describing cinema. As was the case with the recovery of the politics of aesthetics more generally, it is important not to allow cinema's logic of thwarting to be subsumed by questionable notions of cinematic modernity or channeled into a thinking of how it does or does not live up to its supposed essence.

4.4 ALLEGORIES OF MODERNITY: DELEUZE AND THE USE OF HITCHCOCK

Gilles Deleuze's two cinema books are the most important philosophical engagement with the art of the moving image. They sustain many discussions in the loosely defined field of visual studies. Here, attention is focused upon an aspect of those works that has come under scrutiny, partly as a result of Rancière's objections. The issue in question is the general historical rupture upon which the project is premised. In both works, Deleuze argues for an essential break between "classical" and "modern" cinema. This is a distinction that, I argue, Rancière counters for three primary reasons. First, it relies on a highly speculative notion of historical causality that attributes cinematic innovation to the sensory landscape of the Second World War. Next, and most concretely, this rupture is not sustainable in terms of actual films. As such, as Rancière notes, Deleuze is continually forced to present the distinction allegorically. Finally, the narrative this rupture sustains gives rise to an undesirable theory of cinematic incapacity.

In philosophical terms, the break between classical and modern cinema is thought by Deleuze as a reversal of the relationship between time and space, with modernity said to have disentangled time from motion. Whereas classical cinema imparts only an indirect image of time, one gleaned from the procedures of montage and the camera's movement, modern cinema is distinctive in that it provides access to unfettered time-images. Immersing viewers in the experience of becoming, the modern cinema—Deleuze explains he is dealing only with "great" films and directors—advances a new form of consciousness. Deleuze's project is philosophical inasmuch as it attempts to think cinema, without destroying what is unique about its "signs" by equating them with other arts. For Deleuze, "The great directors of the cinema may be compared ... not merely with painters, architects, but also with thinkers. They think with movement-images and time-images instead of concepts."[48] Deleuze thus proposes a semiotics— as opposed to the linguistically based semiology—of the non-verbal signs composing films, in the attempt to preserve in thought the distinctly dynamic nature of the cinematic image.

With a Bergsonian ontology of the image and a taxonomy derived from the work of Charles Saunders Peirce, Deleuze describes two distinct regimes of cinema-signs. The classical system of the movement-image knits together three primary types: the perception-image, the affection-image, and the action-image. They are joined in what Deleuze calls the sensory-motor schema. The essential point about the sensory-motor schema is that it allows for the various elements of a film to be connected into a meaningful whole. The sensory-motor schema, like the Kantian schematization performed by the imagination, joins together perceptions, affects, thoughts, and actions. It is the basic unity according to which each perception, affective response, and action can be understood as contributing to a film's development. The heart of any arrangement of movement-images is the action-image. There is, for Deleuze, a major and minor form of the action-image. In the first case, the SAS' form, there is a situation S that when impacted by action A leads to a transformed situation S'. In the case of the second, the ASA', an action A discloses something unexpected about situation S, which in turn necessitates another action A'. Both forms link actions to situations, with the large form presenting a situation transformed by action and the small form deriving the situation from an action.[49] In both cases, the structure of the movement-image is essentially the tragic form defined by Aristotle: there is a readily discernable arrangement of incidents precipitated by a hero. The ordering of these situations and actions unites perceptions and affects, supplying their *raison d'être*. The world defined by the sensory-motor schema is thus one in which there exists a certain rationality of actions, emotions, and perceptions. Characters respond to a given situation, if not always as one might expect, according to a causality that can be reconstructed in terms of a film's chain of events. Deleuze terms these scenarios movement-images because the viewer's vantage point (on time), results from the unfolding of the plot, the operations of montage, and the camera's mobility.

With the onset of cinematic modernity, this schema comes undone. The resulting time-images outstrip both viewers' and characters' capacity for organizing, arranging, and making sense of what is seen and heard. Modern cinema employs instead irrational cuts, complicated temporalities, disorienting spaces, floating actions, and obscurely linked events. This second regime of signs—opsigns and sonsigns—is thus understandable in terms of the pure sight and sound situations with which it replaces the respective forms of the movement-image. Deleuze describes the cinema of seeing and hearing that overtakes the cinema of action as an event that is "perhaps as important as the conquering of a purely optical space in painting, with impressionism."[50]

The experience is again described in terms of the Kantian problematic. With the breakup of the schema linking perceptions to actions, modern cinema "brings out the thing in itself, literally, in its excess of horror or beauty, in its radical or unjustifiable character."[51] For Deleuze, the time-image's optical and sound situations tear viewers away from traditional ways of ordering and thus avoiding experience, what he calls "clichés," and allow them to experience the becoming of time. They undo our retinal-logical habits, and, much the way he described it in *Difference and Repetition*, "engender 'thinking' in thought." In that work, Deleuze compared the task of philosophy to the gulf separating modern and classical painting, hoping to launch it onto a non-representational plane. "The theory of thought is like painting: it needs that revolution which took art from representation to abstraction."[52] It is this type of thinking that is held to emerge in the encounter with modern cinema, with Deleuze's text, in part, functioning as an account of the mind at work—forging connections, developing problems, displacing itself— and ultimately failing. For Deleuze, with modern cinema, "It is a matter of something too powerful, or too unjust, but sometimes also too beautiful, and which henceforth outstrips our sensory-motor capacities."[53] In philosophical terms one can say that modern cinema marks the cessation of the mind's schematizing operations, thereby yielding a purely sensory experience.

This new experience corresponds to a historical turning point in which the cinema of action was replaced by a cinema of pure sights and sounds. It is one, according to Deleuze, in which characters and viewers alike fail to make sense of images that are henceforth too strong to be processed. The ensuing time-images are those which are no longer supported by a structuring narrative, but rather evolve in a random and disjointed fashion. At the end of *Cinema 1*, the time-image is described as having five distinguishing characteristics: its situations are *dispersive*, rather than synthetic, meaning that there are several types of staging, characters, and times of succession within a single film; second, there are deliberately *weak links* between a film's events, that is, the SAS′ and ASA′ structure is undone; next, the aimless *stroll* in an "any-space-whatever" replaces purposeful and deliberate sensory-motor action; fourth, there is a *consciousness of clichés*—whether they be auditory or visual—and a renewed effort to outmaneuver them; finally, there is what Deleuze terms the *condemnation of plot*, by which he means that there is a heightened awareness of the means of media-support, as in films like Sidney Lumet's *Network* or Robert Altman's *Nashville*.[54]

In *Cinema 2*, Deleuze charts the development of this ontologically distinct form of the image, which, at its most basic level, he describes as a crystal. The time-image unites the actual and the virtual, the real and the imaginary, the past and the present of becoming into a single element where their separation becomes impossible. "It is as if an image in a mirror, a photo or a postcard came to life . . . and passed into the actual, even if this meant that the actual image returned into the mirror and resumed its place."[55] This indiscernibility, constitutive of the time-image, overwhelms sensory-motor connections, offering glimpses of the branching-off of the instant. The two novelists invoked in *Cinema 2* are Robbe-Grillet, cited frequently, and Proust, mentioned in passing. If we think of Proust's complex temporal layering compounded by the ontological confusions imported by Robbe-Grillet's descriptions, those which overtake/create their objects, we have a literary approximation of the time-image. For Deleuze, the time-image looks, feels, and acts like the constant shuttling back and forth between temporal layers found in

Orson Welles' *Citizen Kane*. Its signs are dispersed and relayed from multiple points of view, while being conveyed by different media apparatuses. What Deleuze has in mind is that with the collapse of classical cinema's structure of well-ordered actions, modern cinema gives rise to confusing spaces and times that cease to be linked together by a single, unifying principle. These conditions can, it is thought, thereby be experienced in their own right. It is frequently claimed that the time-image completely effaces the movement-image, and elements of this position can be detected in Rancière's discussions. To be fair, however, Deleuze insists that the movement-image has not completely disappeared from cinema: it "now exists only as the first dimension of an image that never stops growing in dimensions."[56]

It is often said that Deleuze links cinema's transformation to the devastated landscapes of the Second World War. This reading is partially correct. The aftermath of the war created sensory environments that outstripped traditional forms of understanding, thereby laying the ground for the images found in Italian Neorealism, the French New Wave, and New German Cinema. There are in fact two primary causes carrying cinema beyond the movement-image. The first emanates from the history of cinema itself and is what can be called the internal cause. According to Deleuze, Hitchcock surpasses the movement-image by creating mental images that take the connections between thoughts, emotions, relations, and symbolic acts as their object. "The essential point . . . is that action, and also perception and affection, are framed in a fabric of relations. It is this chain of relations which constitutes the mental image, in opposition to the thread of actions, perceptions, and affections."[57] In effect, the claim is not so different from the traditional thesis about the onset of artistic modernity: with an increased self-reflexivity, Hitchcock carries the art form to a new level. Confronted with Hitchcock's suspenseful images, we no longer have a simple causal schema in which actions are recounted; it is now incumbent upon the viewer to forge connections that escape even the film's characters. These mental images can thus in a sense be said to introduce viewers into the film. Deleuze explains that Hitchcock no longer thinks of production as a dualistic affair between director and film, but as a tripartite relationship with an audience, "whose reactions must form an integrating part of the film."[58] Consider the famous images of the photographer L.B. "Jeff" Jeffries (James Stewart), confined to a wheelchair at the start of *Rear Window*, an example to which we will return in our discussion of Rancière's criticism of Deleuze. We learn the cause of the character's incapacity, Deleuze observes, not from dialogue but the subtle connections knit between his leg cast, broken camera, and photos of automobile races.[59] Thanks to a few simple shots, the viewer even deduces the immobile photographer's place within the apartment structure's scopic regime. As we will see, the paralysis of this man of action, for Deleuze, emblematizes the transformation of action cinema into a cinema of pure seeing.[60] For now, however, the point is that with the genesis of the mental image, we leave behind the old logic of a structuring plot to the advantage of a cinema of relations.

The second constitutive moment of modern cinema stems from external causes. Cut off from previous traditions, whether theatrical or cinematic, and finding itself in a completely unprecedented perceptual space, postwar European art cinema reinvented itself. In general, the collapse of the sensory-motor schema mirrors a world becoming more and more incomprehensible, and its films are, for Deleuze, indicative of the deeper forces afflicting human agency, that is, the ability to make connections between seeing, thinking, and acting. On this point, it is worth quoting Deleuze at length, in part because it is one of the least well-developed points of his cinema books, and the thesis Rancière challenges. Deleuze:

> . . . the crisis which has shaken the action-image has depended on many factors which only had their full effect after the war, some of which were social, economic, political, moral and others more internal to art, to literature and to the cinema in particular. We might mention, in no particular order, the war and its consequences, the unsteadiness of the "American Dream" in all its aspects, the new consciousness of minorities, the rise and inflation of images both in the external world and in people's minds, the influence on the cinema of the new modes of narrative with which literature had experimented, the crisis of Hollywood and its old genres. . . . Certainly, people continue to make SAS and ASA films: the greatest commercial successes always take that route, but the soul of the cinema no longer does. The soul of the cinema demands increasing thought, even if thought begins by undoing the system of actions, perceptions and affections on which cinema had fed up to that point.[61]

Rancière poses two basic questions to this Deleuzian hypothesis: first, is it warranted to draw such connections between an artistic rupture and a historical event? Second, can the thesis of an ontological break at the level of the image be sustained by a concrete analysis of films?[62] In these questions we should hear more than just a skepticism regarding a claim about the relationship between art and history, or the effort to provide better, closer readings of canonical films. Rancière takes issue with Deleuze for the way he unnecessarily delimits the sphere of cinematic possibility. In failing to take account of the mixed nature of the cinematic image, one might say, Deleuze reduces to one, the time-image, what has many causes, numerous becomings, and multiple futures. Rancière's critique attempts to restore possibility to the practice and analysis of cinema. It does this by attending to the resources in its arsenal and the possibilities created through the combination of different poetic inheritances. As one would expect, Rancière argues that Deleuze unnecessarily divides the two poetics integral to the history of cinema, making its fables stand for the movement-images of classical cinema, while equating its thwarts with the time-images of modern cinema. Ascribing a historical identity to each ultimately makes it difficult to describe the instances in which both are operative. For Rancière, on the other hand, the distinction between the movement-image and the time-image corresponds to two points of view on this mixed art. "In Deleuzian terms, I would say that each image functions both as movement-image and time-image. Every film is composed not of images but of image functions that both supplement and contradict each other."[63] He thus proposes an understanding according to which Deleuze's ". . . distinction between two images would be strictly transcendental and . . . not correspond to an identifiable rupture."[64] As our experience of the medium verifies, the two poetics are inextricably linked, relying upon their contrasts to make its games visible. Even the most abstract of films orders its elements into a meaningful whole, while moments of passivity and suspension are indeed only recognizable as such when they depart from the logic of the fable.

In essence, Deleuze repeats Epstein's operation of abstracting a pure cinema from the surrounding fable. The problem is compounded, however, when he attempts to map it onto a narrative of historical development and rupture. Ultimately, it becomes difficult to determine empirically the difference between the two forms of the image.

This, Rancière argues, is what accounts for a certain number of contortions in Deleuze's text. Since the distinction between movement- and time-images is ideal, Deleuze must continually present it by means of allegory. There are numerous examples, but let us consider again the curious role Hitchcock plays at the end of *Cinema 1*. He is the director who prepares the way for the time-image, and announces it by inflicting passivity on the lead characters of two of his most famous films: the photographer in *Rear Window* and the detective of *Vertigo*, Scottie (James Stewart), paralyzed by acrophobia. Their respective forms of immobility make literal the idea of images stripped of sensory-motor connections. They place the protagonist in the position of a viewer, "reduced as it were to a pure optical situation."[65] For Rancière, however, Deleuze "goes a bit too fast when he aligns the crisis of narrative action with the disability which transforms the hero into a passive spectator."[66] He turns what is in effect a plot contrivance into a means of paralyzing the fable's action. The problem is, for Rancière, the inverse: the camera already achieves the passivity valorized by the aesthetic age, thereby serving as a means for developing the director's conscious eye. This is what leads cinema, in spite of its theoretical formulations, to rehabilitate the representative conception of artistic activity, making art the conscious shaping of unconscious image-affects. Deleuze's analysis is especially problematic with a filmmaker like Hitchcock who, in Rancière's estimation, "rehabilitates the sovereignty of the central intelligence," by insisting upon the director's role in coordinating visual and narrative evidence.[67]

Reading Deleuze from the vantage point of Rancière's historical poetics, it becomes questionable as to whether or not his texts function as an accurate account of the history of cinema. Deleuze's work is obviously not intended as such, but rather as a cartography of the forms of thought it generates. It is debatable nevertheless whether or not failing to adequately grasp the historical situation of the art undermines this endeavor. More seriously, I contend, separating these two poetics and describing them in the way that Deleuze does advances an undesirable conception of the spectator's passivity, for the cinema of seeing is nothing if not a loss of agency. The problem is more acute than simple art history since, as Rancière notes, with the Bergsonian equation of image and real, Deleuze recognizes no distinction between the history of an art and history more generally.[68] His project, as many commentators attest, is the attempt to plumb the twentieth century for its forms of consciousness. To discourse on an art is thus to simultaneously advance a conception of world, thought, and subjectivity. Despite Deleuze's insistence on the possibility of a new image of thought emerging from the ruins of the sensory-motor schema, it ultimately remains unclear how this could translate into a theory of human capacity. Indeed, the long passage from Deleuze cited above culminates in this conclusion: "We hardly believe any longer that a global situation can give rise to an action which is capable of modifying it—no more than we believe that an action can force a situation to disclose itself, even partially. The most 'healthy' illusions fall."[69] And while it is almost certain that Deleuze intends to describe a certain state of cinema, the point to be made from Rancière's perspective is that such descriptions are themselves political. They shape the meaning of what presents itself to sense, and indicate what is possible with respect to what is seen and heard. Cinema is more than simply the reflection of a pre-established reality; it is one of the means by which we discover and contest the boundaries of what is sensible, thinkable, and possible. It distributes and redistributes the sensible. Through our encounters with this art, we inhabit new worlds, ones that, although fictional, can be brought into conflict with the world as ordained. As Ranciere has said, "an art is never simply an art; it is always at the same time the proposition of a possible world."[70] Exiting from the logic of incapacity, the question thus becomes: what kind of world do we want to fashion, and how can we sustain it in our theoretical endeavors?

4.5 CINEMA AND ITS CENTURY: GODARD AND THE ABUSE OF HITCHCOCK

Before concluding with a positive account of cinema's aesthetico-political potential, we must look briefly at one more of Rancière's critical encounters. He has returned frequently enough to the work of Swiss filmmaker Jean-Luc Godard that something of his own position can be gleaned from the criticisms to which he subjects Godard's theoretical, historical, and cinematic work.[71] In these engagements, we see again a familiar strategy: Rancière follows to its conclusion a certain line of thinking that culminates in a discourse of incapacity. With respect to Godard, he explains that it is a question of diagnosing the logic of a position that, at first glance, appears radical but turns out to be conservative. "It's a matter . . . of recognizing the paths by which the apparent iconoclast of the Sixties has slowly changed into one of the most rigorous servants of the icon (*iconodules*)."[72] By outmaneuvering these theoretical-practical dead ends, Rancière's thought may allow us to escape many of the discourses and practices of the image that restrict its capacities for dissensus.

There are two primary criticisms in Rancière's discussions of Godard, both of which take exception with the latter's monumental video project, *Histoire(s) du cinéma*, a montage of classic film sequences, theoretical texts, and voiceovers, originally undertaken for French television. The first is the diagnosis and rejection of the conversion of the image, with its various functions of resemblance and representation, into an icon, an image construed solely as the immediacy of self-presence. This transformation is recognizable in those practices that treat the image as, in Rancière's words, ". . . the mark of the true, the face on Veronica's veil, the face of the Word of our savior the son of God."[73] The legacy of Hitchcock is once again at stake, for Godard builds his case for the meaning of cinema with an argument about the nature of some of the former director's most famous images. In his montage, Godard isolates, slows down, and enlarges certain memorable objects, such as the glass of milk in *Suspicion* or the purse containing stolen money in *Psycho*. Separating images from their narrative context, Godard attempts to make each, in their visual purity, stand not only for the whole of the film, but also for the essence of the medium. The problem of course is that these images gain significance by serving as relay points for the film's plot. For Rancière, Hitchcock's most memorable visual forms are "model examples of the representative tradition," inasmuch as they move viewers "by playing with the shifting relations of pleasure and pain through the relationships between ignorance and knowledge."[74] That is, these images are elements within a plot that stimulate, center, and carry the emotions necessary to achieve catharsis. What is interesting, however, is that these images are often counter-effectual. At the same time as they advance the plot's chain of events, they suspend and thwart it.[75]

As easy as it is to refute, Godard's practice of the icon nevertheless serves his dramaturgy of the rise, fall, and rebirth of cinema. *Histoire(s) du cinéma* is an essay on cinema that uses these icons to illustrate, on the one hand, cinema's fundamental rapport with painting, and, on the other, the degree to which cinema failed to bear witness to its century. Godard describes the history of cinema as a missed encounter; it is guilty of failing to capture the horrors of war and the extermination camps. *Histoire(s)* thus tells the story of the twentieth century with the benefit of hindsight, condemning its images—the rabbit hunt in Jean Renoir's *The Rules of the Game* and Charlie Chaplin's *The Great Dictator*, for example—for not having been fully conscious of what they foretold. In this sense, the turning icon of the image and the missed encounter are joined: if for Godard cinema is guilty of failing to fulfill its duty, it is because it renounced its fundamental connection with presence, serving instead Hollywood and Soviet fantasies. Rancière explains:

> Godard wants to show that cinema betrayed its own ability to prophesy the future because it had already betrayed its presence to the present. Like Peter who denies the Word made flesh, cinema betrayed the loyalty it owed to this word made flesh called the image.[76]

Cinema is nevertheless, for Godard, redeemed by the fact that George Stevens, the director of *A Place in the Sun*, managed to tear away from the oblivion of history a few images of the cruelty experienced in the camps. He thereby opens the possibility for cinema to reconnect with the pictorial tradition and recover its powers of testimony. "If George Stevens had not used the first sixteen-millimeter color film at Auschwitz and Ravensbrück, undoubtedly Elizabeth Taylor's happiness would never have found a place in the sun," Godard explains, accompanying these words with an iconized-image of Elizabeth Taylor emerging from the water to be crowned by a Mary Magdalene borrowed from Giotto.[77] As Rancière reads it, the addition of this saint, released "from a plastic dramaturgy," signifies the Godardian faith in the image's redemptive powers and the resurrection of postwar European cinema.[78]

We thus have in *Histoire(s)* a complicated structure according to which Godard attempts to prove cinema guilty in order to prepare the way for its reconciliation with itself. Godard needs cinema to be culpable in order for it to assume its "sacred mission."[79] Cinema missed its century because it misunderstood its capacity for presence, and it can recover its powers by resisting the seductions of narrative. Advancing the essence of this art as icon allows Godard to re-screen the images of the century, so to redeem the cinematic endeavor.

Rancière's second refusal pertains precisely to the way Godard construes the relationship between film and the century. It is, for him, too obviously laden with the melancholy that makes art impossible after Auschwitz. While not discounting the very real ethical and political catastrophes of the twentieth century, Rancière proposes turning our energies in the other direction. Rather than lamenting what was or was not filmed, or invoking the sacredness of the screened image, he proposes instead an investigation of the capacities cinema has at its disposal. Primarily this consists of the ability to make and undo connections, to slow down and stop a causal order, and to thwart and undermine a distribution of the sensible. While there is nothing inherently progressive about these operations, the workings of montage remind us that a given configuration of sense is far from natural, much in the way that the polemical verification of equality sets itself in opposition to all established powers.

CONCLUSION

If Rancière's writings on cinema contain these many rejections—the standard avant-garde idea of a cinema of pure forms, Deleuze's insistence upon a rupture that would usher in a cinematic modernity, Godard's practice of the icon and idea of the century—it is because his analyses are oriented toward what becomes possible without them. It can be said that what unites these disparate endeavors is that they each rely on strong hypotheses regarding the nature of the filmic medium. These delimitations restrict in advance what can be seen and said about the cinema, in turn yielding undesirable sensible-political consequences. Rancière's topographical analysis demonstrates the advantage of taking leave of these accounts. Freed from such perspectives, it becomes possible to describe new forms of experience, analyze the type of dissensus at work in the poetics of film, and knit new connections between cinema and politics.

It has rightly been noted that Rancière's writings on cinema implicitly sidestep two common ways of politicizing this art: the first, represented by Siegfried Kracauer, according to which cinematic realism gives birth to images of a common humanity, and the second, pioneered by Walter Benjamin, which construes film as a "mass art."[80] What Rancière's topographical analysis offers is both more restrained, in theoretical terms, and integrally related to the poetics of individual films. The recent essay "The Politics of Pedro

Costa" indicates that grasping the politics of cinema requires us to avoid thinking politics in the customary ways. It means, first of all, that one must take account of the connections between art and politics at the level of what is perceptible, and secondly, that we be more creative in describing and shaping our collective world. This activity of course is centered on the axiom of equality. It involves identifying its functioning with analytical writings and looking for ways to insinuate its presupposition into the general *aisthēsis* by means of artistic practices. Costa is perhaps a model because he avoids the traps that would ensnare other filmmakers working with marginalized subjects.[81] He creates images in which one can begin to see an equality of capacities emerge. Rancière explains that "Pedro Costa does not film the 'misery of the world.' He films its wealth, the wealth that anyone at all can become master of."[82] In this sense, the images he composes rely more on aestheticization than they do on indignation. Rather than presenting themselves as explanations regarding the sources of his subjects' misery, Costa's images instead locate hidden capacities, powers of speech and vision, and forms of relation that elude the dominant distribution of the sensible. These films thus make it possible to imagine otherwise what are certainly degrading conditions.

With respect to analysis and commentary, Rancière's position allows us to appreciate the more delicate achievements of the cinematic art. It enables us to attend to how, because of its aesthetic heritage, the thwarts of cinema can be linked to notions of freedom, idleness, equality, and the possible. In fact, one might argue that the poetic moments in cinema are some of our most tangible experiences of dissensus. They are an indication of what it looks like when one logic, one set of assumptions, counters another. Thwarts themselves function like the polemical scenes analyzed in Rancière's political writings, separating the sensible from itself and demonstrating that other meanings and directions are always possible. Moreover, the thwarts are created and insinuated into spaces where one ordinarily expects to find hierarchy. Cinema's poetic moments counter and contest the codes of representative poetics, in much the same way that political dissensus creates a world in conflict with the dominant distribution of the sensible. Rancière mines this space, offering astute discussions of how thwarting inserts "deviant lines" into the structure of well-ordered events.[83] His topographical analyses politicize films from the inside, seizing upon the moments of idleness, capacity, and equality that destabilize otherwise hierarchical arrangements. Charting the means by which images pass from one regime to another is indeed to compose an account of how the sensible can be split and its direction diverted. In this sense, cinema's images are a reminder of how it is always possible to play one tension within the sensible off against another in order to redistribute the coordinates of the world. The cinema's counter-effects, equivocal gestures, and unexpected connections indicate that the dominant meanings that are made of sense are not inevitable. They show that by means of invention it is possible to depart from a direction perceived to be natural.

It is important to remember that Rancière lays no claim to having exhausted the techniques by which cinema elaborates its freedom, and he offers no prescription for how the game is to proceed. His idea is that these inscriptions of happiness, and the longings they inspire, serve as an indictment of our prevailing distributions. They are propositions for possible worlds that, even though they may not be explicitly political in content, inspire our vision and provide us with indications about how to bring about change.

CHAPTER 5

BEYOND RANCIÈRE

INTRODUCTION

Rather than concluding in a definitive manner with a statement about Rancière's place within the history of European philosophy or the limitations of his project, I instead want to indicate some of the questions raised by his thought, as well as to explore some of the avenues that can be opened up by taking a broader view of the aesthetic regime. Such is in keeping with the general spirit of his work, oriented as it is by the domain of the possible. In order to provide further resources for clarifying, critiquing, and redistributing the sensible, it will be necessary to continue fleshing out the aesthetic regime. This task should not fall to Rancière alone. Indeed, given the nature of his work, the undertaking will be an indisciplinary undertaking, involving the reserves of the fields—literature, philosophy, psychoanalysis, art, aesthetics, and history—from which he draws. From my perspective—that hesitant space between art and philosophy known as aesthetics—it will be necessary to counter Rancière's presentation of this regime in terms largely drawn from Schiller. Doing so may allow us to describe a richer and more complex tapestry from which to create resources for dissensus.

My efforts here, critical though they may be, are thus intended to contribute to Rancière's project of reinvigorating art and politics by defining capacities for the contestation of our sensible world. As such, I identify two key areas of inquiry. The first pertains to the articulation of the relationship between aesthetics and politics, specifically, the democratic form of politics Rancière espouses. Here, I question his reading of the texts of the aesthetic regime in terms of equality. This is obviously not to claim that Rancière hasn't described the ways in which certain forms of art rely upon equality for their functioning; it is to challenge his reading of aesthetic theory as the place where this experience is codified. For while the latter texts no doubt describe disruptions of sense and counterworldly propositions, it remains to be seen to what extent the experiences described therein are political by the exacting standards of Rancière's own conception of politics. In the second instance, I contend that Rancière's thought enables us to shed new light on the phenomenon of the imagination, and that charting its role in the texts composing the aesthetic regime can provide resources for art and politics. Even though Rancière is skeptical of traditional philosophical strategies such as ontology, I submit that reckoning with the imagination will enable us to describe in more detail the process by which the sensible is distributed and re-distributed. In conclusion, then, I propose to re-conceptualize the imagination not as a subjective faculty, but as a collective power of dissensus.

5.1 SENSING EQUALITY?

At various points Rancière attempts to move the aesthetic tradition away from the accounts of freedom that it reads from the aesthetic experience, towards a consideration of the new relations of equality woven by the regime. While this allows him to define the plane on which art and a specifically democratic form of politics meet, the position itself needs to be more clearly announced and rigorously verified through a close reading of the texts of the aesthetic regime. Why, in the final analysis, should aesthetic experiences be understood in terms of equality, rather than, as they were by thinkers such as Kant, Schiller, Schelling, and Hegel, instances of human freedom? Needless to say, equality is central to Rancière's politics, and providing an account of the ways in which aesthetic experience relies upon and/or demonstrates equality would allow us to state precisely the extent to which aesthetics is truly political. The problem is that the texts Rancière claims as part of the aesthetic regime are hardly uniform on the question of equality. One need simply to undertake a genealogy of the concept of taste or recall the name of Friedrich Nietzsche in order to see that aesthetics also divides the world in two. Likewise, and closer to Rancière's own concerns, one could cite the problem of the Romantics themselves, many of whom became staunch conservatives in old age. Intimations of this are to be found even in the young Friedrich Schlegel, who, despite his enthusiastic embrace of the French Revolution, Fichte's philosophy, and Goethe's *Meister* as "the greatest tendencies of the age," maintained the rhetorical habit of separating the world into those who get it and those who don't.[1] The concept of genius announced in Kant's philosophy as an "innate" mental capacity presents a similar problem.[2] On the one hand, it allows for an understanding of creativity that breaks with the rule-based notions of production proffered by rationalism. On the other hand, it posits two distinct forms of humanity. The point of course is not that the politics of these authors are in conflict with the politics of aesthetics. It is that there are divisions in the aesthetic texts themselves at odds with Rancière's project of reading aesthetic theory as the inscription of equality in sense. Aesthetic theory cuts both ways, and a more concerted effort is needed to direct it away from its reliance on hierarchy.

Given these complications, which Rancière tends to downplay, how can we draw out the relations between aesthetics and equality? How can we describe, both with the texts that shape the aesthetic regime and in terms of Rancière's own position, the connections between aesthetic experience and the experience of equality? Can the traditionally articulated experience of freedom play a role, as it does with Rancière's discussion of politics, in creating the connection?

It is difficult to make the argument in terms of theoretical texts, and this is perhaps why Rancière reads particular works, such as those of Flaubert and Pedro Costa, as well as Schiller's description of the *Juno*, itself a sort of novelistic interlude in an otherwise theoretical exposition, as examples of a sensible form of equality. These analyses allow him to re-describe and transfigure our understanding of the aesthetic experience, which is perhaps Rancière's own original contribution to the aesthetic tradition. As we saw in Chapter 3, equality first manifests itself in the practices of art as indifference, an indifference to subject matter and stylistic form. In its displacement of the hierarchical system of values that formed the representative regime, the aesthetic idea of art affirmed that anything could become the subject of art and that there is no necessary way in which a subject must be presented. Literature, for example, cancels the hierarchies found within the *belles-lettres*, investing its powers in stylistic innovations. It circulates its signs in an indeterminate space resistant to definitive interpretations. Rancière not only describes the network of historical *a prioris* accounting for the birth of literature, he analyzes the procedures by which words are removed from hierarchical regimes of sense in order to be outfitted with new forms of affectivity in a different, more egalitarian economy of meaning. With Flaubert, for example, he describes the process of "petrification," which converts words from acts structured by the principles of representation into a prose that breaks up the space of well-ordered action.[3] Flaubert's abstractions, close descriptions, and recalcitrant phrasings create blocks of sense in which meaning is no longer subordinate to action, but relies instead upon the reader to compose a synthetic whole out of conflicting worlds of sense. Critics in the nineteenth century, Rancière reminds, well understood what was at stake in these gestures. "The absolutization of style was the literary form of the democratic principle of equality."[4] According to Rancière, such stylizations direct language away from one regime of sense into another in which equality would be detectable. To these analyses, however, two series of questions can be posed: Is indifference to subject matter and style a rich enough notion of equality? Does it provide us with an active and polemical form of equality capable of undoing and remaking our world? Is indifference not simply indifference? And, is it really the case that the moments of reverie and idleness found within films, literary fables, and other works are instances of egalitarian promise? Do the deviant lines opened up within the Aristotelian order signal the equality of anyone with everyone else?

Likewise, in Chapter 3 we argued that the rehabilitation of spectatorship that Rancière proposes is premised upon the idea that some forms of art rely upon equality for their functioning. We mined Rancière's account of Jacotot's pedagogical practices in order to contend that art objects—loosely understood to include plastic, literary, and theatrical forms—can be a means of verifying equality. Such experiences, Rancière contends, allow for the discovery of an equality of capacities at odds with the dominant distribution of the sensible. Nevertheless, given that aesthetics—the system of intelligibility according to which these works are thought—frames their production, reception, and functioning, it is necessary to have a clear articulation of the connections between aesthetic art and equality. If equality is so integral to these works, why is it not (directly) expressed within the theoretical texts that delineate their reception? Is there a gap between the experiences of art, described by Rancière, and the manner in which they have been codified by the aesthetic tradition? Rancière attempts to reconcile the two by reading aesthetic theory as describing a form of equality. We have seen throughout that he conceives of aesthetic experience as instantiating equality between the faculties of sense and reason, thus canceling the customary domination of the former by the latter. Instead of experiencing himself at odds with himself, in the aesthetic experience the human being discovers a harmony between the two sides of his nature. Indeed, essential for Rancière are Kant's description of the "free play" of the faculties and Schiller's discussion of the mediating influence of the play impulse. Both detail a condition of the subject at odds with the dominant configuration of sense where the free relation of the faculties betokens a new distribution of the sensible. It can be argued that these thinkers articulate a distribution that contradicts an order based on the inevitability of mastery and the necessity of work. They could be seen as inscribing a heterogeneous element that provides the inspiration for the political task of transforming our world. In this sense, Rancière reads Schiller's *Letters* as an "anthropological" and "political" translation of the Kantian account, one which functions as an allegory of equality.[5] He explains, "If aesthetic 'play' and 'appearance' found a new community, it is because they are the sensible refutation of this opposition between intelligent form and sensible matter, which is really the difference between two humanities."[6] Aside, however, from the equal importance of the faculties, it is difficult to see how the overall lesson of the aesthetic experience is equality. Schiller is clear on this point: man is fully human when he plays, precisely because it is the first time in which he is not compelled by the sense and form impulses. He describes beauty—for Schiller the very essence of the aesthetic experience—as annulling both compulsions, to "set man free both physically and morally."[7] Schiller: "As our nature finds itself, in the contemplation of the Beautiful, in a happy midway point between law and exigency, so, just because it is divided between the two, it is withdrawn from the constraint of both alike."[8] In Rancière's reading, however, freedom plays an under-defined role. The function of free play is too quickly assimilated to the suspension of a world of two distinct natures.[9] Is not another argument regarding the nature of this freedom needed? Is it correct to read this scene as an allegory? Why is the mind's freedom with respect to itself also a promise of equality with others? Does aesthetic freedom serve, as it did for the Greek experience of democracy, as the transitive property by means of which we move from subjective experience to universal equality? It is clear in Kant as well, despite the strongly democratic impulses of his theory of taste, that the primary lesson of aesthetic experience is freedom. As is well known, beauty for Kant functions as the symbol of the moral not because it imbues us with a reverence for others, but because it provides a glimpse of morality's condition of possibility. "In this ability [taste], judgment does not find itself subjected to heteronomy . . . as it does elsewhere in empirical judging—concerning objects of such a pure liking it legislates to itself, just as reason does regarding the power of desire."[10] One could make similar arguments with respect to Hegel and Schelling as well as German, French, and British romanticism. In terms of the theoretical texts that define the aesthetic regime of art, it is difficult to argue that the primary import of such an experience is equality.

Given that Rancière's case is best made with individual works, do we need, then, to be more empirical, describing specific works in terms of whether or not they presuppose equality? Or, is it possible to make an argument at the theoretical level, in terms of the poetics that shape a given regime of intelligibility? In truth, these endeavors are not separate. One can imagine a three-fold strategy: first, the careful description, discussion, and evaluation of specific works—both contemporary and those of historical importance—in terms of their abilities to serve as a means for the verification of equality; second, an analysis of the manner in which the democratizing dimension of the art of the past two hundred years has been either discussed or neglected by artists' writings, criticism, and aesthetic theory; finally, a correction to the existing ways of understanding and framing art. It will be important to pinpoint, as I have been arguing, where equality can and cannot be located within the texts of the aesthetic regime, and to gauge to what extent it is preferable to freedom for describing the aesthetic experience.

My own position is that equality is implicit in many artistic practices, although it is often obscured by the tradition's conceptualization of the aesthetic experience. Rancière does us a great service by making equality central to our conversations, even if the picture is more complicated than his writings lead us to believe. His approach to joining aesthetics with equality is preferable to other such attempts, notably Elaine Scarry's, in that: (1) it does not rely, as Scarry does, on treating beauty as the central element of the aesthetic experience; (2) it conceives of equality as an explicitly political notion, rather than an ethical one; (3) it is more sensitive to historical ruptures, understanding art, aesthetics, and beauty not as atemporal phenomena with innate links to equality, but as historically constituted forms that maintain unprecedented and yet limited links with the value that reshapes the distribution of the sensible.[11]

Of course we cannot expect art or aesthetic philosophy to carry the weight of our politics, which as we have seen consists of presupposing, verifying, and inscribing equality into arrangements set up to deny it. Nor can we expect that the experience of equality will be the same in these two domains. Rancière himself has indicated that despite the congruence he analyzes, art and politics are distinguishable in that the former alters the framework of what is perceptible, while the latter is a struggle for the constitution of a collective subject, an "us," that would alter forms of part-taking. While the two endeavors sustain one another, they are not synonymous. Politics asserts equality, and attempts to extend its reach in a world hostile to its functioning. Art allows us to have a sensible intimation of what it is we struggle for. It is debatable to what extent aesthetic philosophy has recognized and denied this form of equality. And even though a more methodical account is wanting, Rancière's contribution consists of reading these texts in terms of their possible openings to the presupposition and verification of equality.

5.2 THE CENTRALITY OF THE IMAGINATION

It is curious that in his readings of the aesthetic regime, Rancière discounts the significant role played by the imagination. For him, aesthetics articulates a new relationship between the sensuous and rational aspects of human life, rupturing the tyranny of the everyday distribution of the sensible. For thinkers such as Kant, Schiller, Hegel, and the Romantics, however, the vehicle of that transformation was the imagination. Indeed, it is the free functioning of the imagination that not only accounts for and defines the uniqueness of art, but which breaches the dominant distributions of the sensible. The aesthetic encounter is nothing less than the imagination functioning independently of the constraints imposed by, depending upon the thinker in question, the other faculties, the natural world, or historical, political, and economic forces. Hegel affirms the imagination's importance as follows: ". . . the source of works of art is the free activity of fancy which in its imaginations is itself more free than nature is."[12] Hegel here cites the imagination to support his contention, against Kant, that man-made beauty is "higher" than natural beauty; however, Hegel's position could well be taken as indicative of the relative importance of the imagination for the aesthetic regime itself.[13] That faculty's functioning explains the unprecedented forms of relation opened up by works of art and scenes of natural beauty, providing the basis for the notions of freedom claimed for aesthetic arrangements.

One can argue that the hallmark of the aesthetic regime is that it is the place where the longstanding philosophical and religious hostility to this faculty is overcome. Previously considered a source of error and an impediment to sound moral judgment, it is here that thinkers begin to reinterpret the imagination in a positive light. It is within the aesthetic regime that the imagination's products are deemed worthy of serious consideration in that they reflect the full range of human capacities and emancipate the mind from an otherwise banal existence. "Art has at its command not only the whole wealth of natural formations in their manifold and variegated appearance," Hegel explains, "but in addition the creative imagination has power to launch out beyond them *inexhaustibly* in productions of its own."[14] Considered in its productive capacity, the imagination refuses to recognize conventional boundaries of sense and barriers of thought. The imagination, taking an expansive view of the aesthetic regime, is the reserve from which the sensible configuration of our world is contested, reinterpreted, and altered. Many such discussions praise the imagination's disruptive and even subversive character. It is, in sum, the point at which the distribution of the sensible is surpassed.

Rancière's thought relies upon an implicit account of the imagination and an unacknowledged debt to the texts, or more precisely the portions of the aesthetic texts, in which the imagination plays a crucial role. One could rightly say that his work describes the fruits of the imagination, measured in terms of their ability to overcome obstacles to collective action, polemically inscribe equality into the institutions of oligarchy, and to challenge the sensible coordinates of our world. On this score, one could read his analyses of political and aesthetic dissensus as the inventions of this capacity. While Rancière is particularly adept at isolating the disruptive capacities of artistic and literary practices, politics, and film, one can sometimes lament that he neglects to provide a fuller account of how such acts are possible. Given that it is increasingly urgent for politics and art to take account of the resources they have at their disposal, it should be asked: whence springs dissensus? How, given the overwhelming tendency of the world to naturalize its distinctions, distributions, silences, and prejudices, do people manage to conceive the world otherwise? What enables subjectivities to create connections, affirm equality, and depart from the overall sensory logic of the day? What distributes and redistributes the sensible? What, in short, drives the processes of politics and artistic invention?

To state it clearly, my point is twofold: (1) in terms of the presentation of the texts of the aesthetic regime, a thorough reckoning with the imagination is wanting; and (2) such an investigation can facilitate the project of human emancipation. The position sketched in what follows holds that highlighting the role of the imagination within these texts not only allows for a fuller and richer understanding of the aesthetic regime, but it enables us to invent a locus of energy, a capacity, from which to create art and politics.

The first claim is relatively easy to verify by means of a reading of the texts in question. There is a consistent movement in Rancière's thought away from investigating the role played by the imagination within the thinkers under consideration, as is evidenced by prioritizing Schiller over Kant and Hegel, and even the *Letters* (1794) over Schiller's *Kallias or Concerning Beauty* (1793), where the Kantian faculties are more central. There is a similar discounting of the imagination at work in his invocation of romanticism, according to which it is presented as giving rise to a new set of aesthetic principles pertaining to the relationship between art and life, and not, as many readings would have it, a valorization of the faculty of invention. One could present a host of texts, as with Hegel above, and show how the imagination, in its unfettered freedom, is the defining feature of the aesthetic relationship. The second part of my claim, that it is *advantageous* to investigate the role of the imagination, and even that it is possible to advance a tentative theory of the imagination, requires more explanation. It must show not only that such an undertaking is politically and aesthetically desirable but also in keeping with the general framework advanced by Rancière.

As we have seen, Rancière's position cannot be understood as philosophy in the traditional sense. It is a form of analysis that attempts to set out the conditions of historical possibility for a discourse, literary form, political process, or artistic practice, while isolating what is most innovative and egalitarian about its deployment. He quite systematically rejects interpreting such events in the language of psychology, anthropology, or by means of categories inherited from German idealism and phenomenology. He shares with Foucault the effort to de-transcendentalize thought by studying the historical constitution of experience in terms of *common* principles and sensible parameters. Accordingly, Rancière attempts to translate the mentalistic language of German idealism into general political and aesthetic propositions. Customarily, this involves reading "faculties" as "capacities," and mental relations as allegories for a more generalized distribution of the sensible. He likewise tends to set aside the truth-value of the texts and thinkers in question, marshalling them instead as tools for dismantling sensible and intellectual orders at odds with equality. Thus, as is frequently noted, Rancière seeks to avoid ontology, and, depending upon how one reads him, speculative positions and prescriptive statements. In this sense, even though he is no longer immersed in the archives, he remains true to the impulses of this approach, displacing the traditional postures of philosophy by means of history. There are, then, two primary obstacles to a retrieval of the imagination: first, the general suspicion of the pretense to mastery inherent in more traditional forms of philosophical theory; and secondly, Rancière's well-founded preference for treating textual and visual events as evidence of a social capacity, rather than expressions of a subjective faculty.

To overcome the general suspicion of philosophical inquiry it suffices to ask: upon what basis can one rigorously distinguish philosophical reflection from the fictive acts that redistribute the sensible? Can one provide this distinction without betraying the methodological distrust of philosophy's attempts at mastery? Why would philosophical pursuits necessarily be different from literary, artistic, cinematic, and political dissensus? Rejecting philosophy's traditional claims of scientificity, one could construe it along the lines of art: it too intervenes in the general ordering of bodies, sensations, and capacities, allowing us to reconfigure what is possible. Philosophical reflection, even in some of its more traditional manifestations, can be conceived and practiced as a way of doing and making that provides us with the necessary distance from the shared distribution of practices such that they can be transformed. Philosophy, then, simply becomes, and in fact always has been, one technique for investigating and provoking the current meanings assigned to sense. Such a position frees up the history of philosophy and can allow us to construe it, much as Rancière does in practice, as a resource for dissensus. Philosophy, more than simply conceptualizing existence, invents new forms of relation, new modes of being, and new sensible configurations. It can open up as many possibilities as it has at times foreclosed.

It is likewise possible to counter the faculties/capacities obstacle by arguing that the distinction is more apparent than real, while granting the need—and this will be a crucial component of my account of the imagination—to conceive capacities in de-subjectized terms, that is, as social capacities. The point is simultaneously historical and practical. In the first place, the imagination has traditionally been construed as a power or capacity, in the sense of "making possible" or "able to do." For example, in Kant, to whom all modern debates about the imagination return, it should be understood less as an innate part of the mind or a "part of a whole," as reading Kant through the lens of nineteenth-century faculty psychology suggests, and more as a force that creates possibilities.[15] This power not only renders cognition possible, but continually undermines the stability of sensible configurations. Kant's formulation in the *Anthropology*, "*facultas imaginandi*," invokes the then-standard Latin translation of the Greek word *dunamis* [capacity].[16] It indicates thus that Kant conceived of the imagination as a power or potentiality, and that his discussions should be viewed as investigations of what resources the subject has at its disposal.[17]

In the critical writings, this capacity is named an "*Einbildungskraft*," or "power of fantasy." In the first *Critique*, it plays an indispensable role in cognition. In the first instance, the imagination is charged with the task of unifying the manifold of sensible intuition, and, in the second, creating the schema through which representations meet the categories of the understanding.[18] More colloquially, one can say that the imagination composes the influx of sensory information into discrete units, while also providing the bridge between sense and reason. As is well known, Kant is notoriously elliptical on this latter point, describing the imagination as a "blind but indispensable function [*Funktion*] of the soul [*Seele*], without which we should have no knowledge whatsoever, but of which we are scarcely ever conscious."[19] In the attainment of knowledge, the imagination serves the understanding. It provides it with unified representations and the means of introducing them to the categories. In more general terms, it can be understood, according to Kant, as the power of making present what is absent. One need not turn to Heidegger for a discussion of this capacity's intimate links with the domain of possibility, for it was Kant who articulated both the imagination's function in memory and its indispensable role in opening possible futures. For him, it alone allows the mind to present itself with objects that were previously encountered, to anticipate possible objects of experience, and even to produce images independently of experience.[20]

More than simply offering a different vantage point on the same power, the third *Critique* is the culmination of Kant's wholesale reappraisal of the imagination. His position develops from a somewhat conservative castigation of its illusory influence in the precritical writings, to a recognition of its importance for cognition, and, lastly, an appreciation of its products. In its *productive* capacity, the imagination functions outside of the understanding's strictures. As Kant explains the difference:

> When the imagination is used for cognition, then it is under the constraint of the understanding.... But when the aim is aesthetic, then the imagination is free, so that, over and above that harmony with the concept, it may supply, in an unstudied way, a wealth of undeveloped material for the understanding which the latter disregarded in its concept.[21]

The idea is simple: the imagination, when functioning in its freedom, is capable of creating a special type of representation, referred to by Kant as aesthetic ideas, which exceed the parameters of both sensible experience and the understanding's conceptual reserve. These ideas strain the understanding to continually produce a concept adequate to the wealth of its sensible presentations. Considered both in terms of its production and reception, art is frequently the source of such a relationship. In the case of the former, genius, a sort of hyperactivity of the imagination, is the mental disposition that allows for the creation of representations that prompt much thought, while resisting the finality of a concept. In transcendental terms, one can say that successful artistic presentations are those that refuse to be reduced to a single, determinate interpretation, thus prompting the understanding to greater heights.[22] Considered from the spectator's perspective, the work of art is the occasion for a "quickening" of both cognitive faculties. Upon encountering something unprecedented, the mind struggles, first, to adequately represent it to itself, and, second, to cognize it. It quickly discovers the limits of conceptual understanding and therewith the freedom of the imagination. The judgment that this feeling is universally shareable is the occasion of pleasure. Fine art is, in short, the ability to generate products that, while tasteful, conduct the understanding to its limits and provide the imagination with an occasion for its freedom. As we have seen throughout, Rancière encourages us to interpret this novel relationship of the faculties as a disruption of the dominant configuration of the sensible world.

While the primary source of these experiences is either scenes of natural beauty or the workings of art, the aesthetic relation of the faculties is not, for Kant, limited to these spheres alone. The third *Critique* describes the natural tendency of the imagination to transfigure the sensible world. Kant explains:

> For the imagination ([in its role] as a productive cognitive power) is very mighty when it creates, as it were, another nature out of the material that actual nature gives it. We use it to entertain ourselves when experience strikes us as overly routine. We may even restructure experience; and though in doing so we continue to follow analogical laws, yet we also follow principles which reside higher up, namely in reason. . . . In this process we feel our freedom from the law of association (which attaches to the empirical use of the imagination); for although it is under that law that nature lends us material, yet we can process that material into something quite different, namely, into something that surpasses nature.[23]

While in the experience Kant describes here the imagination is linked to reason, it is not governed by it. In fact, the imagination provides reason with material for consideration, ideas, only by surpassing experience. Taking up the various strands of Kant's position, then, we can understand the imagination as the power of producing, reproducing, and, as described by the third *Critique*, contesting the sensible. Because of its role in cognition, the imagination is the function of sensibility that moves beyond the sensible in order to create, one might say in more contemporary language, a virtual mediation between representations and the categories of thought. The imagination is thus at once a part of sensibility and capable of departing from it. Indeed, one can say that the imagination is the place where the sensible separates from, departs from, and surpasses itself.

In this respect, the imagination has the same essential structure as that which Rancière describes as dissensus. It is the manifestation of a sensible that is continually being opened by a difference from itself. Extrapolating from Kant, we can describe dissensus as generated by the imagination's power for creating different senses of sense. The imagination is that capacity, located on this side of sensibility, which prevents the sensible from becoming closed and static. It continually transgresses previously constituted distributions by de-realizing the world. Its first movement consists of suspending and invalidating a given distribution of the sensible. It then sketches, using what it has otherwise gathered from experience, alternative configurations. It subjects the world to a process of fictionalization which it treats as the raw material for its own compositions. The kingdom of the imagination is the domain of possibility, and it continually prompts itself with the simple thought of what might be. In so doing, it awakens the power of reason, which begins to contemplate, evaluate, and perhaps enact that which is not present. The imagination is dissensual in that it is the capacity which allows sensibility to depart from sense because something in the latter proves intolerable. Even if it is only because the world is too constant and predictable, the faculties are always on the verge of revolt. Their rebellion can be prompted, but not determined, by the undertakings of others. These gestures normally carry the names of art and politics. They allow the faculties to become unstructured, and for the pleasures of freedom to become concrete. When this energy becomes concentrated, it gives rise to more systematic re-orderings of the possible, such as those found in the worlds of art. When these become the basis of collective challenges to the hierarchical infrastructure of our world, we have entered into the process of politics. We need to find more ways to elicit the insubordination of our faculties, and to channel their errancy into concrete, sensible political inscriptions.

5.3 INVENTING THE TRANS-SUBJECTIVE IMAGINATION

Until this point we have proceeded in largely Kantian terms, portraying the imagination as a capacity of sensible-political dissensus. It is necessary to depart from the strictly Kantian line, however, inasmuch as it relies upon an untenable notion of the subject, one which prevents us from discovering the nature of creativity and the full power of the imagination. As the history of philosophy attests, and deconstructive critics have recently pointed out, the imagination is not reducible to one of the subject's properties.[24] It is, for example, conspicuously absent from Kant's inventory of the mind's powers in the *Critique of Judgment*, and accordingly resists a simple account of its nature when framed in terms of the subject.[25] An investigation of the creative imagination need not place us within the economy of the *cogito*, and it is possible to reinterpret its textual legacy along the lines Rancière has created for the aesthetic regime. It is evident that Rancière operates in an intellectual space cleared by poststructuralism's critiques of the subject, along with its concomitant sensitivity to the forces created by redeploying archival positivities. The retrieval of the imagination thus follows this general methodological approach, where the insights of the philosophy of consciousness are retained after a process of critique, revision, and extension. The imagination is one such concept that, given what we know about the nature of language, the educational relationships conducive to learning, and the formats that foster creativity, is overdue for such an update. Here, I do not intend to endorse the latest trends in the human sciences, pedagogical theory, or the uncritical embrace of communications technology, but rather to describe, in philosophical terms, this capacity that I see operating in dissensus. Doing so allows not only for a fuller understanding of the aesthetic regime, but can enable us to see, more concretely, its potential import for contemporary artistic and political practices.

It is necessary to retain from the preceding section the sense in which the imagination is a force that breaks from and disturbs sense. The imagination is a type of sensual recalcitrance that, when pursued systematically, enters the subject into insurrection. Joining with Rancière, however, it is necessary to connect this capacity to the generative effects of equality. Doing so allows us to begin to formulate an account of the imagination as a social capacity. Describing the imagination as a social capacity does not mean, as is often thought, that it is the faculty that makes social interaction possible. It is not "social" in the sense that it founds intersubjective relationships by allowing for the mutual adoption of different points of view. It is not, as certain phenomenologies would have it, the capacity for empathy that permits one to move from one subjective position to another. Neither is the social imagination reducible to psychoanalytic or Bachelardian archetypes, nor Deleuzian notions of group fantasy. The position I am advocating begins with the realization that the imagination cannot be understood simply as a power of the subject. It rejects, as with Rancière's conception of the aesthetic regime, the traditional priority accorded to the will. Emphasizing the subject's will in creation covers over the concert with others that stands as the imagination's foundation. The imagination is a trans-subjective capacity whose force is created through the assumption and practice of radical equality. When we presuppose it, find it, or fabricate it, equality engenders and spurs the process of creativity. It breaks the habitual sensory frameworks that prevent the full flourishing of human capacities, ushering them into new space-time configurations. The presupposition of equality literally transfigures the world: arrangements, objects, persons, and ourselves appear different under its assumption, and we cannot help assuming an aesthetico-normative stance with respect to the rest of existence. It is in this space opened up with others that the imagination luxuriates in its freedom, celebrating its distance from the everyday by composing new forms.

The imagination, as we verify daily through experience, requires others in order to be activated. We must, therefore, reject the traditional perspective according to which the imagination allows us to move outward toward others, and recognize instead how the imagination is created in practices of solidarity. We imagine through the assumption of equality, that is, only on the condition that we have already broken from thought's strictures by identifying with others. How much easier it is to write a book, compose music, and develop new visual forms when one can locate their becomings in shared concerns, collective emotive responses, conversations, and unspoken complicities. In theoretical terms, we need to account for the feelings of empowerment we gain in straying from ourselves. And we need to update our notions of creativity to keep pace with the new forms of collective production and action spawned by the aesthetic regime. For while the world of art has come to embrace practices of collectivity, sometimes resembling the structures of activist political organizations, the philosophy of art, even when it engages with the texts of aesthetics proper, remains mired in notions of creativity inherited from the representative regime. In contrast to the subject-centered accounts of inspiration, we should affirm that creation takes place between individuals who, through processes of collaboration—whether artistic, intellectual, or political—cease being individuals through the practical assertion that the world is not divisible into two different types of intelligence. One could justify such an account on

Rancière's terms by returning to the analyses of the forces created by the will-on-will relationship of universal teaching described in *Schoolmaster*. Accordingly, one could claim that what Jacotot discovered is the trans-subjective space in which discoveries occur because of the relationships of intellectual equality presupposed between two or more people. Such, I submit, enables us to describe how equality not only destabilizes established orders, but produces new configurations.

It is necessary to endorse something of the conception of creativity forged by German idealism and romanticism, while forcing it to remain true to its most radical insights. In a sense, both can be said to have recognized the de-subjectifying pull that founds the imagination when they identified genius with nature, and made creation itself dependent upon a new regime of signification. As it was pondered so deeply by the young Nietzsche, creation does not spring from the "I," but takes place outside of oneself. In the *Birth of Tragedy*, he affirms Schiller's suggestion that images, loosely understood to include discursive forms, emerge from a sundering of the ego. Hence the importance of music: creation follows upon a musical mood that ruptures the "principle of individuation," scattering fragments of the individual among the "primal unity" of existence.[26] Faced with this dissolution, and indeed because of it, art breaks away from nature through the creation of a second nature, the pleasing illusions that restore the individual.[27] With this dynamic, Nietzsche counters the tendency, also inherited from romanticism, of locating the source of creation in the particularities of subjectivity. Nietzsche:

> We contend . . . that the whole opposition between the subjective and objective . . . is altogether irrelevant in aesthetics, since the subject, the willing subject, the willing individual that furthers his own egotistic ends, can be conceived only as the antagonist, not as the origin of art. Insofar as the subject is the artist . . . he has already been released from his individual will, and has become . . . the medium through which the one truly existent subject celebrates his release in appearance.[28]

The important point is that, for Nietzsche, the first movement of invention entails a transgression of the habitual boundaries of experience and the paradoxical identification of the self with what is other than the self. It is here, outside of the self, that the imagination is in full force, with the return to self in the second moment serving only to cement the discoveries made elsewhere. Obviously, Nietzsche's account remains unsatisfactory to the extent that it can only hint at the dynamic processes of dis-identification and subjectivation that lead the individual beyond his allotted role within a distribution of the sensible. The essential insight, however, is that the imagination functions through contact with someone or something different. Individuals cannot dream, create, imagine, or produce without this paradoxical identification with others.

In the end, it will be necessary to retain something of Kant's transcendental approach to the imagination. We can describe and study its activities and products, but a definitive conceptual account will elude us. On the one hand, this is because the imagination distributes the sensible, thinkable, and possible, and, on the other, because completely conceptualizing the imagination in its productive capacity, that is, in its freedom from the restraints of the understanding, would subordinate it once again. We are a long way from knowing what the imagination is capable of, and the investigation of its powers must be both philosophical-transcendental and political-experimental. In this sense, it is fair to say that the imagination is the capacity for resisting the distribution of the sensible, and that to study it is to test and develop our powers for establishing worlds of sense. We should resist the effort to explain away the imagination by evoking crass materialisms that reduce it to expressions of class, gender, identity, historical context, and geographic locale. In its practice, dissensus rejects precisely this version of the world, and an account of the imagination should as well. The imagination transcends these limitations by creating connections between individuals at different positions within the distribution of the sensible.

Even as something about the imagination—that power which breaks from experience—remains ideal, it is essential to advance, as far as possible, a materialism of the imagination. It would be naïve to theorize the imagination as a completely oppositional power. Even though it breaks from and disrupts the distribution of the sensible, it too is subject to its divisions. The Kantian account is instructive in this regard as well: the imagination is a sensible faculty and is thus touched by the world's distributions. It is, therefore, necessary to reverse the position according to which the imagination, responsible for unifying the sensible manifold, rests outside of space and time. Location within the distribution of the sensible provides the imagination with its raw material, and, to some degree, dictates the range of its functioning. We need a deeply empirical account of the transsubjective conditions that permit and/or block its activation. Such an undertaking would analyze the spatial and temporal configurations of our world in order to determine which are conducive to the imagination's flourishing and which have been created in order to squelch its functioning. These inventories would catalogue the practices that affirm equality, either through textual, visual, or political practices, and then measure their results in terms of the advance of concrete inscriptions. Art today already carries too much of the burden of redistributing the sensible. While we can well learn its lessons in altered perception—a looking removed from the everyday distribution of the sensible—we must not come to be overly reliant on it for our moments of reverie. It cannot seriously be put forward as a substitute for political action, and there is a danger in describing art as a series of "micro-utopias," whether palliative or antagonistic, without critiquing the social, political, and economic structures that relegate art to readily predictable places within the division of labor. We must study the specific distributions of space-time that preempt the encounters required for activating this capacity of the imagination, everything from the rhythms of the school and work day, to the compositions of neighborhoods and cities, and the circuits of artistic display. We must be indefatigable critics of the privileges that enable some to imagine, while convincing others that it is a luxury they cannot afford. Not all are allotted equal opportunities to engage this capacity, and it will therefore be necessary to challenge the distribution of the sensible *with* and *on behalf of* the imagination.

CONCLUSION

It could be said that the above analysis unnecessarily multiplies the terms of Rancière's thought. Why spend so much time reworking the imagination when equality itself is a sufficiently rich political notion? Is not the affirmation of equality capable of effectively destabilizing the hierarchical distributions of our world? What is to be gained by muddying the waters with a concept whose history is so disputed and problematic?

In this very line of questioning, however, we can see reasons for introducing the imagination into the discussion. Its complicated history is precisely what allows it to be seized upon by new interpretive forces and put to work in new and varied contexts. Likewise, its indeterminate role within the philosophy of consciousness means that it continually destabilizes, from the inside, philosophical and theoretical systems. For the same reason, it moves us beyond the province of philosophy into experimental terrains where unclassifiable thoughts give rise to unforeseeable discourses, gestures, and actions. It is an indisciplinary capacity that can never be exhaustively codified, and which requires continual experimentation in order to verify its existence. It is evoked, when we are together, in art and politics.

The multiplication of the names for dissensus need not overly concern us. In fact, there is much to be gained from the process of multiplication itself in that it allows us to define new resources, capacities, forms of intervention, and sources of normativity. One cannot always predict the institutional, historical, and economic obstacles we will face, just as one cannot always envisage the machinations the police will undertake on behalf of oligarchy. At times, it may be more advantageous to inscribe the freedom of the imagination than to resort to equality outright. Indeed, one of the paradoxes of the contemporary work situation, as many authors attest, is that it demands collaboration, spontaneity, and invention. Championing the rights of the imagination may be one way to smuggle into the policed distributions of sense the destabilizing power of equality.

Returning to the founding texts of the aesthetic regime with an eye towards the imagination may enable us to elaborate, in more precise terms, the connections between art, freedom, aesthetics, and equality. As we have argued, the experience of freedom is central to idealist and romantic aesthetics. When these authors describe the aesthetic—the process of creation, the encounter with, and even works of art themselves—they are unanimous in describing it in terms of freedom, whether it be the appearance of freedom, as it was for Kant, or as the actual manifestation of freedom, as thinkers like Schelling, Hegel, and later the Romantics contended. The imagination is the locus of that freedom. It remains only to describe, by means of a rigorous archaeology, the imagination as a faculty of equality. I have begun that task here, indicating how the imagination can be reframed as a capacity that relies upon others for its activation, that is, one which requires the assumption of intellectual, social, and political equality.

Aside from providing us with a more complete, but by no means exhaustive, understanding of the aesthetic regime—its texts and meta-politics—the focus on the imagination will allow us to advance with a more sensuous account of politics' operative terms. This is not to say that Rancière's thinking is not sensible, for indeed it is. The position that politics is about counting, concepts such as consensus and dissensus, and the framing of these in terms of a distribution of the sensible, allow him to elaborate well the idea that politics is first and foremost about struggles over spaces and times, as well as the voices and bodies that occupy them. In terms of art, film, and literature, he is likewise attentive to how minor displacements of sense can be translated into political propositions. Nevertheless, the operations of dissensus and equality themselves remain abstract. To say that they open worlds does not provide a fully embodied sense of what it is like to invent art and politics, nor do these concepts themselves prompt action. Recourse to the imagination, along with other faculties, can provide for richer notions of dissensus and equality, and allow us to describe our experiences of art and politics more fully. Since the imagination occupies a position between sense and reason, attending to it will facilitate the composition of descriptions, themselves already political operations, and, more importantly, instill in us the desire for equality.

NOTES

CHAPTER 1

1 Jacques Rancière, *The Philosopher and His Poor*, trans. John Drury, Corinne Oster, and Andrew Parker (Durham: Duke University Press, 2004), 217.
2 Ibid.
3 I acknowledge my gratitude to Professor Rancière for his time in conversation, during which he stressed this point.
4 Jacques Rancière, "Jacques Rancière and Interdisciplinarity: An Interview with Marie-Aude Baronian and Mireille Rosello," *Art & Ideas: A Journal of Ideas, Contexts and Methods* 2, no. 1 (2008): 3.
5 Ibid.
6 Didier Eribon claims that because of Althusser's frequent illnesses, his influence was primarily restricted to personal interactions with students during office hours. Didier Eribon, *Michel Foucault*, trans. Betsy Wing (Cambridge: Harvard University Press, 1991), 33.
7 François Dosse, *History of Structuralism, Volume 1: The Rising Sign, 1945–1966*, trans. Deborah Glassman (Minneapolis: University of Minnesota Press, 1997), 290.
8 Étienne Balibar, "Althusser and the rue d'Ulm," *New Left Review* 58 (2009): 96.
9 Dosse, *History of Structuralism*, 290–291.
10 Karl Marx, Preface to *A Contribution to the Critique of Political Economy*, in *The Marx-Engels Reader*, 2nd ed., ed. Robert C. Tucker (New York: W. W. Norton & Company, 1978), 5.
11 At the opening of *For Marx*, Althusser attributes the notion of the problematic to Jacques Martin, a little-known philosopher who, before his death in 1963, was close to Althusser and Foucault. See Louis Althusser, *For Marx*, trans. Ben Brewster (New York: Verso, 2005), 32. Althusser frequently credited Martin, to whom *For Marx* is dedicated, with "having discovered the road to Marx's philosophy."
12 Ibid., 34–35.
13 See Louis Althusser, "Contradiction and Overdetermination," in *For Marx*, 87–128.
14 Louis Althusser, *Lenin and Philosophy and Other Essays*, trans. Ben Brewster (New York: Monthly Review Press, 1971), 40.

NOTES

15 Louis Althusser, "Philosophy as a Revolutionary Weapon," in *Lenin and Philosophy*, 15.
16 Louis Althusser et al., *Lire Le Capital* (Paris: Presses Universitaires de France, 1996), 390–411.
17 Ibid., 345–362.
18 Ibid., 25. Italics in original.
19 Rancière was integral to the planning and implementation of the seminar. His contribution "*Le concept de critique et la critique de l'économie politique des Manuscrits de 1844 au Capital,*" which was to become a matter of contention after Rancière's break with Althusser, is not contained in the English translation published by New Left Books in 1970, or the recent reissue *Reading Capital*, trans. Ben Brewster (New York: Verso, 2009). The translation is based on the abridged, second edition of 1968, in which Rancière's text was not included as it was intended for another volume of this edition. When, in 1973, the completion of this edition was proposed, Rancière wanted his contribution to be preceded by a short, self-critical essay in which he repudiated the project for its "reactionary political foundations." This essay was initially accepted and then rejected by Althusser. It was subsequently published as "*Mode d'emploi pour une réédition de Lire Le Capital,*" *Les temps modernes* 328 (Nov. 1973): 788–807. Throughout, I have made use of the complete, single-volume third edition, which more closely reflects the plan of the seminar itself.
20 Althusser, "Philosophy as a Revolutionary Weapon," 21.
21 Ibid., Italics in original.
22 Althusser, *Lenin and Philosophy*, 60–63.
23 Rancière, *The Philosopher*, 223.
24 Jacques Rancière, "*Entretien avec Jacques Rancière,*" 6. Available from: http://www.armand-gatti.org/fichiers/_cat2_27831_chantierranciere.pdf. Accessed on February 13, 2010. (Pages 1–26).
25 Jacques Rancière, *La leçon d'Althusser* (Paris: Gallimard, 1973), 10.
26 It is the version of this article reprinted as an appendix to *La leçon* (227–277) that I quote in what follows.
27 Jacques Rancière, "*Pour mémoire: Sur la théorie de l'idéologie,*" in *La leçon d'Althusser*, 237.
28 Ibid.
29 Ibid., 240.
30 Ibid., 241.
31 Rancière, *La leçon*, 9.
32 See Rancière, "*Sur la théorie de l'idéologie,*" 242, 250, and 255–257.
33 Rancière, "*Entretien avec Jacques Rancière,*" 8. *La leçon* describes the complex set of historical conditions that rendered Althusserian discourse possible. It is an important document for understanding the history of postwar Marxist groups in France. Rancière contends that Althusserianism functioned by playing the *gauchisme* of the Maoist student groups against the revisionist tendencies of the Communist Party. Exploiting the disarray opened up by Khrushchev's program of de-Stalinization, Althusserianism was able to present itself as the true voice of Marxism in France, where

NOTES

Party leadership had begun collaborating with Socialists, Social Democrats, and left-leaning Catholics. In adopting much of the Maoist rhetoric, Althusserianism framed itself as a radical alternative to the conservatism of the PCF; however, Althusser never fully endorsed the Maoist positions on the Cultural Revolution, remaining close to the Party on practical matters and distancing himself from the priority students accorded to politics over Party organization (63–64). It was in this context that the project of restoring the truth of Marxism through a reading of *Capital* was undertaken. Rancière contends the endeavor can be viewed as having had a twofold aim: first, it attempted to influence Party politics with theory, and second, it sought to restore order to the student milieu with a reading lesson. Althusser's lesson is thus ultimately that of orthodoxy, one that served the party not by recapitulating its positions, but by assimilating opposing doctrines and restoring traditional pedagogical arrangements (74–86).

34 Rancière, *La leçon*, 11–15. Rancière's articulation of this project bears a resemblance to the archeological language used by Michel Foucault. *La leçon* is described not as a refutation of Althusserianism, but as the study of "the positivity of its functioning" and as a "genealogy" of the connections it articulates between theory and political practice.
35 Ibid., 14.
36 Ibid., 121.
37 John Lewis, "The Althusser Case (Part 1)," *Marxism Today*, 16, no. 1 (January 1972): 23–28; "The Althusser Case (Part 2)," *Marxism Today*, 16, no. 2 (February 1972): 43–48; "On the Althusser Discussion," *Marxism Today*, 18, no. 6 (June 1974): 168–174.
38 Louis Althusser, "Reply to John Lewis," in *Essays in Self-Criticism*, trans. Grahame Lock (London: New Left Books, 1976), 53. While John Lewis is ostensibly the object of Althusser's polemic, the more general target is existential Marxism. In Lewis' "man," Althusser denounces the fiction of the "little Sartrean god . . . endowed with the amazing power of 'transcending' every situation . . ." (45).
39 Ibid., 64. Translation modified.
40 Ibid., 65.
41 Rancière, *La leçon*, 36.
42 Ibid., 34.
43 Ibid., 35.
44 Ibid., 21–32.
45 *Les LIP—l'imagination au pouvoir*, writ. and dir. Christian Rouaud, 1 hr. 58 min., Les Films d'Ici, 2007.
46 Quoted in Rancière, *La leçon*, 157.
47 Ibid., 161–171.
48 Ibid., 169.
49 Rancière's contributions have been republished as Jacques Rancière, *Les scènes du people: Les Révoltes logiques, 1975/1985* (Lyon, Horlieu éditions, 2003). A historical account of *Les Révoltes logiques* can be found in Kristin Ross, *May '68 and Its Afterlives* (Chicago: University of Chicago Press, 2002), 124–137.

NOTES

50 Jacques Rancière, "Preface to the Hindi translation of *Nights of Labor.*" Available at: http://hydrarchy.blogspot.com/2009/01/ranciere-2-new-preface-to-hindi.html. Accessed on March 2, 2010.
51 Donald Reid, "Introduction," to Jacques Rancière, *The Nights of Labor: The Worker's Dream in Nineteenth-Century France*, trans. John Drury (Philadelphia: Temple University Press, 1989), xxx.
52 Jacques Rancière, "The Myth of the Artisan: Critical Reflections on a Category of Social History," *International Labor and Working-Class History*, No. 24 (Fall, 1983): 10. See also, Jacques Rancière, "A Reply," *International Labor and Working-Class History*, No. 25 (Spring, 1984): 42–46.
53 Rancière, *The Philosopher*, xxvi.
54 Jacques Rancière, "From Politics to Aesthetics?" *Paragraph* 28, no. 1 (2005): 13.
55 Ibid., 14.
56 Jacques Rancière, *Malaise dans l'esthétique* (Paris: Éditions Galilée, 2004), 38.
57 Rancière has collected and published the most significant of Gauny's writings as Gabriel Gauny, *Le philosophe plébéien*, ed. Jacques Rancière (Paris: La découverte-Maspéro, 1983). For the texts on the "cenobitic economy" see section two, "*Économie de la liberté*," 89–138.
58 Gabriel Gauny, "*Le travail à la tâche*," in *Le philosophe plébéien*, 45–46. This passage is frequently employed by Rancière as an example of the indiscriminate nature of the aesthetic relationship and its ability to disengage one from a given distribution of the sensible. See his commentaries in *Nights*, 80–86, and Jacques Rancière, *The Emancipated Spectator* trans. Gregory Elliott (New York: Verso, 2009), 70–73.
59 Rancière, *Emancipated Spectator*, 71.
60 Rancière, "Preface to Hindi translation."
61 Plato, *Republic*, IV, 433a, 7–9.
62 Rancière, *The Philosopher*, 33.
63 Plato, *Republic*, IV, 433a, 5–7.
64 Rancière, *The Philosopher*, 48.
65 Ibid., 17.
66 Ibid.
67 Ibid., 52–53.
68 Ibid., 206.
69 Ibid., 52. Italics in original.
70 Ibid., 51.
71 For an extended treatment of the confrontation between Bourdieu and Rancière, see Charlotte Nordmann *Bourdieu/Rancière: La politique entre sociologie et philosophie* (Paris: Éditions Amsterdam, 2006).
72 Kristin Ross, "Translator's Introduction," to Jacques Rancière, *The Ignorant Schoolmaster: Five Lessons in Intellectual Emancipation* (Stanford: Stanford University Press, 1991), x.
73 Ibid., ix–x.
74 Rancière, *The Philosopher*, 179.
75 Ibid., 215.

NOTES

76 Ibid., 171. Italics in original.
77 Ibid., 170–171.
78 Pierre Bourdieu, *Distinction: A Social Critique of the Judgement of Taste*, trans. Richard Nice (Cambridge: Harvard University Press, 1984).
79 Rancière, *The Philosopher*, 184. Italics in original.
80 Ibid., 185.
81 Ibid., 186–189.
82 Ibid., 197.
83 Ibid., 199.
84 Ibid., 217.
85 The phrase was used by Félix and Victor Ratier to describe Jacotot's method. It is quoted in Rancière, *Schoolmaster*, 2.
86 Ibid., 46.
87 Ibid., 47.
88 Ibid., 60–65.
89 Ibid., 50.
90 Ibid., 13.
91 Ibid., 6.
92 Ibid.
93 Ibid., 13 and 20–25.
94 Ibid., 27. Italics in original.
95 Ibid., 39.
96 Ibid., 65. Italics in original.
97 Ibid., 137. Italics in original.
98 Ibid., 133.
99 Rancière, *The Philosopher*, 207–217.

CHAPTER 2

1 Alain Badiou, *Metapolitics*, trans. Jason Barker (New York: Verso, 2005), 116.
2 Jacques Rancière, "*Dix Thèses Sur La Politique*," in *Aux bords du politique* (Paris: Gallimard, 1998), 233–237.
3 Jacques Rancière, *Disagreement: Politics and Philosophy*, trans. Julie Rose (Minneapolis: University of Minnesota Press, 1999), 9.
4 Ibid., 124.
5 Rancière, "*Dix Thèses*," 240–241.
6 Rancière, *Disagreement*, 29.
7 Jacques Rancière, *Chroniques des temps consensuels*, (Paris: Éditions du Seuil, 2005), 7–10.
8 Rancière, *Disagreement*, 132.
9 Rancière, *Aux bords*, 56–59.
10 Rancière, "*Dix Thèses*," 244.
11 Rancière, *Disagreement*, 136. "Politics today must be immodest in relation to the modesty forced on it by the logics of consensual management."
12 Ibid., 35.

13 Ibid., 22–23. Italics in the original.
14 Aristotle, *Politics*, I, 1254b, 1–15.
15 Ibid., I, 1245b, 20–22.
16 Rancière, *Disagreement*, 33.
17 Ibid., 39.
18 Jean-Philippe Deranty, "Rancière and Contemporary Political Ontology," *Theory and Event* 6, no. 4 (2003).
19 Rancière, *Disagreement*, 14.
20 Ibid., 27.
21 Aristotle, *Nicomachean Ethics*, V, 1131a, 20–25.
22 Ibid., V, 1131a, 25–30.
23 Rancière, "*Dix Thèses*," 232.
24 Claude Mossé, "How a Political Myth Takes Shape: Solon, 'Founding Father' of Athenian Democracy" in *Athenian Democracy*, ed. P. J. Rhodes (Oxford: Oxford University Press, 2004), 242–259.
25 Rancière, *Disagreement*, 8. Italics in original.
26 Jacques Rancière, *Hatred of Democracy*, trans. Steve Corcoran (New York: Verso, 2006), 38–49.
27 Todd May, *The Political Thought of Jacques Rancière: Creating Equality* (University Park: The Pennsylvania State University Press, 2008), 73.
28 Rancière, *Schoolmaster*, 46–49.
29 Rancière's account of the plebeian revolt builds upon the interpretation put forward by Pierre-Simon Ballanche. Rancière discusses Livy in a number of places. Most notably: *Schoolmaster*, 96–99; *Aux bords*, 159–160; *Disagreement*, 23–27; and Jacques Rancière and Davide Panagia, "Dissenting Words: A Conversation with Jacques Rancière," *Diacritics*, 30, no. 2 (2000): 116.
30 Rancière, *Aux bords*, 140.
31 Rancière, *Hatred*, 48.
32 Rancière, *Aux bords*, 163. Here, I make recourse to Liz Heron's fine translation, Jacques Rancière, *On the Shores of Politics*, trans. Liz Heron (New York: Verso, 1995), 84.
33 Rancière, *Aux bords*, 160.
34 Rancière, *Hatred*, 48.
35 Jacques Rancière, "Literature, Politics, Aesthetics: Approaches to Democratic Disagreement," *Substance* 29, no. 2 (2000): 19.
36 Jacques Rancière, "Politics, Identification, Subjectivization," *October* 61 (Summer, 1992): 60.
37 Ibid.
38 Ibid.
39 Rancière, *Aux bords*, 157–174.
40 Rancière, "Politics, Identification, Subjectivization," 60. Italics in the original.
41 Rancière, *Disagreement*, 118.
42 Ibid., 42.
43 Peter Dews, "The *Nouvelle Philosophie* and Foucault," in *Michel Foucault: Critical Assessments, Volume III*, ed. Barry Smart (New York: Routledge,

1994), 125–161. For a historical perspective on the development of the New Philosophers, see Ross, *May '68 and Its Afterlives*. See also Rancière's critique of Bernard-Henri Lévy, "Reply to Lévy," *Telos: A Quarterly Journal of Radical Thought* no. 33 (1977): 119–122.
44 Rancière, *Disagreement*, 31–32.
45 Ibid., 32.
46 Herbert Marcuse, *The Aesthetic Dimension: Toward a Critique of Marxist Aesthetics* (Boston: Beacon Press, 1978).
47 For Rancière's critique of Habermas, see *Disagreement*, 44–87.
48 On the debates between phenomenology, psychoanalysis, and structuralism regarding the subject, see Paul Ricoeur, "The Question of the Subject: The Challenge of Semiology," in *The Conflict of Interpretations: Essays in Hermeneutics*, ed. Don Ihde (Evanston: Northwestern University Press, 1974), 236–266.
49 Louis Althusser, "Ideology and Ideological State Apparatuses" in *On Ideology*, trans. Ben Brewster (New York: Verso, 2008), 44–51.
50 Michel Foucault, "The Subject and Power," in *Power: Essential Works of Foucault, 1954–1984, Volume Three*, ed. James D. Faubion (New York: The New Press, 2000), 326–348.
51 Rancière, *Disagreement*, 140.
52 Rancière, "Politics, Identification, Subjectivization," 61.
53 In *Disagreement*, Rancière laments that this last name can no longer be construed in anything besides an identitarian fashion. He claims that it has been deprived of its original, subjectifying capacity by the logic of "law and order" that "accept[s] as legitimate only those claims made by real groups that take the floor in person and themselves state their own identity" (127). His argument is that police operations make difficult names that were previously occasions for solidarity.
54 Ibid., 59. Italics in original.
55 Ibid., 139.
56 Rancière, "Politics, Identification, Subjectivization," 61.
57 Foucault, "The Subject and Power," 336. "Maybe the target nowadays is not to discover what we are but to refuse what we are. . . . We have to promote new forms of subjectivity through the refusal of the kind of individuality that has been imposed on us for several centuries."
58 Rancière, "Politics, Identification, Subjectivization," 59.
59 Rancière, *Disagreement*, 117–118.
60 Ibid., 102. Italics in the original.
61 Jacques Rancière, "Postface" to *La parole ouvrière*, ed. Alain Faure and Jacques Rancière (Paris: La Fabrique éditions, 2007), 342.

CHAPTER 3

1 Michel Foucault, *The Order of Things: An Archaeology of the Human Sciences* (New York: Vintage Books, 1994), ix–xxiv. Also, Michel Foucault, *The Archaeology of Knowledge and The Discourse on Language*, trans. A. M. Sheridan Smith (New York: Pantheon Books, 1972).

NOTES

2 Jacques Rancière, "Jacques Rancière and Interdisciplinarity," 2.
3 Jacques Rancière, "Interview for the English Edition," in *The Politics of Aesthetics: The Distribution of the Sensible*, trans. Gabriel Rockhill (New York: Continuum, 2006), 50.
4 Rancière, *Politics of Aesthetics*, 103–104.
5 Ibid., 103.
6 Aristotle, *Poetics*, 1449b, 22–30.
7 Rancière, *Malaise*, 16–17.
8 Rancière, *Politics of Aesthetics*, 22.
9 Ibid., 16.
10 Rancière, *Malaise*, 17.
11 Ibid., 22.
12 Jacques Rancière, *The Emancipated Spectator* (New York: Verso, 2009), 60.
13 Ibid., 62.
14 Rancière, *Politics of Aesthetics*, 25.
15 Rancière, *Malaise*, 14.
16 Ibid., 18.
17 Ibid., 53.
18 Jacques Rancière, "The Aesthetic Dimension," plenary lecture at the annual meeting of the Society for Phenomenological and Existential Philosophy, October 31, 2009.
19 Jacques Rancière, "Thinking between disciplines: an aesthetics of knowledge," *Parrhesia*, no. 1 (2006): 4.
20 Rancière, *Malaise*, 24.
21 Ibid.
22 Immanuel Kant, *Critique of Judgment*, trans. Werner S. Pluhar (Indianapolis: Hackett Publishing Company, 1987), 45–46.
23 As we have seen, Rancière takes exception with the central thesis of Bourdieu's *Distinction*. Rancière notes how sociology itself presupposes the conception of signification imported by the aesthetic revolution, and contends that the discipline is a "war machine invented in the age of the aesthetic which is also the age of democratic revolutions, as a response to the troubles of this age." Rancière, "Thinking between disciplines," 6–9. See also the critique of Bourdieu in the introduction to *Malaise*, 9–27.
24 Rancière, *Schoolmaster*, 60–67.
25 Ibid., 69. Italics in the original.
26 Ibid., 70–71.
27 Rancière, "Art of the Possible: Fulvia Carnevale and John Kelsey in Conversation with Jacques Rancière," *Artforum*, March 2007, 267.
28 For the former discussion, see "Art of the Possible," 264–266. The latter is in Rancière, *Emancipated*, 26–30.
29 Rancière, *Malaise*, 65.
30 Rancière, *Emancipated*, 8.
31 Ibid., 7–9.
32 Ibid., 12. Translation modified.

NOTES

33 Ibid.
34 Ibid., 13.
35 Ibid.
36 Ibid., 14–15.
37 Clement Greenberg, "Modernist Painting," in *Modern Art and Modernism: A Critical Anthology*, ed. Francis Frascina and Charles Harrison (New York: Harper & Row Publishers, 1982), 5.
38 Jacques Rancière, "The Aesthetic Revolution and Its Outcomes," *New Left Review* 14 (2002): 133 and 138.
39 Ibid., 134. Italics in the original.
40 Friedrich Schiller, *On the Aesthetic Education of Man*, trans. Reginald Snell (Mineola, New York: Dover Publications, Inc., 2004), 81.
41 Rancière, "Aesthetic Revolution," 142–143.
42 Schiller, *Aesthetic Education*, 27.
43 Ibid., 80. Italics in the original.
44 Ibid., 75.
45 Ibid., 80.
46 Ranciere, *Malaise*, 47.
47 Ibid.
48 Schiller, *Aesthetic Education*, 80.
49 Clement Greenberg, "Avant-Garde and Kitsch," in *Art and Culture* (Boston: Beacon Press, 1989), 7. This is a conservative gesture that allows Greenberg to contend that modern painting is not a rupture with, but a continuation of traditional painting. See Greenberg, "Modernist Painting," 5.
50 Rancière, *Politics of Aesthetics*, 24. See also "Painting in the Text," in *The Future of the Image*, trans. Gregory Elliott (New York: Verso, 2007), 73. In the latter Rancière explains, "Those who regard *mimesis* as simply the imperative of resemblance can construct a straightforward idea of artistic 'modernity' as the emancipation of the peculiarity of art from the constraint of imitation: the reign of coloured beaches in the place of naked women and war horses. This is to miss the main thing: *mimesis* is not resemblance but a certain regime of resemblance."
51 Jacques Rancière, *La parole muette: Essai sur les contradictions de la littérature* (Hachette Littératures, 1998).
52 Jacques Rancière, *Mallarmé: La politique de la sirène* (Paris: Hachette Littératures, 2006).
53 For Rancière's discussion of Mallarmé and Behrens see, "The Surface of Design," in *The Future of the Image*, 91–107. Rancière explains that the commonality he locates in the work of Mallarmé and Behrens exemplifies the tendencies of the aesthetic regime more generally.
54 Rancière, *Malaise*, 23–24. "Aesthetics is the thought of a new disorder. This disorder is not only that the hierarchy of subjects and publics becomes blurred. It is that the works of art no longer relate to those who have commissioned them, whose image they fix and grandeur they celebrate. They relate to the 'genius' of peoples and offer themselves, in theory at least, to the gaze of anyone."

NOTES

55 Rancière, *Politics of Aesthetics*, 28.
56 Jean-François Lyotard, *The Postmodern Condition: A Report on Knowledge*, trans. Geoff Bennington and Brian Massumi (Minneapolis: University of Minnesota Press, 1984).
57 Kant, *Critique of Judgment*, 106. Italics in the original.
58 Lyotard, *Postmodern Condition*, 81.
59 Ibid.
60 Jean-François Lyotard, *Heidegger and "the jews,"* trans. Andreas Michel and Mark Roberts (Minneapolis: University of Minnesota Press, 1990), 45.
61 For an account of art's duty to bear witness to the unrepresentable, see the first half of *Heidegger and "the jews,"* 3–48.
62 Rancière, "Aesthetic Revolution," 150. See also "Are Some Things Unrepresentable?" in Rancière, *The Future of the Image*, 109–138.
63 Rancière, "Aesthetic Revolution," 148.
64 Rancière, *Malaise*, 140.
65 Rancière, "Art of the Possible," 261. Rancière uses the idea of the "discreet affect" to describe Alfredo Jaar's installation on the Rwandan genocide. It is contrasted with the "shopworn affect" of indignation. I find this phrase helpful, even if underdeveloped, for understanding more concretely the kinds of approaches that Rancière favors. See also *Emancipated Spectator*, 103–105.
66 Rancière, *Malaise*, 133.
67 Ibid., 48.
68 In this section I have drawn upon Rancière, *Malaise*, 41–55 and 129–133.

CHAPTER 4

1 Jacques Rancière, *"Le cinéma, art contrarié,"* interview with Stéphane Bouquet and Jean-Marc Lalanne, *Cahiers du cinéma*, no. 567, April (2002): 57.
2 Rancière, "Jacques Rancière and Interdisciplinarity," 6–7.
3 Jacques Rancière, *"L'historicité du cinéma,"* in *De l'histoire au cinéma*, ed. Antoine de Baecque and Christian Delage (Bruxelles: Éditions Complexe, 1998), 57.
4 "Oldest Programme for a System of German Idealism," in *Classic and Romantic German Aesthetics*, ed. J. M. Bernstein (Cambridge: Cambridge University Press, 2003), 186.
5 Rancière, *"L'historicité du cinéma,"* 49.
6 Rancière, *"Le cinéma, art contrarié,"* 59.
7 Ibid.
8 Jacques Rancière, *Film Fables*, trans. Emiliano Battista (New York: Berg Publishers, 2006), 15.
9 Rancière, "Jacques Rancière and Indisciplinarity," 5.
10 Rancière frequently makes reference to the film theory of the 1920s even though many of the themes that he points to—the unity of opposites, an

NOTES

electric-sensible form of writing, and the opposition to narrative—are present in prewar and interwar discussions of the medium, most notably in Ricciotto Canudo and Blaise Cendrars' writings. See Richard Abel's insightful essays in his *French Film Theory and Criticism, Volume I: 1907–1929*, (Princeton: Princeton University Press, 1988), 4–34 and 94–124. It is likely that Rancière focuses on the 1920s because it was during this period of systematization that the anti-narrative themes became the most pronounced.

11 Jean Epstein, "The Senses I (b)" in *French Film Theory and Criticism, Volume I: 1907–1929*, 242.
12 Abel, *French Film Theory*, 205.
13 Rancière, *Film Fables*, 5. The melodrama in question is *The Honour of His House* (1918). It was directed by William C. De Mille, not, as Rancière's text implies, Thomas Ince.
14 Jacques Rancière, "L'inoubliable," in *Arrêt sur histoire* (Paris: Éditions du Centre Pompidou, 1997), 54.
15 Rancière, *L'inconscient esthétique*, 31.
16 Ibid., 25–32.
17 Ibid., 27.
18 Kant, *Critique of Judgment*, 174–176.
19 Rancière, *L'inconscient esthétique*, 36.
20 Ibid., 35.
21 Ibid., 41–42.
22 Rancière, *The Future of the Image*, 17.
23 Ibid.
24 See the important first essay in *The Future of the Image* where Rancière distinguishes between the naked image, the ostensive image, and the metaphorical image—three ways of combining the powers of signification and presence (22–31). See also "The Pensive Image" in *Emancipated*, 107–132.
25 Rancière, "L'inoubliable," 54.
26 Epstein, "The Senses I (b)," 243.
27 Rancière, *Film Fables*, 2.
28 Ibid., 11.
29 Ibid., 4.
30 See "Painting in the Text" in *The Future of the Image*, 69–89.
31 Rancière, *Film Fables*, 3.
32 Ibid., 19.
33 Rancière, *The Future of the Image*, 11. For Rancière, the image is not unique to the visual arts. He frequently cites the descriptive, imagistic interludes that suspend the action of modern novels as examples of literary "images."
34 Rancière, *Film Fables*, 13–17.
35 Ibid., 41.
36 Ibid., 40.
37 Ibid., 42.
38 Ibid., 43.
39 Ibid.

40 Ibid., 73–93.
41 Ibid., 102.
42 Ibid., 103.
43 Ibid., 96.
44 Ibid., 97.
45 Ibid.
46 Ibid., 96–97.
47 Ibid., 100.
48 Gilles Deleuze, *Cinema 1: The Movement-Image*, trans. Hugh Tomlinson and Barbara Habberjam (Minneapolis: University of Minnesota Press, 1986), xiv.
49 Ibid., 141–177.
50 Gilles Deleuze, *Cinema 2: The Time-Image*, trans. Hugh Tomlinson and Robert Galeta (Minneapolis: University of Minnesota Press, 1989), 2. I leave it to the reader to decide whether the comparison with Impressionism is warranted. For my part, I follow Foucault's analysis of Manet as providing the essential rupture that inaugurates a more exclusively visual space for the practice of painting. See Joseph J. Tanke, *Foucault's Philosophy of Art: A Genealogy of Modernity* (London: Continuum, 2009), 52–92.
51 Deleuze, *Cinema 2*, 20.
52 Gilles Deleuze, *Difference and Repetition*, trans. Paul Patton (New York: Columbia University Press, 1994), 276.
53 Deleuze, *Cinema 2*, 18.
54 Deleuze, *Cinema 1*, 207–211.
55 Deleuze, *Cinema 2*, 68.
56 Ibid., 22.
57 Deleuze, *Cinema 1*, 200.
58 Ibid., 202.
59 Ibid., 201.
60 Ibid., 205.
61 Ibid., 206.
62 Rancière, *Film Fables*, 108.
63 Jacques Rancière, "Godard, Hitchcock, and the Cinematographic Image," in *For Ever Godard*, ed. Michael Temple, James S. Williams, and Michael Witt (London: Black Dog Publishing, 2007), 227.
64 Rancière, *Film Fables*, 114.
65 Deleuze, *Cinema 1*, 205.
66 Jacques Rancière, "Cinematographic Vertigo: From Hitchcock to Vertov and Back." I am here quoting my notes of a lecture that Rancière delivered on May 21, 2008 at Roehampton University, London, England.
67 Rancière, *Film Fables*, 118.
68 Ibid., 108–109.
69 Deleuze, *Cinema 1*, 206.
70 Rancière, "Cinematographic Vertigo."
71 One of the earliest reflections on Godard is contained in "*L'image fraternelle: Entretien avec Jacques Rancière*," *Cahiers du cinéma*, no. 268–269, juillet–août, (1976): 7–19. In this early interview, Rancière detects a certain

NOTES

ambiguity within what is ostensibly the most radical phase of Godard's output. He praises *Ici et ailleurs* for, on the one hand, "dividing" contemporary political consensus, and yet suspects Godard of liquidating history, thereby risking, in his pedagogies of sound and image, "a pacifistic response to the violence of the bourgeoisie's images" (11). Rancière argues it is necessary to develop creative means beyond Godard, for in his work there is an "*aristocratisme un peu suicidaire*" (19).

72 Jacques Rancière, "The Saint and the Heiress: A propos of Godard's *Histoire(s) du cinéma*," *Discourse* 24.1 (2002): 118.
73 Ibid., 116.
74 Rancière, *Film Fables*, 173–174.
75 Rancière has described this capacity to both advance and suspend the plot in terms of literature's double poetics. See, for example, his discussion of the famous image of the glass of milk from *Suspicion* in Rancière, "Godard, Hitchcock, and the Cinematographic Image," 217–221. Whereas in the representative regime of the arts, pity and fear would be induced by the arrangement of events and conveyed by the words and gestures of the performers, the aesthetic regime transfers this capacity to objects. The glass of milk is thereby endowed with speech and, because it is an object, resistance to signification. In the context of the film, it can thus function "akin to the words possessing a double meaning in Greek tragedy" (220).
76 Rancière, *Film Fables*, 182.
77 Godard, *Histoire(s) du cinéma*, quoted in Rancière, *Film Fables*, 183.
78 Rancière, "The Saint and the Heiress," 117.
79 Ibid., 119.
80 Philip Watts, "*Images d'égalité*," in *La philosophie déplacée*, ed. Laurence Cornu and Patrice Vermeren (Paris: Horlieu Éditions, 2006), 361–363. Watts provides a helpful account of the connections between cinematic montage and distribution of the sensible that informs my understanding of the politics of cinema. In addition to equality, however, I think it is necessary to describe Rancière's analyses in terms of causality, suspension, idleness, and freedom. Likewise, I understand the encounters between the representative and aesthetic poetics as dissensus, that is, as moments where the meaning and direction of the sensible is separated from itself. The resulting experience is thus about the creation of capacities and the domain of the possible as well as equality.
81 Pedro Costa's films revolve around the lives of people inhabiting the slums of Lisboa. His productions blur the boundary between fiction and documentary by using a method of collaboration that enables his "subjects," non-actors, to participate in telling their own stories.
82 Jacques Rancière, "The Politics of Pedro Costa." Forthcoming essay. I am grateful to Emiliano Battista for making his translation available to me.
83 Jacques Rancière, "Image, Narration: The Tensions of Fiction." I am here quoting my notes of a lecture Rancière delivered on June 4, 2009 at Bauhaus-Universität, Weimar, Germany. This lecture concluded with a reading of Robert Bresson's *Mouchette*, in which Rancière analyzed the

ways in which the lead character's playful actions both advanced and suspended the overall logic of the plot. He compared these "descriptions" with those found in literary texts, arguing that conditions of equality are created by these moments of thwarting.

CHAPTER 5

1 Friedrich Schlegel, "Athenaeum Fragments," in *Classic and Romantic German Aesthetics*, 251.
2 Kant, *Critique of Judgment*, 174.
3 Jacques Rancière, *Politique de la littérature* (Paris: Éditions Galilée, 2007), 16–17.
4 Ibid., 19.
5 Rancière, *Malaise*, 46.
6 Ibid.
7 Schiller, *Aesthetic Education*, 74.
8 Ibid., 78.
9 Rancière, *Malaise*, 47–50.
10 Kant, *Critique of Judgment*, 229.
11 Elaine Scarry, *On Beauty And Being Just* (Princeton: Princeton University Press, 1999). See in particular part two "On Beauty and Being Fair" where Scarry, with classical and medieval sources, sketches an account of beauty as a form of symmetry that aides the quest for justice (55–124).
12 G. W. F. Hegel, *Aesthetics: Lectures on Fine Art, Volume I*, trans. T. M. Knox (Oxford: Oxford University Press, 1998), 5.
13 Ibid., 2–5. The priority of the imagination accounts for a number of Hegel's more vexed positions, including the hierarchy he erects in terms of the arts with the least amount of spiritual content, such as architecture, to those with the most, like poetry, as well as the differences between the symbolic, classical, and romantic forms.
14 Ibid., 5. Italics in the original.
15 On this point I am indebted to conversations with Colin McQuillan, as well as his outstanding dissertation "Critical Philosophy: Immanuel Kant and the Critique of Pure Reason" (Ph.D. diss., Emory University, 2009).
16 Immanuel Kant, *Anthropology From a Pragmatic Point of View*, trans. Robert B. Louden (Cambridge: Cambridge University Press, 2006.) 60.
17 Readers interested in fuller genealogies of the imagination should consult: Richard Kearney, *The Wake of the Imagination* (New York: Routledge, 1998); Richard Kearney, *Poetics of Imagining: Modern to Post-Modern* (New York: Fordham University Press, 1998); and John Sallis, *Force of Imagination: The Sense of the Elemental* (Bloomington and Indianapolis: Indiana University Press, 2000).
18 Immanuel Kant, *Critique of Pure Reason*, trans. Norman Kemp Smith (Boston: Bedford/St. Martin's, 1933), 180–187. (A137–147/B176–187).
19 Ibid., 112. (A78/B103).
20 Kant, *Anthropology*, 60–62.

NOTES

21 Kant, *Critique of Judgment*, 185.
22 Ibid., 181–189.
23 Ibid., 182.
24 Sallis, *Force of Imagination*, 44–45. See also, Rodolphe Gasché, "Leaps of Imagination," in *The Path of Archaic Thinking: Unfolding the Work of John Sallis*, ed. Kenneth Maly (Albany: State University of New York Press, 1995), 35–48.
25 Kant, *Critique of Judgment*, 38.
26 Friedrich Nietzsche, *The Birth of Tragedy Out of the Spirit of Music*, in *Basic Writings of Nietzsche*, trans. Walter Kaufmann (New York: The Modern Library, 2000), 45.
27 Ibid., 59.
28 Ibid., 52.

BIBLIOGRAPHY

Abel, Richard, ed. *French Film Theory and Criticism, Volume I: 1907–1929*. Princeton: Princeton University Press, 1988.
—. *French Film Theory and Criticism, Volume II: 1929–1939*. Princeton: Princeton University Press, 1988.
Althusser, Louis. "*Problèmes étudiants.*" *La nouvelle critique* 152 (January 1964): 80–111.
—. *Lenin and Philosophy and Other Essays*. Translated by Ben Brewster. New York: Monthly Review Press, 1971.
—. *Essays in Self-Criticism*. Translated by Grahame Lock. London: New Left Books, 1976.
— et al. *Lire Le Capital*. Paris: Presses Universitaires de France, 1996.
—. *For Marx*. Translated by Ben Brewster. New York: Verso, 2005.
—. *On Ideology*. Translated by Ben Brewster. New York: Verso, 2008.
Aristotle. *The Basic Works of Aristotle*. Edited by Richard McKeon. New York: Random House, 1941.
Badiou, Alain. *Metapolitics*. Translated by Jason Barker. New York: Verso, 2005.
Baecque, Antoine de, and Christian Delage, eds. *De l'histoire au cinema*. Bruxelles: Éditions Complexe, 1998.
Balibar, Étienne. "Althusser and the rue d'Ulm." *New Left Review* 58 (2009): 91–107.
Beiser, Frederick C. *The Romantic Imperative: The Concept of Early German Romanticism*. Cambridge: Harvard University Press, 2003.
Bernstein, J. M., ed. *Classic and Romantic German Aesthetics*. Cambridge: Cambridge University Press, 2003.
Bourdieu, Pierre. *Distinction: A Social Critique of the Judgement of Taste*. Translated by Richard Nice. Cambridge: Harvard University Press, 1984.
Comolli, Jean-Louis, and Jacques Rancière. *Arrêt sur histoire*. Paris: Centre Georges-Pompidou, 1997.
Cornu, Laurence, and Patrice Vermeren, eds. *La philosophie déplacée*. Paris: Éditions Horlieu, 2006.
Davies, J. K. *Democracy and Classical Greece*. 2nd ed. Boston: Harvard University Press, 1993.
Debord, Guy. *La Société du Spectacle*. Paris: Éditions Gallimard, 1992.
Deleuze, Gilles. *Cinema 1: The Movement-Image*. Translated by Hugh Tomlinson and Barbara Habberjam. Minneapolis: University of Minnesota Press, 1986.

—. *Cinema 2: The Time-Image*. Translated by Hugh Tomlinson and Robert Galeta. Minneapolis: University of Minnesota Press, 1989.

—. *Difference and Repetition*. Translated by Paul Patton. New York: Columbia University Press, 1994.

Deranty, Jean-Philippe. "Rancière and Contemporary Political Ontology." *Theory and Event* 6, no. 4 (2003).

Dosse, François. *History of Structuralism, Volume 1: The Rising Sign, 1945–1966*. Translated by Deborah Glassman. Minneapolis: University of Minnesota Press, 1997.

—. *History of Structuralism, Volume 2: The Sign Sets, 1967–Present*. Translated by Deborah Glassman. Minneapolis: University of Minnesota Press, 1997.

Engels, Friedrich, and Karl Marx. *The Marx-Engels Reader*. 2nd ed. Edited by Robert C. Tucker. New York: W. W. Norton & Co., 1978.

Eribon, Didier. *Michel Foucault*. Translated by Betsy Wing. Cambridge: Harvard University Press, 1991.

Faure, Alain, and Jacques Rancière, eds. *La parole ouvrière*. Paris: La Fabrique éditions, 2007.

Foucault, Michel. *The Archaeology of Knowledge and the Discourse on Language*. Translated by A. M. Sheridan Smith. New York: Pantheon Books, 1972.

—. *The Order of Things: An Archaeology of the Human Sciences*. New York: Vintage Books, 1994.

—. *Power: Essential Works of Foucault, 1954–1984, Volume Three*. Edited by James D. Faubion. New York: The New Press, 2000.

Frascina, Francis, and Charles Harrison, eds. *Modern Art and Modernism: A Critical Anthology*. New York: Harper & Row Publishers, 1982.

Gauny, Gabriel. *Le philosophe plébéien*. Edited by Jacques Rancière. Paris: La découverte-Maspéro, 1983.

Greenberg, Clement. *Art and Culture*. Boston: Beacon Press, 1989.

Hegel, G. W. F. *Aesthetics: Lectures on Fine Art, Volume I*. Translated by T. M. Knox. Oxford: Oxford University Press, 1998.

—. *Aesthetics: Lectures on Fine Art, Volume II*. Translated by T. M. Knox. Oxford: Oxford University Press, 1998.

Houlgate, Stephen, ed. *Hegel And The Arts*. Evanston: Northwestern University Press, 2007.

Kant, Immanuel. *Critique of Pure Reason*. Translated by Norman Kemp Smith. Boston: Bedford/St. Martin's, 1933.

—. *Critique of Judgment*. Translated by Werner S. Pluhar. Indianapolis: Hackett Publishing Company, 1987.

—. *Anthropology from a Pragmatic Point of View*. Translated by Robert B. Louden. Cambridge: Cambridge University Press, 2006.

Kearney, Richard. *Poetics of Imagining: Modern to Post-Modern*. New York: Fordham University Press, 1998.

—. *The Wake of the Imagination*. New York: Routledge, 1998.

Laclau, Ernesto. *On Populist Reason*. New York: Verso, 2005.

Lewis, John. "The Althusser Case (Part 1)." *Marxism Today* 16, no. 1 (January 1972): 23–28.

BIBLIOGRAPHY

—. "The Althusser Case (Part 2)." *Marxism Today* 16, no. 2 (February 1972): 43–48.
—. "On the Althusser Discussion," *Marxism Today* 18, no. 6 (June 1974): 168–174.
Löwy, Michael, and Robert Sayre. *Romanticism against the Tide of Modernity.* Translated by Catherine Porter. Durham: Duke University Press, 2001.
Lyotard, Jean-François.. *The Postmodern Condition: A Report on Knowledge.* Translated by Geoff Bennington and Brian Massumi. Minneapolis: University of Minnesota Press, 1984.
—. *Heidegger and "the Jews."* Translated by Andreas Michel and Mark Roberts. Minneapolis: University of Minnesota Press, 1990.
Maly, Kenneth, ed. *The Path of Archaic Thinking: Unfolding the Work of John Sallis.* Albany: State University of New York Press, 1995.
Marcuse, Herbert. *The Aesthetic Dimension: Toward a Critique of Marxist Aesthetics.* Boston: Beacon Press, 1978.
May, Todd. *The Political Thought of Jacques Rancière: Creating Equality.* University Park: The Pennsylvania State University Press, 2008.
McQuillan, Colin. "Critical Philosophy: Immanuel Kant and the Critique of Pure Reason." Ph.D. dissertation, Emory University, 2009.
Nietzsche, Friedrich. *Basic Writings of Nietzsche.* Translated and edited by Walter Kaufmann. New York: The Modern Library, 2000.
Nordmann, Charlotte. *Bourdieu/Ranciere: La politique entre sociologie et philosophie.* Paris: Éditions Amsterdam, 2006.
Plato. *The Collected Dialogues.* Edited by Edith Hamilton and Huntington Cairns. Princeton: Princeton University Press, 1989.
Rancière, Jacques. *La leçon d'Althusser.* Paris: Gallimard, 1973.
—. "Mode d'emploi pour une réédition de Lire Le Capital." *Les temps modernes* 328 (November 1973): 788–807.
—. "L'image fraternelle: Entretien avec Jacques Rancière." *Cahiers du cinéma* no. 268–269 (July–August 1976): 7–19.
—. "Fleurs intempestives (*sur La communion solennelle*)." *Cahiers du cinéma* no. 278 (July 1977): 17–20.
—. "Reply to Lévy." *Telos: A Quarterly Journal of Radical Thought* no. 33 (1977): 119–122.
—. "The Myth of the Artisan: Critical Reflections on a Category of Social History." *International Labor and Working-Class History* No. 24 (Fall 1983): 1–16.
—. "A Reply," *International Labor and Working-Class History* No. 25 (Spring 1984): 42–46.
—. *The Nights of Labor: The Worker's Dream in Nineteenth-Century France.* Translated by John Drury. Philadelphia: Temple University Press, 1989.
—. "Politics, Identification, Subjectivization," *October* 61 (Summer 1992): 58–64.
—. *The Names of History: On the Poetics of Knowledge.* Translated by Hassan Melehy. Minneapolis: University of Minnesota Press, 1994.
—. "Les mots de l'histoire du cinéma: Entretien avec Antoine de Baecque." *Cahiers du cinéma* no. 496 (November 1995): 48–54.
—. *On the Shores of Politics.* Translated by Liz Heron. New York: Verso, 1995.

BIBLIOGRAPHY

—. *Aux bords du politique*. Paris: Gallimard, 1998.
—. "Le cinéma de Marie." *Cahiers du cinéma* no. 527 (September 1998): 42–44.
—. "De la difficulté d'être un personnage de cinéma." *Cahiers du cinéma* no. 529 (November 1998): 42–45.
—. *La parole muette: Essai sur les contradictions de la littérature*. Hachette Littératures, 1998.
—. *Disagreement: Politics and Philosophy*. Translated by Julie Rose. Minneapolis: University of Minnesota Press, 1999.
—. "Dissenting Words: A Conversation with Jacques Rancière." *Diacritics* 30, no. 2 (2000): 113–126.
—. "Literature, Politics, Aesthetics: Approaches to Democratic Disagreement." *SubStance* 29, no. 2 (2000): 3–24.
—. *L'inconscient esthétique*. Paris: Éditions Galilée, 2001.
—. "The Aesthetic Revolution and Its Outcomes." *New Left Review* 14 (March–April 2002): 133–151.
—. "Le cinéma, art contrarié." *Cahiers du cinéma* no. 567 (April 2002): 56–61.
—. "The Saint and the Heiress: A propos of Godard's *Histoire(s) du cinéma*." *Discourse* 24.1 (Winter 2002): 113–119.
—. *Les scènes du peuple: Les Révoltes logiques, 1975/1985*. Lyon: Éditions Horlieu, 2003.
—. *Short Voyages to the Land of the People*. Translated by James B. Swenson. Stanford: Stanford University Press, 2003.
—. *The Flesh of Words: The Politics of Writing*. Translated by Charlotte Mandel. Stanford: Stanford University Press, 2004.
—. *Malaise dans l'esthétique*. Paris: Éditions Galilée, 2004.
—. *The Philosopher and His Poor*. Translated by John Drury, Corinne Oster, and Andrew Parker. Durham, NC: Duke University Press, 2004.
—. *Chroniques des temps consensuels*. Paris: Éditions du Seuil, 2005.
—. "From Politics to Aesthetics?" *Paragraph* 28, no. 1 (2005): 13–25.
—. *Film Fables*. Translated by Emiliano Battista. New York: Berg Publishers, 2006.
—. *Hatred of Democracy*. Translated by Steve Corcoran. New York: Verso, 2006.
—. *Mallarmé: La politique de la sirène*. Paris: Hachette Littératures, 2006.
—. *The Politics of Aesthetics: The Distribution of the Sensible*. Translated by Gabriel Rockhill. New York: Continuum, 2006.
—. "Thinking Between Disciplines: an Aesthetics of Knowledge." *Parrhesia* no. 1 (2006): 1–12.
—. "Art of the Possible: Fulvia Carnevale and John Kelsey in Conversation with Jacques Rancière." *Artforum* XLV, no. 7 (March 2007): 256–269.
—. *The Future of the Image*. Translated by Gregory Elliott. New York: Verso, 2007.
—. *Politique de la littérature*. Paris: Éditions Galilée, 2007.
—. "Aesthetics against Incarnation: An Interview by Anne Marie Oliver." *Critical Inquiry* 35, no. 1 (Autumn 2008): 172–90.
—. "Art is Going Elsewhere: Interview with Sudeep Dasgupta." *Krisis* no. 1 (2008). http://www.krisis.eu/content/2008-1/2008-1-09-dasgupta.pdf.

BIBLIOGRAPHY

—. "Charlie Chaplin: La machine et son ombre." *Trafic* 65 (March 2008): 34–44.
—. "Jacques Rancière and Indisciplinarity." Interview with Marie-Aude Baronian and Mireille Rosello, translated by Gregory Elliott. *Art & Research: A Journal of Ideas, Contexts and Methods* 2, no. 1 (2008). http://www.artandresearch.org.uk/v2n1/jrinterview.html.
—. *Le spectateur émancipé*. Paris: La Fabrique éditions, 2008.
—. *The Emancipated Spectator*. Translated by Gregory Elliott. New York: Verso, 2009.
—. "Entretien avec Jacques Rancière," 1–26. Available from: http://www.armand-gatti.org/fichiers/_cat2_27831_chantierranciere.pdf. Accessed on February 13, 2010.
—. "Preface to the Hindi translation of *Nights of Labor*." Available at: http://hydrarchy.blogspot.com/2009/01/ranciere-2-new-preface-to-hindi.html. Accessed on March 2, 2010.
—. "The Politics of Pedro Costa." Translated by Emiliano Battista. Forthcoming.
Rhodes, P. J., ed. *Athenian Democracy*. Oxford: Oxford University Press, 2004.
Ricoeur, Paul. *The Conflict of Interpretations: Essays in Hermeneutics*. Edited by Don Ihde. Evanston: Northwestern University Press, 1974.
Rockhill, Gabriel. "The Silent Revolution." *SubStance* 33, no. 1 (2004): 54–76.
—, and Philip Watts, eds. *Jacques Rancière: History, Politics, Aesthetics*. Durham: Duke University Press, 2009.
Ross, Kristin. *May '68 and Its Afterlives*. Chicago: University of Chicago Press, 2002.
Rouaud, Christian. *Les LIP—L'imagination au pouvoir*. 1 hr. 58 min., *Les Films d'Ici*, 2007.
Sallis, John. *Force of Imagination: The Sense of the Elemental*. Bloomington and Indianapolis: Indiana University Press, 2000.
Scarry, Elaine. *On Beauty And Being Just*. Princeton: Princeton University Press, 1999.
Schiller, Friedrich. *On the Aesthetic Education of Man*. Translated by Reginald Snell. Mineola, New York: Dover Publications, Inc., 2004.
Smart, Barry, ed. *Michel Foucault: Critical Assessments Volume III*. New York: Routledge, 1994.
Stockton, David. *The Classical Athenian Democracy*. Oxford: Oxford University Press, 1990.
Temple, Michael, James S. Williams, and Michael Witt, eds. *For Ever Godard*. London: Black Dog Publishing, 2007.
Tanke, Joseph J. *Foucault's Philosophy of Art: A Genealogy of Modernity*. New York: Continuum, 2009.
Winckelmann, Johann Joachim. *History of Ancient Art Among the Greeks*. Translated by Giles Henry Lodge. London: John Chapman, 1850.

INDEX

XIth thesis on Feuerbach 12

activity–passivity schema 92, 107, 115–16, 119
aesthetic experience 85, 86–7, 94–5, 96, 102, 105, 107, 116, 143–4, 146–7
aesthetic regime 5–6, 142, 143, 144, 148, 149, 150, 156–7, 161, 175n. 75
   of art 73, 74, 76, 81–6, 88, 90–9, 103, 105, 108, 147
   of cinema 111, 112, 115, 116, 117
Aesthetic Unconscious, The 117
aesthetic-political action 26
aesthetics 25, 26, 34, 42, 73–109
   see also art
   of counting 48–55
   and equality 144–9
   and imagination 149–56
   and modernity 93–9
   of politics 49
aisthēsis 5, 50, 55, 62, 75, 80, 81, 104
Althusser, Louis 10–15
   agrégation in philosophy 11–12
   For Marx 11, 12
   on Lewis 19
   on Marxism 12–13
   subjectivation 66
Althusserianism 16–18, 19, 20, 28, 164–5n. 33

Altman, Robert
   Nashville 131
Anderson, Edward 124–5, 126
   Thieves Like Us 125
Anthropology 152
appearance 30, 92
archaeology 76–7, 161
archives 22–7, 40, 151
aristocratic lockup of philosophy 30, 31
aristoi 51
Aristotle 44, 48, 53, 81, 111, 113, 129–30
   arkhē 53, 54, 55, 78, 79
   dēmos 4, 43–5, 52–5, 67, 68, 71–2
   logos 57
   mimēsis 79
   on natural slavery 50
   Poetics 50, 78–9
art *see also* aesthetics
   analysis of 74–7
   aesthetic idea of 146
   as dissensus 104–8
   and distribution of the sensible 83
   equality in 85–93
   and life 83–4
   otherness 103
   regimes of 77–85 *see also* aesthetic regime; ethical regime of images; representative regime

INDEX

artisan 28, 29, 30–1, 39, 104
artistic stultification 89
auto-emancipation 20, 26, 31

Bachelard, Gaston 11, 14, 156
Badiou, Alain 43
beauty 96–7, 146, 147, 149, 154
Benjamin, Walter 49, 77, 139
Bergsonian ontology 129, 135
Birth of Tragedy 158
Bonjour Cinema 115
Bourdieu, Pierre 28, 31–4
  Distinction 33
  The Inheritors and *Reproduction* 32
  on taste 33
  sociology 33–4, 36
bourgeoisie 21

capacity and imagination 152–3
Capital 11, 12, 13–14
capitalism 13
Chaplin, Charlie 138
  Great Dictator, The 138
cinema 110–41
  activity–passivity schema 92, 107, 115–16, 119
  in aesthetic age 115–21
  allegories of modernity 128–36
  historical poetics of 112–15
  and its century 136–9
  logic of thwarting 121–8
Cinema 1 131, 135
Cinema 2 131
Citizen Kane 132
class 11, 14, 15, 16, 20, 23, 32–4, 53
Classical Age 79, 81
communication 37, 39, 42, 88, 90–1
community of equals 1, 57, 58, 61, 89
consensus, political *see* politics of consensus
Costa, Pedro 140, 144

counter-logics 10
counting 44, 68, 71, 162
  aesthetics of 48–55
Critique of Judgment 94, 152, 153, 154, 156

Daney, Serge 110
Debord, Guy 91, 92
defigurative descriptions 120
Deleuze, Gilles 120, 128–36
  Cinema 1 131, 135
  Cinema 2 131
  Difference and Repetition 139
  on *Rear Window* 133, 135
  on *Rules of the Game, The* 138
democracy 4, 32, 44, 47–8, 49, 53–5, 61, 66, 146
  after the demos 71
demonstrations 25, 35, 49, 51, 56, 58–62, 65, 69
dēmos 4, 43–5, 52–5, 67, 68, 71–2
Dews, Peter 63
Difference and Repetition 139
Disagreement 44
dissensus 4, 5, 6, 31, 47, 66, 74, 137, 140, 149, 151, 155
  art as 103–7, 108
  and imagination 155, 159
  politics as 61–5, 85, 140
Distinction 33
distribution of the sensible 1–3, 8, 10, 30, 65, 139, 140, 148, 149, 151, 155, 159–60
  aesthetics 5, 26, 34
  and art 73, 74, 75, 80, 81, 84, 86–7, 92, 94, 97, 104, 106, 107
  and philosophy 39–40
  and politics 45, 48, 52, 61, 65
division of labor 14, 19, 24, 29, 31, 32, 33, 40, 56, 75, 78, 160
Documenta 11, 90
domination 18, 20, 44, 50, 54, 57, 63, 83, 87, 97, 102, 104, 107

INDEX

egalitarian 4, 10, 51, 61, 145, 150
Emancipated Spectator, The 91
emancipation 10, 18, 20, 21, 38, 56, 63, 69, 70, 76, 90, 93, 102–3, 108, 109, 150
  auto-emancipation 20, 26, 31
Engels, Friedrich 11, 12
episteme 76–7
epistemological rupture 11
Epstein, Jean 115, 118, 120, 134
equality 15, 35–40, 44, 61
  aesthetics 144–9
  in art 85–93, 107
  community of equals 1, 57, 58, 61, 89
  geometric equality 53
  of intelligences 36–7, 40, 56, 61, 89
  logic of 55, 65
  natural equality 53
  sensing of 144–9
  social equality 57
  supposing, verifying, and demonstrating 55–61
ethical regime of images 74, 76, 77–8
ethics 69–70
exclusion by homage 23
explication 1, 35, 37–8, 39, 89, 90

Faure, Élie 120
Feuerbach, Ludwig 12, 92
Fichte, Johann Gottlieb 144
Film Fables 113, 114, 116, 121
film *see also* cinema
  aesthetic logic of romanticism 112
  artistic logic 112
  representative idea of art 112
film theory 119 *see also* cinema
fine art 154 *see also* aesthetics
Flaubert, Gustave 144, 145
For Marx 11, 12

Foucault, Michel 14, 63, 69, 151
  archeological method of 76–7
  on subjectivation 66
free citizenship 53
free play *see* freedom
freedom 6, 26, 33, 54, 68, 96, 140, 143, 144, 149, 155, 161
  aesthetic 146–7
French Revolution 83, 96, 99, 106–7, 144
Future of the Image, The 98, 117

Gaullist bureaucrats 16
genius 116, 144, 153
geometric equality 53
German idealism 5, 11, 111, 151, 158
Godard, Jean-Luc 114, 120, 136–9
  Histoire(s) du cinéma 114, 137–8
Goethe, Johann Wolfgang
  Meister 144
governance 47, 50
Great Dictator, The 138
Greek democracy 4, 44
Greek ethics 69
Greek philosophy 44, 48
Greenberg, Clement 94, 97

Habermasian models of communicative action 63
Hegel, Georg Wilhelm Friedrich 63, 73, 111, 115, 143, 148–9, 150, 161
  Lectures on Aesthetics 83, 116
  "Oldest Programme for a System of German Idealism" 111
Heidegger, Martin 78, 153
hermeneutics of depth 3
heterogeneous sensible 95, 98, 105
hierarchical divisions of labor 21, 51
Histoire(s) du cinéma 114, 137–8
History of Rome 56
Hitchcock, Alfred 132, 135, 137

INDEX

Hölderlin, Friedrich 111
"Oldest Programme for a System of German Idealism" 111
hybrid culture 23

identifications 52, 64, 67–8
ideology 10, 16, 18, 20, 21, 36, 46, 66
ideology/science distinction 12, 14–19
Ignorant Schoolmaster, The 4, 7, 32, 35, 91, 158
imagination 6, 21, 26, 27, 100, 129, 143, 160, 161–2
   as capacity of sensible-political dissensus 148–55
   Einbildungskraft (power of fantasy) 152
   facultas imaginandi 152
   trans-subjective 155–60
imitation 28, 29, 30, 78, 79, 80, 81, 97, 104
immigrants 69–70
individual will 158
inegalitarian 4, 10
inequality 2, 8, 15, 32, 36, 51–2, 57, 58, 61, 65, 106 *see also* equality
   and equality 58
   logic of 46
   social inequality 29, 52, 56
intelligence 15, 37–8, 41, 91, 135, 157
   equality of 36–7, 40, 56, 61, 89
   and poetry 39
   types of 3
interpretation of sense 46, 61

Jacotot, Joseph 35–40, 44, 56, 57, 61, 88–93, 145, 158
   Ignorant Schoolmaster, The 4, 7, 32, 35, 91, 158
   on *Télémaque* 35, 38, 93
Juno Ludovici 95–6, 105, 116, 144

Kallias or Concerning Beauty 150
Kant, Immanuel 6, 25, 33, 34, 73, 83, 87, 97, 100–1, 102, 106, 115, 116, 129, 143, 144, 146, 147, 148, 149, 152–4, 161
   Anthropology 152
   Critique of Judgment 94, 156
   knowledge 9, 10, 14, 18, 19, 67, 90, 92, 100, 137
Kracauer, Siegfried 139

La leçon d'Althusser 7, 16, 18, 20, 28
La parole muette 98
L'Atelier 24
Lectures on Aesthetics 83, 116
Les Révoltes logiques 22
Letters on the Aesthetic Education of Mankind 94, 96, 146, 150
Lewis, John 19, 20, 21
L'historicité du cinéma 113
LIP watch factory 16, 22, 62, 165n. 45
   workers' experiment in self-management 21–2
literary texts 64, 123
Livy 56, 58
   History of Rome 56
logic 8
   of *arkhē* 53
   of cause and effect 90, 93, 105
   counter-logics 10
   of counting 68, 71
   of equality 55, 65
   of inequality 46
   of thwarting 121–8
logos 49–50, 51, 57, 60, 80, 104, 111, 116, 117–18, 119
Louvre 83
Lumet, Sidney
   Network 130
lying 29, 30–1
Lyotard, Jean-François 99–103

INDEX

Mallarmé, La politique de la sirène 98
"man" 19, 21, 25, 96, 146
Mann, Anthony 114, 125
Marcuse, Herbert 64
Marx, Karl 11–13, 63, 92
Marxism 10, 12–13, 18–19, 23, 64
master, need for 3, 37–8, 89
materialism 12, 13, 17, 159
May 1968 14, 15–22, 63, 68, 73, 78
May, Todd 55
McCarthy, Paul 90
Meckseper, Josephine 90
Meister 144
mimēsis 79, 80, 81–2, 97–8
modern painting 79, 97, 171n. 49
modernity
 aesthetic 93–9
 cinematic 128–36
movement-images 129–30, 132, 134
Murnau, F.W.
 Tartuffe 123–4

Nashville 131
natural beauty 148–9, 154
natural equality 53
natural slavery 50
Network 131
Nietzsche, Friedrich 143, 158–9
 aesthetics 116
 Birth of Tragedy 158
Nights of Labor, The 4, 7, 22–4, 26, 27–8, 33, 65, 74, 104
noble lie 29, 31
nouveaux philosophes 63
Novalis 115, 117

"Oldest Programme for a System of German Idealism" 111
oligarchs 49, 52, 54, 68

panecastic method 39
partage 1–2, 17, 114

part-taking 48, 49, 53, 59, 67, 148
passivity–activity schema 92, 107, 115–16, 119
pathos 80, 116, 118, 119
Peirce, Charles Saunders 129
petrification process 145
Philosopher and His Poor, The 4, 7, 20, 22, 28, 31–2, 34, 75
philosophers 27–35, 48, 111
philosophical practice 14, 22, 41
photogénie 118
Place in the Sun, A 138
Plato 20, 23, 28–30, 31, 44, 48, 74, 75, 78, 79, 92
 Republic 28–9, 48, 78, 104
play 95, 96
playing 30
Poetics 50, 78–9
poetry 29, 39
poiēsis 78, 80, 81
polemical universal 4, 59
police, the 4, 43, 45–8, 51–2, 55, 56, 58, 61–3, 65, 67–9, 70, 72, 104, 107, 161
polis 43, 45, 68, 69, 71, 78, 105
political action 26, 107, 160
politics 16, 39, 43–72
 of aesthetics 73–109
 of consensus 45–8, 62
 as dissensus 48, 61–5
 and distribution of the sensible 26
 and the police *see* police, the subjective process
 of 65–70
 universality in 59
polling 71
poor 28, 31, 52, 75
postmodernism 4, 94–5, 99, 100, 108
postmodernity 99–103
proletariat 20, 21, 68, 71
Psycho 137

Racine, Jean 89
racism 69
Ray, Nicholas 114, 124–5, 126
  They Live by Night 124, 127
Reading Capital 12, 13, 14, 164n. 19
realism 4, 46–7, 61, 81, 126, 139
Rear Window 133, 135
Reid, Donald 23
relational art 91
Renoir, Jean
  The Rules of the Game 138
representative regime 74, 76, 78, 80–2, 84–7, 90, 97, 105, 111, 118, 144, 157
Republic 28–9, 48, 78, 104
revolutions 18, 23–4, 27
  aesthetic revolution 73, 79, 82–3, 106, 170n. 23
  French Revolution 83, 96, 99, 106–7, 144
Rhoades, Jason
  Shit Plug 90
romanticism 5, 81, 111, 113, 118, 125, 147, 150, 158
Romantics 116, 143–4, 161
Ross, Kristin 32
rue d'Ulm 11, 18
Rules of the Game, The 138

Scarry, Elaine 147
Schelling, Friedrich Wilhelm Joseph 111, 115, 116, 143, 147, 161
  "Oldest Programme for a System of German Idealism" 111
  System of Transcendental Idealism 116
Schiller, Friedrich 34, 73, 83, 95–7, 102, 105, 106, 107, 143, 148, 158
  Kallias or Concerning Beauty 150
  Letters on the Aesthetic Education of Mankind 94, 96, 146, 150
  sensorium 95

Schlegel, Friedrich 144
Schopenhauerian aesthetics 116
science 12, 13, 24–5, 29, 31
science/ideology distinction 12, 14–19
self 69, 70, 158–9
self-management 21, 62
sensibility
  and imagination 154–5
  passive 83, 97
sensorium 27, 82, 83, 90, 95, 105, 111
sensory-motor schema 129–30, 131
Shit Plug 90
silent speech 98, 117–18, 119
slavery, natural 50
social equality 57 *see also* equality
social harmony 29
social imagination 156
sociology 28, 31, 32, 33–4, 36, 75, 87
Socrates 29
Solon 54
space-time of occupation 25
spectatorship 88, 90–3, 145
Stendhal 82
Stevens, George 138
strikes 15, 60, 61, 62, 103
structural causality 13, 19
stultification 35, 38, 90–1, 92, 93
subjectivation 4, 49, 52, 65–70, 72, 87
subjective process of politics 65–70
subjectivities 33, 64, 67–8, 150
Sur la théorie de l'idéologie: Politique d'Althusser 16
Suspicion 137
System of Transcendental Idealism 116

Tartuffe 123–4
technai 79
Télémaque 35, 38, 93
theoreticism 18, 20

INDEX

They Live by Night 124, 127
Thieves Like Us 125
thinking 17, 22–3, 30, 31, 36, 40, 82, 86, 101
thwarted fables 121–8
time-image 129–2, 134–5
topographical analysis 3, 8, 17, 20, 31, 47, 74, 121, 139
tragedy 79, 80

universal teaching 37–8, 40, 88, 89, 158

universality in politics 59

Vertigo 135
visual essentialism 122

Welles, Orson 132
  Citizen Kane 132
workers 15, 16, 19, 21–33, 44, 45, 46, 49, 50, 54, 60, 67, 74–5, 104

xenophobia 69–70